HOW KINDERGARTEN CAME TO AMERICA

HOW KINDERGARTEN CAME TO AMERICA

Friedrich Froebel's Radical Vision of Early Childhood Education

BERTHA VON MARENHOLTZ-BÜLOW

Translated from the German by Mrs. Horace Mann

THE NEW PRESS

NEW YORK
LONDON

Originally published in the United States as *The Reminiscences of Friedrich Froebel*
by Lee and Shepard, Boston, 1895
This edition published in the United States by The New Press,
New York, 2007
Distributed by W. W. Norton & Company, Inc., New York

ISBN 978-1-59558-154-9 (pbk)
ISBN 978-1-59558-183-9 (hc)
CIP data available

The New Press was established in 1990 as a not-for-profit alternative to the large, commercial publishing houses currently dominating the book publishing industry. The New Press operates in the public interest rather than for private gain, and is committed to publishing, in innovative ways, works of educational, cultural, and community value that are often deemed insufficiently profitable.

www.thenewpress.com

Composition by NK Graphics,
a Black Dot Group Company
This book was set in New Caledonia

Printed in Canada

2 4 6 8 10 9 7 5 3 1

Contents

Series foreword by Herbert Kohl vii

Foreword by Herbert Kohl ix

1. MY FIRST MEETING WITH FROEBEL 1
2. FROEBEL IN LIEBENSTEIN 9
3. DIESTERWEG AND FROEBEL IN LIEBENSTEIN 18
4. MIDDENDORFF 29
5. THE SUMMER OF 1850 IN LIEBENSTEIN 40
6. VISIT OF DR. GUSTAV KÜHNE 50
7. VISIT OF DR. HIECKE 64
8. EDUCATIONAL VALUE OF FESTIVALS 79
9. CHILD-FESTIVAL AT ALTENSTEIN 85
10. HERR VON WYDENBRUGK 101
11. DR. R. BENFEY AND TEACHER HERMANN PÖSCHE 121

12. DR. WICHARD LANGE 134

13. THE LAST SUMMER IN LIEBENSTEIN 141

14. SECOND VISIT OF DIESTERWEG 144

15. VISIT OF HERR BORMANN 158

16. THE PROHIBITION OF THE KINDERGARTEN IN PRUSSIA 161

17. VISIT OF VARNHAGEN VON ENSE 166

18. TEACHERS' CONVENTION 208

19. THE YEAR 1852 223

20. LAST DAYS OF FROEBEL 234

SERIES FOREWORD
Classics in Progressive Education

My first classroom was empty. Not a book, piece of paper, pencil, or stick of chalk was in sight. The principal welcomed me to the school and informed me he had high expectations for each and every student. Crazy. I figured I had to dig into my meager savings and buy pencils, some remaindered typing paper, and discount crayons. Books were out of the question.

It was rough going for my first week of teaching, but during my second, two older female teachers showed up in my classroom after school. It turns out they were watching me and decided I might be a lifer—a life-long progressive education teacher. They brought me boxes of books, material about the United Federation of Teachers, and most of all, some classics of progressive education. Over coffee after school one day, they informed me that both of them would retire in a year but wanted to keep the tradition of democratic, student-centered education alive. These teachers hoped to keep arts in the schools and they hoped that young teachers like me (I was 23 at the time) would keep the tradition going. But, they emphasized, in order to keep a tradition alive, you had to know its history and read its literature. That's why, in addition to all the specific educational material these teachers brought me, they insisted I read Dewey, Froebel, Freinet, Homer Lane, Makarenko, and many other democratic educators whose work has had major influences on educators throughout the world. Their teaching was concrete and their vision for education was large.

I didn't have a chance to thank these two teachers because

they retired in the middle of my first year of teaching without leaving their names or addresses. But I have honored their commitment to children and to progressive education. This series is meant to show them my appreciation for their unsolicited gifts to me.

This series will reissue important but often hard-to-find works of progressive education which are still very useful to people teaching today. It is essential to connect to tradition, to know that you are not alone trying to fight against authoritarian or corporate education. The goal is to energize teachers through a connection to educators who have struggled for democratic and creative education against the demands of governments, the rigidity of some churches, and the complex lives many students are forced to bear. The books reprinted are for teachers of hope who understand the complexities of struggling for their students and who might need a dose of history, a bit of humor, and lots of new ideas.

—Herbert Kohl
February 2007

Foreword

Mary Mann, the translator of this book, called the kindergarten "the free republic of childhood." Mann's husband was Horace Mann, the first U.S. Commissioner of Education, and her sister was Elizabeth Peabody, a feminist and creator of the first English language kindergarten in the United States (there were some German language kindergartens in the mid-West). The very idea of freedom for young children and the sense that they could be self-governing was radical at the time this book was published in the mid-nineteenth century. In the twenty-first century, it is radical once more. *How Kindergarten Came to America* is part of a series of classic works in progressive education that seek to introduce a new generation of readers and educators to seminal works of earlier eras that are newly relevant today. *How Kindergarten Came to America* reminds us of where we came from and is a call to recommit ourselves to the ideas of democratic education and children's lives. The books in this series hope to overcome the radical disconnect between the people who have struggled for progressive and socially responsible ideas in the past and the current caring teachers who have been denied their heritage.

Before creating her "child's garden," Elizabeth Peabody made a trip to Germany to visit with the author Bertha von Marenholtz-Bülow and to observe the kindergarten created by Friedrich Froebel. In fact, Peabody and her sister Mary Mann were instrumental in bringing von Marenholtz-Bülow to the United States to lecture on the need for kindergartens in order to nurture children to think and act intelligently when they become adults in a free democratic society.

This was no small thing in the mid-nineteenth century, nor is it now. An intelligent public is essential to the development of democratic sensibility and to keep democracy vital: the right to speak out and be heard, the skills for thinking through social and personal issues, and the sense that the gifts of being alive should be shared by everyone are all democratic values. The driving force of the work of Friedrich Froebel (1782–1852), Mary Mann, and Elizabeth Peabody was to ensure that creative activity and fulfilling work were part of the education of every child. They were driven not by a desire to serve the state or the economy but to serve children, liberating them to be compassionate, caring members of a newly formed democratic country whose goal was a society free of oppression and autocratic rule.

The central part of this book is its focus on the specific details of developing children for democratic living. It is also a story of the sometimes wonderful and sometimes sad tale of Froebel's life, set in the context of the failed people's uprising in Europe during the 1840s. The struggle for democracy was as difficult and often as bellicose as the struggle of revolution. People with power do no let their control go easily.

Froebel, however, saw the need for revolution not in the streets but in childhood and education. Several overarching concepts inform his pedagogy. The first was that all young children regardless of social class should be provided with a free, playful, loving education. He advocated a concept that we might find somewhat problematic today, but that was truly revolutionary in the mid-nineteenth century: training women to be teachers, on the theory that the nurturance of growth and the free democratic spirit could come only from women. As part of his work, he joined with Bertha von Marenholtz-Bülow, an early German feminist, to develop a program to train women teachers of kindergartens. The goal was to inform women, even poor women, about the theory and techniques of educating young children.

In order to do this Froebel developed a series of what he called learning gifts for children—the polar opposite of training children to perform to state or national norms. He felt teachers of young children should issue an invitation to creativity and open-ended exploration of the wonders of the world. In particular it was an invitation for the poorest of children to become rich in learning. Froebel's school served the most needy of children and did so with no condescension or any sense that being poor precluded being artistic and intellectual. His approach provides an important warning for us now when the children of the poor are regimented and not respected.

One of the most radical of Froebel's ideas was to give children, from the age of three on, a total of twenty gifts that could contribute to their learning through play and experiment. These gifts were given in a pre-planned sequence beginning with the following three:

- Six rubber balls, covered with worsted wool of various colors
- A sphere, cube, and cylinder
- A large cube, divided into eight small cubes

At the end of the list are things such as material for drawing, weaving, paper cutting, paper folding, and clay modeling.

Anyone acquainted with Montessori schools will recognize that all of these manipulables are the materials that Maria Montessori refined and turned into her teaching curriculum. It is also no accident that Montessori began to implement her methods in a poor working-class housing project in Italy and had values very similar to the democratic values of Froebel.

The introduction of Froebel's gifts to kindergartens in the United States had some interesting consequences. One of Elizabeth Peabody's neighbors was Milton Bradley who sold game kits (such as Games for Soldiers) to Union soldiers during the Civil War. He was educated in a Froebelian manner and in 1869 he agreed to publish Edward Wiebe's *Paradise of Childhood: A Practical Guide to Kindergartners*. In addition, Milton Bradley began producing sets of Froebel's gifts and eventually added variations on the gifts to his growing toy line. As a result, many of Froebel's radical ideas were incorporated into the games and toys produced by one of the most successful games manufacturers in U.S. history.

The architect Frank Lloyd Wright went to a Froebelian kindergarten and describes in his autobiography the effect it had on him:

> The strips of colored paper, glazed and matte, [had] remarkably soft brilliant colors. Now came the geometric byplay of these charming colored combinations! The structural figures to be made with peas and small straight sticks; slender constructions, the joinings accented by the little green pea-globes. The smooth shapely maple blocks with which to build, the sense of which never afterwards leaves the fingers: form become feeling.
>
> And the exciting cardboard shapes with pure scarlet face—such scarlet! Smooth triangular shapes, white-black, and edges cut into rhomboids with which to make designs on the flat table top. What shapes they naturally made if only you would let them!
>
> Adding thickness, getting sculpture thereby, the square became the cube, the triangle the tetrahedron, the circle the sphere. These primary forms and figures were the secret of all effects . . . which were ever got into the architecture of the world.*

In fact, some of Frank Lloyd Wright's buildings were loosely modeled after constructions that were part of the program of

*Jennifer Wolfe, *Learning From the Past: Historical Voices in Early Childhood* (Mayerthorpe, Alberta, Canada: Piney Branch Press, 2000), page 122.

building with the Froebel gifts. And in 1916 Wright's son, John Lloyd Wright, incorporated Froebelian ideas in developing Lincoln Logs, one of the most popular construction sets ever.

In order to understand the development of Froebel's ideas it is important to know something of his personal life. He was born in Germany in 1782 and had a hard time growing up. His mother died when he was still a baby and his father, a pastor, neglected him. However, he had a stepmother who nurtured him, and he eventually went to live with one of his uncles.

Then he became an apprentice forester from 1797 to 1799. During his time working in the Thuringian forest, Froebel began to study natural forms, and began to develop a sense of the structures that lead to growth. Accounts tell of constructions he made out of what he observed: rocks, stones, plants, and even cobwebs. It is possible that many of his future educational ideas developed from his observation of nature. In fact, two central ideas of his pedagogy are the unity of nature and the discovery of specific universal natural laws.

These concepts complemented his idea that women should be educators of young children, imbuing them with a love of learning and exploration of the dual worlds of nature and ideas, and redeeming the world from what he saw as masculine tendencies toward war and greed. His mantra was learning by doing, which is at the core of progressive educational practice.

While still a young man Froebel worked for several years at a model school founded and directed by the Swiss educator Pestalozzi. Evidently he was quite brilliant in his work with the children and inspired by conversations with Pestalozzi. He became determined to elaborate on Pestalozzi's pioneering work on the development of a science of learning that freed children to develop their inner selves, creativity, and sense of the natural world.

Froebel held that the same laws must govern people as nature and developed a profound knowledge of natural science. Pestalozzi seemed limited to him. He said Pestalozzi did not "honor science in her divinity." Froebel returned to the university after eleven years of wandering from job to job and, in 1811, he began to study natural science. His studies were interrupted again by the king of Prussia's call "to [his] people" to enlist in the Prussian army. Though not a Prussian, Froebel was heart and soul a German. He responded to the call, enlisted in Lutzow's corps, and went through the campaign of 1813 against Napoleon, writing in his autobiography, "as far as the fatigues I underwent allowed, I carried in my thoughts my future calling as educator; yes, even in the few engagements in which I had to take part. Even in these I could gather experience for the task I proposed to myself."

After his military service, Froebel began teaching kindergarten and set up the first institute to train women teachers at Keilhau, Thuringia, in the early 1840s. Strongly believing that child-rearing skills, though resting on an innate maternal instinct, must nonetheless be developed through training, Froebel developed kindergartens that differed from existing preschool institutions, most of which were church-run day-care centers. These schools provided custodial services for the children of the very poor and their pedagogy was based on traditional Christian doctrines of original sin. Their teaching staff was largely male. Froebel's kindergarten was for children of all classes, though its initial students were mostly middle class. The teachers were women, though Froebel also participated in all activities at the school.

On a chance outing during 1849 in the countryside, Bertha von Marenholtz-Bülow, a feminist who had been working on the development of early childhood education, came upon Froebel playing with children in the woods near his school. She introduced herself to Froebel and they soon became fast friends and colleagues. She became part of his life from that day through the banning of kindergartens by the German state as subversive to the Monarchy (and through the ingenious ways kindergartens were kept alive despite state surveillance). She also participated in many philosophical conversations with Froebel on his ideas and worked with him training kindergarten teachers in his methods. She remained working with him until his death and became a leading promoter of Froebelian kindergartens, first in Europe, and then in the United States.

The story of the amazing personal and pedagogical relationship between Bertha von Marenholtz-Bülow and Friedrich Froebel is at the core of *How Kindergarten Came to America.* In it, both people emerge as complex, sensitive human beings obsessed with building up democratic sensibility through the exercise of creativity, discovery, and free exploration in early childhood. They truly believed that every child needed a garden in which to learn, and their passion informed von Marenholtz-Bülow's personal, philosophical, and very moving book.

—Herbert Kohl
February 2007

1

My First Meeting with Froebel

In the year 1849, at the end of May, I arrived at the Baths of Liebenstein, in Thuringia, and took up my abode in the same house as in the previous year. After the usual salutations, my landlady, in answer to my inquiry as to what was happening in the place, told me that a few weeks before, a man had settled down on a small farm near the springs, who danced and played with the village children, and therefore went by the name of "the old fool." Some days after I met on my walk this so-called "old fool." A tall, spare man, with long gray hair, was leading a troop of village children between the ages of three and eight, most of them barefooted and but scantily clothed, who marched two and two up a hill, where, having marshalled them for a play, he practised with them a song belonging to it. The loving patience and *abandon* with which he did this, the whole bearing of the man while the children played various games under his direction, were so moving, that tears came into my companion's eyes as well as into my own, and I said to her, "This man is called an 'old fool' by these people; perhaps he is one of those men who are ridiculed or stoned by contemporaries, and to whom future generations build monuments."

The play being ended, I approached the man with the words, "You are occupied, I see, in the education of *the people*."

"Yes," said he, fixing kind, friendly eyes upon me, "that I am."

"It is what is most needed in our time," was my response. "Unless the people become other than they are, all the beautiful ideals of which we are now dreaming as practicable for the immediate future will not be realized."

"That is true," he replied; "but the 'other people' will not come unless we educate them. Therefore we must be busy with the children."

"But where shall the right education come from? It often seems to me that what we call education is mostly folly and sin, which confines poor human nature in the strait-jacket of conventional prejudices and unnatural laws, and crams so much into it that all originality is stifled."

"Well, perhaps I have found something that may prevent this and make a free development possible. Will you," continued the man, whose name I did not yet know, "come with me and visit my institution? We will then speak further, and understand each other better."

I was ready, and he led me across a meadow to a country-house which stood in the midst of a large yard, surrounded by outhouses. He had rented this place to educate young girls for kindergartners. In a large room, in the middle of which stood a large table, he introduced me to his scholars, and told me the different duties assigned to each in the housekeeping. Among these scholars was Henrietta Breyman, his niece. He then opened a large closet containing his play-materials, and gave some explanation of their educational aim, which at the moment gave me very little light on his method. I retain the memory of only one sentence: "Man is a *creative* being."

But the man and his whole manner made a deep impression upon me. I knew that I had to do with a true MAN, with an original, unfalsified nature. When one of his pupils called him Mr. Froebel, I remembered having once heard of a man of the name who wished to educate children by *play*, and that it had seemed to me a very perverted view, for I had only thought of *empty* play, without any serious purpose.

As Froebel accompanied me part of the way back to Liebenstein, which was about half an hour's distance from his dwelling, we spoke of the disappointment of the high expectations that had been called forth by the movements of 1848, when neither of the parties was right or in a condition to bring about the desired amelioration.

"Nothing comes without a struggle," said Froebel; "opposing forces excite it, and they find their equilibrium by degrees. Strife creates nothing by itself, it only clears the air. New seeds must be planted to germinate and grow, if we will have the tree of humanity blossom. We must, however, take care not to cut away the roots out of which all growth comes, as the destructive element of today is liable to do. We cannot tear the present from the past or from the future. Past, present, and future are the trinity of time. The future demands the renewing of life, which must begin in the present. In the *children* lies the seed-corn of the future!"

Thus Froebel expressed himself concerning the movements of the time, always insisting that the historical (traditional) must be respected, and that the new creation can only come forth out of the old.

"That which follows is always conditioned upon that which goes before," he would repeat. "I make that apparent to the children through my educational process." (The Second Gift of his play-materials shows this in concrete things.)

But while Froebel, with his clear comprehension, cast his eyes over the movements of the time, neither joining with the precipitate party of progress nor with the party of reaction that would hinder all progress, he was counted by those in authority among the revolutionists, and condemned with his kindergartens. He repeated again and again: "The destiny of nations lies far more in the hands of women—the mothers—than in the possessors of power, or of those innovators who for the most part do not understand themselves. We must cultivate women, who are the educators of the human race, else the new generation cannot accomplish its task." This was almost always the sum of his discourse.

Froebel's Normal Teaching

Already on this first day of my acquaintance with Froebel the agreement was made that I should take part as often as possible in the instruction given to the pupils he was training.

The fire with which he uttered and illustrated his views gave them a peculiar stamp, and the deep conviction with which he demonstrated their justice was sometimes overpowering and sublime. He became entirely another person when his genius came upon him; the stream of his words then poured forth like a fiery rain. It often came quite unexpectedly and on slight occasions; as in our walks, for instance, the contemplation of a stone or plant often led to profound outbursts upon the universe. But the foundation of all his discourses was always his theory of development—the law of *universal* development applied to the human being.

One needed to see Froebel with his class, in order to realize his genius and the strong power of conviction which inspired him. No one could avoid receiving a deep impression of it who saw him in that circle of young maidens, teaching with that profound enthusiasm which only an unswerving conviction of the truth uttered lends to the discourse, with a love for the subject which communicated his enthusiasm to his hearers, and an untiring patience.

The greater number of his scholars may not have fully comprehended his words, for that which he was teaching often far transcended their accustomed sphere of thought, and his strange mode of speech made it difficult for them to understand him; but the spirit of the subject penetrated their hearts, and in the course of his teaching developed a partial understanding of it. This was true only of those who could understand with the heart, and in whom also love for the subject was really awakened. Yet it cannot be denied that some of his scholars carried into their own subsequent activity nothing but the practical occupations of the kindergarten, and often, alas! an assumption of a knowledge which is not real knowledge.

But the learning of the practical occupations and plays in their logical connection, and with their intellectual meaning, gave each of these young maidens at least a limited comprehension of the subject. The full measure of it, indeed, can be appreciated only by the highly gifted and highly developed.

The understanding of his often obscure style was facilitated by the accompanying demonstrations. Tears would often be seen in the eyes of his scholars, when with his overflowing love of humanity he would speak of the helplessness of children, exposed to all harms by the arbitrary way in which they are managed, but whom God has intrusted to the female sex to be moulded into true men and at the same time into children of God, to be led back consciously to him from whom they had come forth. And then he further emphasized the great responsibility which was imposed upon women as educators of the human race—a responsibility doubled in our day, whose problems are so great and difficult to solve that the male sex alone is not able to solve them. "The immature most become mature; the immature are especially the women and children whose human dignity has not been in full measure recognized hitherto," he used to say, when he spoke of the new tasks of the female sex. He was most difficult to understand when he spoke of the application of his "law" through the gifts; and also when he treated of the first impressions of the outward world upon the very young child, which were given by concrete things, symbols, as it were, for the later apprehension of spiritual facts.

Even the most developed of his scholars were hardly capable of clearly reproducing this truly most difficult and obscure side of his instruction. I saw this from their notebooks in which they wrote down the contents of his lessons to them. On this account, therefore, I have ever since conducted this part of the instruction in quite another manner than he was accustomed to do.

But his eyes sparkled with delight when he pointed out to me, here and there, in these notebooks, passages which showed a deeper insight and understanding of the subjects he had treated. Still more would his joy break forth when I would further develop and explain the illustrations which he privately gave to *me*, and when I showed that I had reflected upon what I had received from him.

"How did you know that?" he often asked me when he was explaining the meaning of his play-materials, and I anticipated him. "I have not yet spoken of that." My answer, "I can infer it from my own recollection of the intellectual demands of my earliest childhood," made him quite happy, and he would reply, "You see, then, that it is true."

And so he would say, when I communicated to him at that time some of my own very short notes of his teachings, as, for example, an aphoristical statement like the following: "The first circle in the unfolding of the earliest child-life is unconscious nature bound by necessity."

"Childhood, in this first period of life, can only find its antitype in the external phenomena of the sensible world, from the crudest types of nature onward, which prefigure their organisms. The elementary finds itself again only in the elementary."

"These images wake the soul-germs that are related to all nature, which, on the other hand, is a symbol of the spiritual. The still unthinking mind of the child can be awakened and taught only through symbols or the higher mental images. Natural phenomena furnish these symbols, but not in the elementary form which corresponds with the still unarticulated simplicity of the child's soul. They must first be selected out of the great manifoldness of things by the thinking mind. They must reflect the universal law that gives its form to the smallest as well as to the largest object, to the flowers as well as to the celestial bodies."

"The simplest forms (types), which lie at the foundation of the fabric of the world, lay also the foundation in the minds of children for the understanding of the world, which expresses God's thought (spirit). These simplest and unarticulated forms are the fundamental forms of crystallization." (The solid forms of Froebel's second Gift.)

"The norms of all the organisms and all the phenomena of nature are the universal properties of things, that which is peculiar to them all in spite of the infinite variety of form; and this universe, which expresses itself in form and color, in relations of size and weight, in tone, in number, etc., is to be stamped in the most elementary manner on the child's soul, through his eye, as fundamental form, fundamental color, fundamental tone—archetypes as it were of ideas."

"Definite, clear, and sharply drawn conceptions follow such logically ordered ideas in the subsequent circle of development. A correct comprehension of external, material things is a preliminary to a just comprehension of intellectual relations."

"Only that knowledge furthers the ripening of the mind which mounts up through its own activity and effort from the perception and contemplation of external objects to the thoughts or the conceptions which dwell in things. Only through a gradual climbing up on the ladder of knowledge does the child's mind rise out of its own darkness to the light of its own consciousness. Only from the antitype which makes objective the child's own inner being can this consciousness be gained clearly. So that the A B C of things must precede the A B C of words, and give to the words (abstractions) their true foundations."

"It is because these foundations fail so often in the present time that there are so few men who think independently, and express skilfully their inborn, divine ideas. The instruction forced upon the child's mind, which does not correspond to its inner stage of development and its measure of power, robs him of his own original view of things, and with it of his greatest power and capacity to impress the stamp of his own individuality upon his being. Hence arises a departure from nature which leads to caricature," etc.*

So obscure and difficult to understand were Froebel's distinctions, and so much veiled was his "Idea" by his peculiar mode of speech, that one could cull out the peculiar meaning of it only af-

*What is quoted here is only for those initiated into Froebel's system, and is referred for explanation to my writings, particularly to that which treats of the method. It has found no other relevance here than so far as it concerns the relation mentioned.

ter one had penetrated his method of intuition (*Anschauungsweise*). Single lightning flashes often illuminated the dark way, and the truth which he himself received preeminently by inspiration was communicated to his hearers also intuitively as it were.

I had many opportunities to notice his intercourse with the princes of Meiningen and Weimar, whom I had interested in him and his subject, and who often accompanied me in my visits to him. He was truly modest, but it was a marked trait of character in him that he felt his dignity as a man and his own importance personally as the bearer of an idea. Real appreciation, however, easily misled him to take for granted the full recognition of his "divine idea," and, rejoicing in that, he could undoubtedly appear arrogant and boastful to those who did not know that he never looked upon the idea as his own, but regarded himself only as the God-favored bearer of it; but the haughtiness of mediocrity was wholly foreign to him.

Therefore I was often vexed when some of the frequenters of the baths of Liebenstein, whom I took to see him, allowed themselves to treat him, on account of the plainness of his external appearance, which was not unlike that of an old village schoolmaster, in his old-fashioned long coat, with his hair parted, and of the childlike simplicity of his manners, with a degree of contempt, or indeed as an inferior! But he was seldom moved by what concerned himself personally, though very much so by everything that undervalued or slighted his cause. When in conversation touching his idea, any learned scholasticism undertook to condemn it without having arrived at any understanding of it, a violent indignation was kindled in him. When he had taken for granted a capacity to understand him, and yet met a motiveless opposition, he could come crashing in, as I experienced in one case, when he defended the truth of his views like an enraged lion.

2

Froebel in Liebenstein

Would that men did not always demand of geniuses who bring the Great and Good into the world, that with this extraordinary gift they should unite all human perfections! This unreasonable requisition often causes them to be misunderstood and calumniated when it is discovered that as men they do not always stand upon the height of their genius. We forget that the heavenly light hardly ever illuminates to its possessor anything but the field whereon he is to build, but cannot penetrate through the whole mind; and by the side of the divine inspiration the natural power stands as yet unpenetrated by the light, which leaves room also for the unspiritualized powers (*dämonisches*) and likewise for human weaknesses.

Froebel was no exception to this rule, and not only in his lifetime, but even now, after his death, has had to suffer from manifold unjust judgments, among which are those of some of his earlier pupils in Keilhau (1817–27), who cannot complain enough of what they call the defects of some of his branches of instruction, without considering all that stood in the way of bringing his method immediately into complete working order. The new always stands in opposition to established claims, and has first to clear the ground of what has become obsolete before it can be effective. In the introduction of new ideas, their representatives pay no regard to men and things that oppose them, and therefore often wound sensibly even those who are dearest.

Froebel often made his friends and relatives suffer when their views and interests did not harmonize with what he considered necessary or best for the good of his idea. But one must in this respect discriminate between the lack of sound judgment in a matter of human interest, and that in a matter which serves the end of self-seeking, the latter being the chief motive with the majority of mortals. This vulgar self-seeking is never known to the real genius, the genuine bearer of an idea, for he must offer himself as a sacrifice on the altar of this idea. Through his whole life Froebel sacrificed himself and his personal interests, also the interests of those nearest to him, to the development and propagation of his idea, and knew no other striving. This should not be forgotten by those who have to complain of him for some loss of their own.

In Keilhau, Froebel could only make experiments in order to get necessary data for the working out of this educational idea. The idea itself was grasped by him at first only in the germ, and was still unripe, as well as the means of its accomplishment. In the process of fermentation towards a new form in which Froebel found himself, he could not, in full measure, fulfil all the duties of the practical teacher, any more than could Pestalozzi or others of his predecessors. Therefore some complaints of his pupils as to gaps in their knowledge may be quite justified, since, moreover, the time for instruction was much curtailed by the practical labors superadded, and by excursions in the fields and woods of Keilhau. Yet, not to be unjust, the gain in respect to the formation of character and practical ability must be thrown into the balance. How very much Froebel did influence the moral culture of his pupils is made public by the unbounded love and gratitude expressed by the majority of them at the time of his death. Even on this side it is to be observed that his peculiar mission did not have reference to the improvement of instruction, which had already been turned into the true path by Pestalozzi, but rather consisted in creating a new foundation for education in general, and consequently in working more indirectly for the reform of instruction. The new truth concerning the nature of childhood which he brought out cannot be without influence upon all branches of education, and here it was that Froebel knew no yielding whenever the jewel of the truth entrusted to him was questioned or attacked.

But on the other hand, he would confess ignorance in the most childlike manner, when the application of his idea touched points not yet considered by him. He frequently said, upon such occasions, "I have not yet considered that side of the subject; I will see; it may be so," or "That is new, but it must be right, and we must work it out." etc. He would even learn from children—or others—for he was wholly free from that pride of knowledge which covers so much emptiness. One day when I visited him, he said, his eyes lighting up "Today is a good day; much that is new has come to me; almost every morning when I wake this comes to me uncalled for, but today it was especially bright and clear. Yes, this truth is endless, and cannot be exhausted by thought."

It was generally extremely difficult to hold him fast to one train of thought, for if a new thought struck him he often followed it up without any regard for his particular theme, and without any consideration for his hearers. He was always learning himself as he spoke, and therefore the logic of his discourse suffered exceedingly, so that he gave to many the impression of disorderliness of thought. Added to this, his peculiar manner of expression, the doubling and trebling of words in order to make the matter clear, the often endless interweaving of sentences—all this made him quite unintelligible to the ordinary public, and especially to women.

Sometimes at Liebenstein, when I introduced strangers to him to whom he tried to explain his method without succeeding according to his wish, he would call on me with the request to explain this or that, with the words, "They understand you better."

Now and then the word "confusion," or something similar, fell from the lips of his hearers, but the great majority of them were won by the power of the deep conviction which expressed itself in every word, even before a real understanding of the subject was possible. The great majority of women, especially, could not avoid being moved when he so strongly appealed to the maternal feeling.

Before Froebel was convinced of my deep interest in his cause and of my understanding of it, there were moments of doubt and distrust on his part. He had been deceived so often, both in his expectations of a correct comprehension of his method, and in the assistance promised him for the purpose of its introduction, that he feared dilettanteism, and a quickly blazing fire of straw, and would sometimes unjustly take these for granted. Only after I had written several anonymous articles for public journals which he used to praise beyond their desert, and after our intercourse had convinced him of the earnestness of my interest, was I unreservedly initiated into the subject.

After I had accepted Froebel's educational method in respect to its pedagogical principles and practical means, I still lacked the final basis and point of departure of his views. I begged him to disclose to me in full the deeper basis of his theory of the world; he replied: "No, my last word I take with me into the grave; the time for it has not yet come."

In vain I urged on him the duty of uttering this last word, even if not publicly, until one day at my house he read some leaves of an old manuscript and begged permission to take with him the volume containing them. When I went to see him the next day he said: "Now *you* shall know my last word; I have been reading in your book nearly the whole night, and see that you have my idea and therefore will not misunderstand me."

Although he construed several general theories in the sense of his idea when he found related ideas of others, yet he had found in mine some nearly related original views of things which facilitated a deeper penetration into his idea, and supplied me by degrees with the proper key for the understanding of it. His explanations alone could not bring this about; they were too aphoristic and unintelligible in expression. Only a longer study and my own working led in the course of years to that, and even then only to the first beginnings of the understanding of an idea which still needs centuries for its development and maturity—an idea which Froebel received from the hands of his predecessors as a seed from the flowers of the past, and which he left to the present only in germ, so that legions of thinkers of the following age and in different departments may develop it and bring it to maturity as an element of the general idea of the time. The present has only to make the first practical application to the child in the cradle and in the garden of children, and thus to prepare the ground for future generations, which alone can complete what the present has begun.

The reproach of mysticism applied to Froebel's system has a certain justification so long as the theory lying at the foundation of his educational idea is not completely understood and scientifically established; and thus far there is little prospect that this will really happen very soon, since the great mass of the representatives of the cause can only comprehend its outside. The conflicts of the present must bring more of the problems of the time nearer to their solution before the solution of this problem which concerns mankind most deeply can come upon the stage. In spite of the slight understanding of his idea that Froebel found in his contemporaries, he was thoroughly convinced that the time for it would come.

"If three hundred years after my death my method of education shall be completely established according to its idea, I shall rejoice in heaven," he replied to me once when I was lamenting over its slow and imperfect advance.

Froebel found in Liebenstein a haven of rest for his last days. The residence in large cities had always been harassing and irksome to him.

"I was born for country life and intercourse with nature," he declared very truly. He did not understand the language of the great world. Literary culture, according to the prescription of faculties and authorities, was foreign to his self-taught and original fashion of thought, and he was ill fitted for the discussion of the claims of science in this or that department. Still less was he fitted for the conflicts with intrigue, vulgarity, and malevolence which met him in the great centres. Therefore he was happy to have escaped them when he arranged his farmhouse near Liebenstein, after he had given a course of instruction to kindergartners in Dresden the winter before.

Here he was again surrounded by the home atmosphere of Thuringia, and by beautiful nature, with which he had always held his most intimate and comforting communion; and his trustful, receptive young scholars gave him an opportunity to state his method without meeting with opposition from an imperfect knowledge of the subject. Here he was able to lay the foundation for the general education of the female sex—the educational vocation—and every one who attended his instructions must have seen how the happiness that inspired him was reflected in the enthusiasm of his pupils.

The interest in his cause shown by the princes of Meiningen and Weimar, especially by her Highness, my patroness and friend, the Duchess Ida of Weimar, who so often accompanied me to Froebel's institution, renewed his courage. I was obliged to mediate with the gracious and amiable princess for much that Froebel wished for in the interest of his cause. Through her a suitable location was at last obtained for his institution.

On a walk which I once took with him we came, in the neighborhood of Liebenstein, upon the small ducal shooting-castle of Marienthal, charmingly situated among the green fields. Froebel stood still, and said, "Look round about you, Frau Marenholz. This would be a beautiful place for our institution, and even the name would suit it so well—Marienthal, the vale of the Marys, whom we wish to bring up as the mothers of humanity, as the first Mary brought up the Saviour of the world."

I remarked to him that he might petition the duke to grant him the building which was standing unused, and that I would endeavor to assist him in the matter through the Duchess Ida. So it came to pass, yet only after a long delay, since many objections were raised by the authorities. Through the continual prompting of her brother by the duchess this end was reached only after months. I had the pleasure of surprising Froebel with the official permission after he had almost given up the hope. One circumstance contributed to bring about this permission sooner, by making still more clear to the duchess the inappropriateness of the farmhouse inhabited by Froebel.

Froebel had been invited with me to dine with the duchess, and had put on a coat which had been laid away for a long time in a closet immediately contiguous to the cow-house, and the coat was completely penetrated with the odor of the stable. As this odor also permeated the instruction-room, from which a small door opened into the cow-house, Froebel had not perceived it himself, being accustomed to it, but the duchess noticed it as soon as she came into the dining room. Thinking the smell came from out of doors through the window, she had it closed. The smell still remained. On informing her of the cause in a whisper, she was much amused, and so were the young princesses her daughters. Froebel joined heartily when we told him the cause of our hilarity, and said, "Your Highness sees now how necessary it is to remove our institution to Marienthal."

After dinner the now reigning Grand Duke of Weimar, then heir presumptive, came in with his wife and several ladies and gentlemen to visit the duchess, and Froebel was requested to make a statement of his idea to them. I begged him to speak clearly and briefly, as was appropriate, and was astonished at his unwonted success; indeed, he spoke with an enthusiasm that moved all his hearers. The duke, whom I had already, during his frequent visits to Liebenstein, made acquainted with Froebel's cause, and who had been present at the plays of the children in the institution, retracted his former censure of Froebel's obscure style.

"He speaks like a prophet," he said now.

This expression of acknowledgment pleased Froebel greatly. He said to me, "Do you know what warmed me up so much today? The beautiful harmony of the architecture of that dining hall! I felt as if I were in a temple!"

The marble pillars which supported the vaulted roof had made an impression on his artistic eyes. I constantly observed this feeling for harmony and beauty in Froebel, who had not been educated to the practice of any art. In nature, nothing escaped him; every tree which embellished the surrounding country, every graceful curved line, every blending of color, every lighting up of the heavens, everything, indeed, which expressed beauty and harmony, was perceived by him, and often served, on our walks with the scholars, for some deep interpretation of nature, and some enthusiastic praise of God's creation, which made an indelible impression upon them. But, on the other hand, the smallest want of harmony was annoying to him.

"I miss harmony of color here," he said once as we were passing a bed of dahlias in which all the colors were confusedly mingled.

This sharpness and fineness of sense extended to all his organs. At great distances he perceived the perfume of plants and viands and wines. I looked upon this as a proof of how he was fitted by nature in all respects for the mission with which he was charged from God. Even the facility of speech denied to him, and his lack of literary expression, cooperated to the same end. It is not likely that he would have known how to embody his ideas in *matter* so completely, if he had been able to make himself entirely intelligible in words. A certain one-sidedness and even limitation is often necessary to a reforming genius in order to keep him within the limits of his calling, and prevent him from wandering away from it. Universal geniuses are rare, and Froebel in no way belonged to them. But in spite of this undeniable gift of prophecy, Froebel had a warm heart for his fellow men, irrespective of his work, and helped wherever he could with the same disinterestedness as that with which he served his idea.

Middendorff told me this little anecdote. Froebel came home one day much heated by a walk in the neighborhood, and wished to change his clothes. When his wife opened the wardrobe she exclaimed with alarm, "The closet is almost empty! thieves have been here." Froebel answered, laughing, "I am the thief!" And he then told her that the inhabitants of a neighboring village which had been destroyed by fire had been there that morning and asked for assistance, and as he had no money, he had felt obliged to give them some of his effects. This warm heart was often concealed under a harsh and rude exterior, which is usually the case with those who work most deeply, working inwardly. Children are the least disturbed by this, and know by intuition the hearts that love them. When I went with Froebel through the village streets, the children of the cottages came running to him from the doorsteps, as to their own father; even the smallest, who had hardly learned to walk, clung to him, and accompanied him to some distance. With what love he embraced the little ones! It shone from his eyes and attracted their hearts magnetically. It was the love of humanity, whose germ he beheld in the children. His words, uttered on such an occasion, "I see in every child the possibility of a perfect man," made an undying impression on me.

In Marienthal I saw a mother of two children who had attended Froebel's kindergarten for a time, and had often been with him, come to take leave at the end of her residence at Liebenstein. One of the boys, five years old, clung sobbing on Froebel's neck and would not go. When the mother said he might remain without her, he was quite willing, although he had always shown great love for his mother. Perhaps the child's spiritual and intellectual wants had been fully satisfied here for the first time, and he felt that gratification which all development brings to the human soul.

3

Diesterweg and Froebel in Liebenstein

In July, 1849, Diesterweg came to Liebenstein. Immediately after the greeting with my old friend, I told him of Froebel and of my acquaintance with him, and how he went by the cognomen of "old fool," at which he laughed heartily. "Tomorrow morning," I said, "you must go with me to Froebel's class and make his acquaintance."

"O, you must excuse me," he replied. "I dislike foolery in methods of education."

But when I had said what was necessary to convince him that there was no such "foolery," he consented to accompany me the next day to Froebel's dwelling in the farmhouse.

The instruction had already begun, and Froebel was so much absorbed in his subject, which was presented with much enthusiasm, that, as usual, he did not observe my entrance with Diesterweg by the open door behind him. Diesterweg listened at first with some irony on his countenance, but by degrees this expression entirely vanished and gave place to the deepest attention, and at last his emotion increased till it broke forth in tears. Those who know Diesterweg admit that such an expression of feeling could not be drawn from him by any everyday occurrence.

When Froebel ended his lesson and I introduced Diesterweg to him, the latter greeted him with great heartiness, which was the more gratifying to Froebel because he had heard of a previous expression of Diesterweg's which did not sound very favorable to his cause. The two men felt themselves drawn together, as was apparent on this first interview, and Froebel explained his ideas enthusiastically and with unusual clearness, and I was obliged to remind Diesterweg of the dining-hour, which was about to strike, in order to bring the interview to a close for the time.

On our way back Diesterweg kept stopping every instant to express to me his great satisfaction with what he had heard from Froebel. I felt in every word he said, how his mind, open to everything noble and high, was impressed.

"The man is actually something of a seer," he exclaimed. "He looks into the innermost nature of the child as no one else has done. I am wholly taken captive by him."

"Yes," I replied, "he impresses one like all genuine enthusiasm for truth and human weal."

From that time, almost every morning, Diesterweg came under my window with the *Mother and Cosset Songs* under his arm, calling out to me, "Frau von Marenholz, it is time to go to school!" And as often as possible we went to walk with Froebel in the afternoons, to converse upon "the Idea" or other views. In bad weather the two educators generally came to my house, and we held a council to consider how the new educational method could be furthered. Diesterweg requested of me a first article for his *Weg Weiser*, which he had after two days, and which Froebel enjoyed even to tears, in spite of its trifling importance.

The name of "Eisel and Beisel" given us by one of the guests at Liebenstein, in harmless fun, spread more widely and gave occasion to the Princess Amalia, daughter of the Duchess Ida, afterwards Princess Henry of Netherlands, to bestow a more fitting appellation, as she said. As I was added as the third in the group, we were named, within our private circle of intimacy, after the Bible expression, "The Way, the Truth, and the Life."

One afternoon when we were together, Diesterweg received a letter from Berlin concerning the projected Goethe foundation, which was to date from his hundredth birthday on the 28th of August of that year (1849), for which purpose committees had been organized in various cities. Diesterweg was a member of the Berlin committee, and told us how various were the views concerning the object of the foundation. I suggested an educational institution for the culture of genius, since the unfettering of the powers of genius in mankind was the best tribute that could be paid to Goethe's memory.

At first Diesterweg laughed, but after thinking awhile said, "It is not a bad idea. At the present time it will be for the advancement of the people, and it will also promote art. Donations for young artists are already proposed."

We conversed further on the subject, and Froebel, who had at first kept perfectly silent, kindled more and more as the plan was discussed, and said, "What if you, Frau von Marenholz, should try to win over the Grand Duke of Weimar for our idea? As honorary president of the Weimar committee he would have much weight."

I promised to undertake this commission, and found a willing listener in the prince, who was always enthusiastic for everything beautiful and good. Soon we had the Grand Duke, the Duchess Ida, the Princess Amalia, and others of the nobility of Weimar interested in our plan, which devoted the Goethe foundation to an educational institution, where those children who should manifest artistic gifts of a high order in the kindergarten that was to be connected with it should be furnished a complete education in the art for which they should show talent.

Diesterweg wrote a little essay, entitled "The Goethe Foundation," and I a "Summons" for the newspapers, in order to gain general concurrence in our plan.

Diesterweg said in his article: "We consecrate this institution to general human culture, and to art in particular. A foundation worthy of Goethe must be creative and productive at once, that is, it shall cultivate men into productive beings, who shall bring forth new creations in the field of art." And again: "What might not be the consequences if the dominion of acquired dead notions, and that intellectual servitude which has been propagated from generation to generation hitherto, could be completely banished, and man become once more his own teacher and his own educator?" "What Pestalozzi strove for his whole life long—the restoration of the sanctity of family life, the training of mothers to their educational vocation, the guidance and culture of women in general that they may take the fitting point of view for the educators of the human race—this is what he has accomplished, and for this he has found practical means," etc.

These words are significant of Diesterweg's high recognition of Froebel and his cause. Froebel also added to this paper the following lines:

"It is to be stated with special emphasis that, although art in its ideality is a pure end of itself, it is not disgraced by becoming a means of education. If the human race, above all the German nation, is to be brought to perfect living and likewise to the appreciation and the expression of art, the arts, as the ripe product of creativeness, must be protected by an educational system whose fundamental idea shall be to contemplate and treat man as a creative being. And therefore this educational system is worthy of being named as the object of a Goethe foundation."

This object especially occupied us for a long time, and there was some prospect of a favorable result. Nevertheless, this result was not reached. The majority of the members of the various committees knew too little of Froebel's methods to accept and efficiently support the proposals made by the Grand Duke in Weimar and Diesterweg in Berlin. The decisive majorities in such cases opposed; these majorities unfortunately do much harm to intellectual interests, since ideal aims can hardly be appreciated except by minorities.

At the end of August Diesterweg and I came, by invitation of the Duchess of Weimar, to celebrate the hundredth birthday of Goethe, and found the decision was already made. The money collected for the purpose of the foundation to Goethe was devoted to the aid of young artists of slender means. Through Liszt's influence in Weimar, the donations were specially bestowed upon musical artists. My struggles against it, during a visit on which we met at the Grand Duke's castle at Ettersburg, were all in vain. Liszt ever repeated that "One could not help genius yet in its swaddling clothes." It was not till a later time that I could convince him of the importance of Froebel's method; then he promised he would compose songs for the kindergarten, a promise which yet awaits its fulfilment.

Froebel, accustomed during his whole life to the disappointment of cherished hopes, knew how to comfort himself for the miscarriage of our plans. Besides his gratification at the fulfilment of another wish, he had joyfully informed me already in July, that he expected one of his earlier Keilhau pupils (Fraulein Levin), who would remain with him to undertake the permanent direction of his household and institution. Soon after she arrived, and (as Froebel expressed it) gave to his institution the stamp of family life, which in his view was of the highest importance to an institution for education.

With truly paternal love Froebel embraced all his pupils, who on their part felt the greatest love and gratitude to him. These affectionate relations in the institution touched everyone agreeably who entered Marienthal, and awakened the sympathies even of those standing farther off; and these sympathies were more and more strengthened in the walks taken in common in the beautiful environs of Liebenstein.

When I once expressed to Froebel how much I enjoyed the feeling of real familiarity that I found in our circle, he said, "Yes, you see that it is only possible where there is an idea to bind us together; only an idea can make us spiritually one."

He said this in a drive which we took to Inselsberg in company with his pupils and Diesterweg. We did not return until night, and then in a wagon. The clear, bright, starry heavens prompted Froebel to point out the constellations to his pupils, and to speak of the system of worlds sparkling above us. He said, among other things: "The firmament, if anything leads us to recognize the connection of all that is, and leads us up to unity—God. No one of the heavenly bodies is isolated, every planet has its centre in the sun of its system. All the solar systems are in relation and continual interaction with each other. That is the condition of all life. Everywhere mutual relation of parts. As there above in great things an unbroken connection and harmony rule, so also here below, even in the smallest thing, everywhere is the same order and harmony, because the same law rules everywhere, the one law of God, which expresses itself in thousand-fold many-sidedness, but in the last analysis is one, for God is himself the law. The heavenly bodies are organized like the grains of sand—the macrocosm and the microcosm correspond to each other exactly; both are organized wholes, but the organization rules from the simplest to the most complex. Everywhere in God's creation, in the infinite manifoldness of phenomena, we always come upon unity, and must infer it where we do not perceive it. Unless unity is continued, unbroken connection is not possible."

Diesterweg here said, "That is what people call Pantheism."

Froebel replied: "And very unjustly; the pantheistic view is outgrown, and we have nothing more to do with an inseparable Unity, but with Trinity. Trinity has become the cornerstone which the people have rejected because they do not understand it. The triple Unity of God is obvious in all his works, to eyes that can see. Have we not always and everywhere a trinity of contrasts and their intermedium? And where are the contrasts which somewhere and somehow have not their intermedium and union? These contrasts, which everywhere appear, are the causes of all movement in the universe or in the least organism (action and reaction). Hence for all development there is a necessary struggle, which sooner or later, however, must find its equilibrium. This equilibrium is the intermedium of the contrasts which creates the harmony or accord in all the parts of a whole. This harmony is the flowering-time of every organism, which is found in the intellectual as well as in the material world. Does not every plant show us the connection of contrasts—inner and outer, force and matter, cause and operation, the visible and the invisible, etc.? But I do not say, like the Pantheists, that the world is God's body, that God dwells in it as in a house. But the spirit of God dwells and lives in nature, produces, fosters, and unfolds everything, as the common life-principle. In like manner the spirit of God dwells in his work, produces, fosters, and preserves it. As the spirit of the artist is found again in his masterpieces, so must we find God's spirit (Geist) in his works.*

"We have to open the eyes of our children, that they may learn to know the Creator in his creations. Only when they have found or divined God as the Creator, through visible things, will they learn to understand the 'Word of God'—God in spirit and in truth—and be able to become Christians. First is the visible world, then the invisible truth—the idea. These contrasts of visible and invisible are to be intermediated (connected) for the very young child, not by words, only by phenomena, which at first give him but an impression of it. My 'Mother and Cosset Songs' show how this can be done. [See the "Gilt Bird," the "Weather-Cock," etc.] Through them the mother learns how the soul of the child can be prepared early for the perception of truth. Without religious preparation in childhood, no true religion and no union with God is possible for men. Faith in God is innate in every man, every child; it has only to be awakened in the right way, but it must be awakened, or it remains dead." In this manner we conversed for a long time, and out of all that Froebel said shone the deepest trust in God, the most sincere and religious mind. He concurred very little with the conventional religious training of children, but he had something of his own to put in the place of that to which he did not agree.

Asking Froebel why he chose the tree especially to symbolize organization and the universal process of development even in the intellectual world, he replied: "No more perfect representation of organic life and the mutual relation of its parts can be found in nature than in a tree. The seed (unity) divides in the germ into duality (difference or opposition), and all the various stages of development follow definitely and clearly to full com-

*See further in Froebel's *The Education of Man*. It is only possible here to quote short fragments of our conversations, to which I am led by circumstances of the moment. It is of greater importance not always to be confined to Froebel's often obscure manner of expressing himself.

pletion. The roots and the crown are the opposite equivalents, for the crown planted in the earth forms roots because it lacks the light. The roots turned up and exposed to the light form themselves into a crown. These two related opposites in the tree phenomena are connected by the trunk, which contains within itself the material of the woody root, and the sap which is diffused through the crown. In the articulation of the twigs and leaves we have the type of all articulation, the great and small boughs and twigs, even to the mass of the leaves connected with them and receiving life from them.

"In like manner is expressed the necessary articulation of human society and the organization of the state. The unity which appears in all parts, from the least to the greatest, gives to the tree its individuality. For instance, the peculiar mellowness and delicacy of the odor of the Linden is found again in the tenderness of the leaf-texture, in the flexibility and softness of the wood, and also of the roots; every part expresses the same characteristic; even the taste of the blossoms and leaves. On the contrary, the oak expresses an opposite character. Everything in that bears the mark of power and concentration—the gnarled root, the bark of the trunk, the thick, firm substance of the wood, the hardness of the leaves, and the acrid taste of the fruit. Both of the trees bear the common marks of their kind, the *universal* of the tree, but each in its mode, that is, the *particular.*

"Thus we see unity (that which is common to all the parts), variety (in the diversity of the parts), and a particular (the individual, expressing the personal character of the tree) united and clearly made evident in the phenomenon of the tree. On this account it is the most expressive symbol of all organization, whether of natural or of intellectual life. Jesus also likened humanity to the tree in the expression, 'the tree of humanity.'"

These deeper aspects of Froebel's idea and theory could only be drawn from him occasionally; but as soon as he touched upon the first principles of his conception of the world on which his educational idea rested, his expression and his formula became absolutely precise, as was shown in his letters to myself. He also knew how to express himself in the clearest manner upon Christianity and its most profound dogmas. Concerning the application of his educational idea and the carrying it out in practical life, he was least able to make himself clear, because he attempted it by means of innumerable circumlocutions. One reason for this lay in the fact that his mind was wholly occupied in a labor which he was far from having completed—a labor which will require many lives and long years for its consummation. Another reason might be, that the experience of seldom being correctly understood induced him to add to his already peculiar style of speech frequent repetitions, and various expressions of the same thought, from which the opposite of the intended clearness resulted. For this reason chiefly are Froebel's writings so little intelligible and throughout not popularly written; at the same time it must be remembered that new thoughts and new theories cannot be made equally clear to every one.

Even Diesterweg often found it difficult to understand Froebel's thoughts, but this great educator never permitted himself, like some of his colleagues, to condemn Froebel's cause and to cast it aside because there were some things in it that were not clear to him. He often said to me, "What I understand of Froebel's idea is enough to prevent me from rejecting a subject many sides of which have been but little worked out. There is much still to be made clear in the matter. The material already prepared for its practical application is excellent. In that Froebel's thought is expressed clearly. It must be further worked out into the school where Froebel and Pestalozzi meet."

Sometimes when I urged upon Diesterweg that he should study more deeply Froebel's method and means of work, in order to explain their application in his writings, he replied, "That is not for me, but for others, to do. I, as a schoolman, have my problem to solve in regard to Pestalozzi," (and who will assert that he has not solved it?) He also said, "It is for women—mothers and kindergartners—to carry out Froebel's method in its practical application to earliest childhood. Their fitness to direct in this first step of education is recognized; then comes the second step, the fusing of it with Pestalozzi's method for the school. But I am too old to undertake this. I already have more work than I have strength for. To each his own. But I will help in single cases, if you will tell me where and how."

Froebel and Diesterweg were contrasts not only in personal appearance; their mental gifts and their employment of them showed a certain contrast. Froebel's long, lean form was the opposite of Diesterweg's short, broad, and thickset body. Froebel's features were sharp and angular; Diesterweg's round and full. Both had the arched nose, but Froebel's was more prominent. His expression of countenance was more deeply thoughtful, and absorbed in himself, while a keen observation of outward things and at the same time a jovial expression characterized Diesterweg. Froebel had but little critical faculty outside of his own subject, while Diesterweg possessed it in a high degree in all directions; and although both minds worked in the same field, it was in very different ways. While Diesterweg was recognized master in the field of instruction and its methods, Froebel's special problem was that of education in general, the development of the whole man, and with special reference to the formation of character, the preparation for acting and producing. This aim was with him the most important in creating a new educational beginning in the earlier years of life. Diesterweg worked with Pestalozzi more to form the understanding; Froebel more for forming the will and the active powers. Diesterweg personally influenced the immediate present by his preeminently practical genius in the field of pedagogics; while Froebel's influence will only make itself fully felt in the future. Those who, like Froebel, are favored with a new idea, are a burning-glass for higher inspirations, for which they have to wait; and their work is so wholly inward it rarely allows them, in their lifetime, to have great authority in the outside world. Besides, Froebel was a discoverer, and such must always work in silence till everything is perfected for outward application.

If these two great souls were in many respects contrasts to

each other, they were yet inwardly united in other respects. Both were men of deep feeling, warm beating hearts, profound, original natures, who knew that they had accepted service in the ranks of humanity, and who, with entire self-renunciation, worked and suffered for it throughout their whole lives.

I have always looked upon my intimacy with these two lofty minds and excellent men, and my association in their great and noble work of education, as a rare happiness.

4

Middendorff

I looked forward with great interest to Middendorff's visit, knowing of him already from Froebel's account, and that he possessed in him his truest friend and companion, who had accompanied him on his life-path, and had shared labor and pain with him for more than thirty years. "He is a childlike man," said Froebel, "who understands me with his heart." Both had been soldiers in Lutzow's free corps, and at the beginning of the campaign of 1813 had found each other out and established a friendship—one of those rare friendships which endure for life, and therefore will last beyond it.

One afternoon in September Froebel came to my house and introduced his friend with the words: "Here is Middendorff." Who that had once seen that presence, simple, plain, and yet arousing full sympathy, could ever forget it? With the first glance of the eyes and clasp of the hands we were friends.

Like Froebel, Middendorff belonged to that class of men who are represented in our time only by rare types; who appear in the modern world as forms out of the past, and not belonging to the present. This type expresses in its nature the honest, true, steadfast, genuine German, combined with that innocent childlikeness and heartiness, knowing no guile because incapable of deceiving, and forms the sharpest contrast to the worldly craftiness, and empty, critical intellectualism of the men of our day. A beautiful simplicity in the highest sense of the word, the inheritance of a bygone generation, characterized Middendorff. Great tenderness of nature gave him an almost feminine stamp. To conquer all opposition with love, to harmonize discords, to veil faults when they could not be cured, to see the better side in dark days, to trust the all-powerful Providence with pious devotion—all this, united with a childlike cheerfulness, gave him the ideal stamp of a soul-keeper, that floats before us out of the past, and here and there may still be seen by us in some real village pastor.

Therefore was Middendorff truly Froebel's good angel during his earthly pilgrimage; he always tried to soothe and to equalize, and was a peacemaker in the wide family circle when that was necessary.

In spite of these characteristic traits of the past, yet Middendorff was one of the spirits longing for a renovation; one of those so completely penetrated with that modern impulse for higher development, that no youthful spirit could pursue promising inducements with more fire, or give himself up to them with more ideal elevation. Froebel's motto, "the renovation of life," had taken complete possession of Middendorff's soul; and the disappointments which at that time followed so closely after this elevation could not rob him of his fair hopes, that, even if they had to traverse a wilderness first, the promised land of a better time and an ennobled humanity would nevertheless be reached. His hopes rested on children—"children worthily educated in truth," who would in the future victoriously maintain the contest against all kinds of savagery, rudeness, vice, and cowardice, and thus be enabled to gain freedom through morality, and to behold the dawn of more beautiful days. This was to him an incontestable certainty, of which he was often able to convince doubters by his inspiring words. He could not doubt the grandeur of human nature, which mirrored itself in his own soul.

How would this fresh, youthful old man have rejoiced had he lived to see the victories of Germany of today!

But he was happy, nevertheless, in his own day, since it was given to him to see everything in the shimmer of beauty—everywhere, in great and perfected things as well as in the smallest and most hidden, God's holy creation and his guidance. His communion with nature, like Froebel's, as always worship of God, and awakened in him the poetical mood, which on our walks often took the form of verse. These I would find the next morning upon my table. Without being masterpieces in form, such a truly poetical nature was expressed in these unassuming little poems that they warmed up the recipient and lighted up the little incidents and impression of our Liebenstein circle. In this little circle, where from all sides streamed upon him honor, love, and trust in full measure, he was always well and happy.

And Froebel, too, was always happy and exhilarated in Middendorff's presence. He exchanged with him every feeling of the soul, every thought upon all the circumstances of their life. Nothing could destroy that intimate friendship, not even occasional undeniable disagreements, or rather incomplete comprehension of Froebel's idea and its consequences on the part of Middendorff. Froebel used to say, "Middendorff seizes everything with his feelings, even the idea. He is all devotion. Without him we could not have attained what we have attained." These were words of deep acknowledgment out of Froebel's mouth. Yes, without Middendorff, Froebel perhaps would not have come out unbroken from the storms and disappointments of his life.

Middendorff, in this union of souls, was the feminine half, which, comforting and softening, stands by the side of the manly strength, so that the storm may not break it, and it may learn to bow to the immutable. Good judgment of things, severe criticism of men and circumstances, were often out of proportion to this predominance of benevolence and goodness of heart. He was hardly capable of understanding evil in others, for he always brought forward extenuating circumstances. Even in judging Froebel's scholars, both he and Middendorff were not seldom deceived by their hopeful and embellishing benevolence. They thought they saw much significance and many promising capacities where at most a lively sympathy and devotion to the cause existed.

But certainly not one of the pupils of the Liebenstein or Marienthal schools has forgotten how Middendorff's visits always brought an innocent, poetical serenity, one might say, a holy state of mind, and how well he knew the way at once to enliven and to elevate them. When, in our customary walks, we saw the sun go down, Middendorff would take out a little songbook and intone a hymn to the sun, in which the young girls would all join, or at least sing the *refrain*. If plants and flowers were woven into wreaths and crowns, he used their admiration and wonder to interest them in the wisdom of creation, and to apply its laws to human life.

The symbolism of things was always attractive to Middendorff, and his explanations and comparisons were always sensuous. It was his deep—and, for a man, rare—sensibility that gave him so great power to influence the female mind, and made him the best interpreter of Froebel's genius. What Froebel created was adopted by Middendorff, worked out with the deepest devotion, and generally given back in an intelligible form; and with what perseverance, with what unflinching courage and unwavering fidelity, did he defend Froebel's idea from the very beginning, even in the narrowest circles, where he found only a glimpse of understanding, and against the often mocking or entirely condemnatory criticism of some teachers and pedagogical authorities, who had never given themselves the trouble to learn the theory and the praxis of Froebel's method! If ever anyone understood how to bring out the ideal of the peculiar nature hidden in every man, then Middendorff knew how to draw Froebel's into the light, and to overlook the human weaknesses and separate them from the genius. Every utterance of this genius he accepted as an oracle; and if there were some things not entirely clear to him, he used to say, "There must be something in that; I will work it out: it will fit in with the rest," etc.

In one of my evening walks with Middendorff I said to him, "By means of Froebel's doctrine and education men will be brought to understand the visible creation as a symbol of the mental, and find the confirmation by experience of what we call *revelation*. Truth is always the same, whether science digs it out of the things of nature, the material world, or a mind of higher enlightenment receives it through the immediate inspiration of genius. It only needs that we learn to understand the language of things (i.e., the original nature of things) in order that we may compare them with that which is original in the mind—with thought. Then we can explain contradictions which are only apparent. This solution abolishes the dualism which exists in the first theory, which is valid only with respect to the incomplete, the relative of all actuality, but not with respect to the truth, *as such*—the absolute.

"An education which, at the start, enables the human mind to see the connection and the originating and finally effective unity of things, must contribute to abolish that dual mode of perception which is called forth by the antitheses and contradictions in the facts of real life, and its incomplete and changing phenomena. This education by and with things themselves, this dealing with the concrete, will help to build the bridge between the material and the intellectual, between the real and the ideal, the universe and God; and in that way will lay the foundation in the childish mind for a religious view of the universe.

"It is certainly a great defect in the present religious teaching that it dwells always, by preference, upon the apparent difference or opposition of nature and spirit, instead of making prominent in the child's mind at first, at least, the harmony and the resolution of differences, which is the goal set by God. The child's eye always, at first, seizes the analogous, the point of union, the whole connection of things, and only after that begins to discern differences and opposition.

"In our time men seem to have forgotten nature in favor of spirit, and objects in favor of abstractions; the word is separated from the thing, and governs; and generally, only as a mere empty word, is not understood. It is quite clear to me that Froebel's method and doctrine will reverse this process, and first connect facts with the outer and inner experience as their root and their cause. Thus only can the spirit of truth, which is the spirit of God, again be recognized as one and the same, in nature and in the mind. Froebel's idea of education strives to bring to the full consciousness of men their relations to nature (the divine nature), and thereby must the relation of men to God (in the spirit) and to all that is divine, as Christianity teaches, be lifted to higher and clearer recognition. One side of truth verifies and explains the other side.

"The ruling tendency of our time towards nature and things, and the interests of actual life, will be obliged to serve identical purposes. In spite of the reverse side, the errors and coarse degeneracy bound up therewith, this tendency is one necessary for the process of development, willed by God, and it will reach its goal, even though in a roundabout way, through a deeper knowledge of human nature, and bridge over the great gulf between the spiritual and material world.

"This agreement of the idea of Froebel with the needs and the legitimate and higher strivings of the present day for progress and reform signalizes it as a *divine idea*. The right carrying out of this new idea of education will, more than anything else, help to conquer crude materialism, and to break the path for idealism to harmonize with the practical actuality, and bring the real and ideal life again into accord."

Middendorff looked at me with beaming eyes, and replied: "You have spoken to me out of the soul; so have I also explained the idea. I will now give you a view which I have never before expressed in words to anyone. This idea of the unity of nature could only have been worked out and prepared for an educational application by a mind that had experienced this truth within itself and lived it out. Froebel has lived in unbroken union with nature; the human weaknesses and defects which are also his inheritance have not hindered this union. Only through God's special ordering could this happen, and therein lies an inexpressible comfort, in view of the evils and woe of humanity. You are right. One truth must ever confirm another; the recognized truth will be more clearly and deeply understood through every new one discovered. The spirit of Christianity, so very much misunderstood and mistaken at present, will awaken to new life in children, and appear in a new and a higher light when Froebel's idea of education has been practically applied. This is my deepest conviction."

"But how," I replied, "can we make this connection between the greatest and the smallest intelligible by means of child's play? how connect the deep idea with so insignificant a form? I confess that I do not see. As the world is at present, it would laugh at us if we should express such views aloud, and yet I own that I cannot be satisfied with the mere practical external side of the subject if I am to devote myself entirely to it."

Middendorff replied: "This is, however, the only way; in all humility to nourish the smallest, and scatter seed which in the future, perhaps long after we shall be no more, will spring up. But to tend the human germs in a constantly progressive manner, in every new stage of human development, is certainly no mean calling, but the greatest and most important for every generation."

"I see this very well," was my answer, "but every mind needs to unfold and live itself out, and would like to leave behind in this life some work of its own, either small or great, according to the measure of its powers. The highest satisfaction, it seems to me, is given by an independent work of beauty, in which one's own mind has mirrored itself. Everyone who bears something in his soul which he is driven by inner impulse to express—an impulse he cannot silence, for it always awakens anew with irresistible power, demanding a hearing—is bound to utter that word; it is the command of God; and if one has desired and striven for this work without appending his own name to it, we may be sure that the motive of it is a higher one than personal vanity. Ought one, however, to sacrifice one's own idea, the children of one's own mind, to represent the ideas of another? Yet, on the other hand, I see plainly that it is far more useful to work for human society on a large scale, and to educate for it in the young generation of this and the following age better men, braver citizens, and greater geniuses. Instead of offering the work of one mind, a thousand greater and more various works will be prepared, if the divine spark of creativeness shall be awakened and more perfectly fostered in the present and future generations than has hitherto been done. All this is undeniable; but it requires in some degree the sacrifice of our own growth and progress, and hence the decision is not easy."

Just at this moment Froebel joined us, and asked the subject of our long conversation. We told him the last part of it, upon which he said, turning to me, "In such questions the inner necessity decides. Whoever has actually recognized a truth that concerns mankind as a whole, must confess and serve it, whether he wishes to or not. This inner necessity will compel you, as you will find. Nothing in the world is attainable without sacrifice; and when one can promote a universal good, the individual (Froebel called it the *particular*) must yield, even if it were the best and the highest accomplishment. When our country is in danger, all those capable of bearing arms must enter into the conflict, however much of intellect and talent is lost by it; and to work in the service of humanity stands higher than to perform any individual thing."

"You are right," said I. "The whole is indeed better than a part. No one can estimate more highly than I do the idea which will awaken creative power in mankind in every direction, and lift thoughts into *deeds*. But will it ever be possible to rid the world of *Philistines* and puppets? I do not believe it."

"By no means," replied Froebel; "that must not be. Every ship needs its ballast, and if we had no Philistines (as you call them), how could the world go on? who would attend to everyday cares and business? Every work needs special powers. Nature provides all necessary powers, and human education must develop them, each one according to its kind, forbidding that the most and best be lost, as hitherto; and that shall prevent men from working like beasts of burden, unconscious of their dignity. An education which does not try to raise roses from thistle-bushes will wisely use all talents and dispositions, and bring each man into his proper place, out of which he will not desire to go. My educational method, in its right application, can surely attain this end—that is to say, gradually, step by step. If we do not force nature, or drive it in a direction opposite to its peculiar bent; if we recognize its general law, and give each particular power its free development, and all the support and care it needs, as an intelligent gardener does with his plants, then will the human powers be better able to bring forth their blossoms. But as the plant grows through its own vital power, so also must human power become great through its own exercise and effort. Only let there be no outside forcing or supporting. Everything in nature remains in its own place, and there fulfils its destiny; the grass will not become a tree nor the insect a bird. The same harmony can be reached in the human world, so that every one can follow his own calling, can work and live. To reach the unconscious harmony of nature with consciousness in the human sphere, is the goal which God has set for man. Battle, strife, war, dissension, pain, error, *sin*, are all to be means to this end. There is no lack of conflict in nature; no intermediation without opposites; no harmony without resolution of discords; no perfection without labor, and without effort to overcome impediments and obstacles. All this Jesus has taught us. But teaching and insight alone do not reach it; it must be enacted as Jesus enacted it. We must educate the children to doing and acting if they are to become in truth Christians."

"And the greatest share in such education belongs to women; in that we are all agreed," said Middendorff. "Women must make of their educational calling a priestly office."

We had now arrived at the door of my dwelling, which brought our conversation to an end. And far into the night I was writing supplementary and explanatory commentaries upon it.

"Your Middendorff is a glorious man," said the Duchess Ida, after she had heard him speak on kindergartens the first time; "he speaks from his heart so warmly that one has to agree with him."

We were especially indebted to this warm impression for the lottery, whose proceeds were to serve for the foundation of a kindergarten in Liebenstein. This was so richly sustained with presents and sympathy that it soon gave actual life to the undertaking, and the largest gifts were from the Princesses, the Duchess of Meiningen, her sister Caroline of Hesse, and the Duchess Ida.

When Froebel and Middendorff saw the table covered with the gifts, some of which were beautiful works of art, Middendorff said, with great feeling, "These gifts of love should encourage us to hold firmly by the faith that the work will not fail of its necessary support, though we may often ask in many places in vain. Even the very small encouragement which my memorial on the kindergarten received from the National Association at Frankfort did not discourage me.* The time will come when they will know that the education of the people from the earliest period of childhood is the first necessary condition of bringing about the political and moral freedom of nations."

"Yes, the time will come," I replied, "when the immediate connection between the political reforms that are striven for and these demands of education will be recognized and appreciated; but we can scarcely live to see it, since politics have so much absorbed the minds of men that this modest planting for the sake of childhood has been overlooked."

"Then we must plant so many of these nurseries all over Germany that they cannot be overlooked," said Middendorff.

"I will give you my hand to work for that," I said, "and whoever understands the time knows that work is not mere talking, or even thinking, but includes *acting*. Let us go and see a house that I think will do for our kindergarten."

Weimar, too, has to thank Middendorff for the interest taken by the court in the kindergarten. Through my influence he received an invitation to come up from Keilhau for a few days in the fall of 1849, and give two lectures. One of these, in a public meeting,

*Middendorff had read a paper before the National Association of 1848; and later his son-in-law, Dr. W. Lange, edited it under the title, "Wilhelm Middendorff upon the Kindergarten"; and it was published in Hamburg, by Hoffman & Co., in 1861.

aroused the interest of a large number of hearers to a high pitch, and laid the foundations for the support of a kindergarten opened in Weimar in the following year. The other lecture was delivered at the Grand Duke's, in the select court circle, and helped me to gain this support of their Highnesses for the furthering of Froebel's cause, and especially for the introduction of his "occupations" into the asylums under the protection of the then reigning Grand Duchess (a Russian princess).

When Middendorff stood in the private court circle for the first time, so simple, so unaffected, and yet so firm, and, according to his habit, with half-closed eyes, uttering those words which well up from the heart and penetrate to the hearts of all, and in that circle so unaccustomed to plain simplicity, the Grand Duke, who was himself so easily interested in all that is good, exclaimed, "What an excellent, inspiring man!"

"Did I do it properly?" asked Middendorff of me, when he had ended. With my whole soul I could say, "Yes."

In the following summer (1850) we met again at Liebenstein, to know each other still better. The course of these reminiscences will again lead us back to Middendorff, and some beautiful things have been contributed to the characterization of him by W. Lange; and still later by Hanschmann, in his *Memoirs of Friedrich Froebel*. Diesterweg also, in his *Rheinische Blättern*, published some fragments upon Middendorff, one of which I myself contributed at Diesterweg's request.

5

The Summer of 1850 in Liebenstein

After having returned to Liebenstein in June, 1850, I found Froebel settled with his school at Marienthal, and among his scholars was a daughter of Diesterweg. Already in the spring of this year he had mentioned to me his removal, and written to me with delight of his new home, ornamented with flowers and wreaths by the hands of his scholars, and in which he felt truly happy and full of hope.

But there is upon earth no light without a shadow, and shadows were not wanting here. Froebel had accepted an invitation from the Women's Union of Hamburg, and had spent the past winter months in that city, and given a course on his educational method. Middendorff had paved the way for him, as he so often did, by some essays which awakened a lively interest there, and Froebel had received the liveliest welcome from a very large circle. His letters to me had acknowledged this and extolled the zeal of his pupils. But what was disagreeable and disturbing to him, and affected him painfully, was the founding of a high school for the female sex, which struck out other paths for the advancement the time demanded for them than those he had pointed out to be the true ones for that purpose.

At that time, and for a quarter of a century, the idea of the emancipation of women had stirred the minds of many women in a high degree, and often drove even the best into false directions, though they were not, however, on that account guilty of the absurdities and perversities of the so-called "emancipated." It is certain that the best and most distinguished women of our country have felt an intense longing after advancement out of the subordinate position formerly assigned to them, and they greeted with joy the movement of our day for enfranchisement.

But at that time the requisite means for the end were not yet seen with clearness. Too much was aimed at at once, without due consideration of the actual development in the majority of women. A demand was made from many sides for a complete external equality of women with the male sex, without considering that the difference of the sexes, so clearly designed by nature, pointed out a different destiny for each, and that only the higher fulfilment of the duties of this destiny would bring them up to the position of equality with men, without, however, involving the same rights, duties, and functions. External independence without corresponding self-poise and self-command leads to destruction. Moreover, there was an attempt to counterbalance the deficient formation of the understanding by a mere increase of knowledge, without the requisite foundation of intellectual habits, which only brings *sham knowledge*, and takes away the greatest treasure of womanhood, her originality and innocence. Even philosophical studies belonged to the proposed programme of the high school, which, even if they could be given to exceptional persons, in an exceptional manner, were only suited to years of intellectual maturity, not to the youthful age to which is natural only belief in truth.

It was, meanwhile, very conceivable that then, when the solution of the woman question was yet in its first beginning, the right track should not be immediately found by the able directors of the institution (Professor Karl Froebel, a nephew of Froebel's, and his wife, with the members of the Women's Union), although they were full of intellect, energy, enthusiasm, and practical ability.

There was yet necessary a longer experience, which might modify and make clear the prevailing views; and this is, indeed, still needed, for at present the woman question is to be decided, more or less, only by experiments, which are demanded for the development of everything new; and on the threshold of this subject a continual pressing external necessity has directed the first attention to women's skill in work, and the material side of the subject. The school is still seeking for the improved cultivation of the female mind, to meet the demands of the time, but without having yet perfectly found them. So there is more need of trials and experiments. Undeniably much good has already been reached, many good steps have been taken; but also many a shadow has fallen, and among these—a not always agreeable *realism*—also an accumulation of trivial acquirements, which has injured genuine womanhood.

Certainly by every forward step the inevitable one-sidedness of all progress much gradually be vanquished, if the female sex is to be lifted according *to its inner nature* into the proper place for it, at the present stage of human development. But one of the necessary requisites for this is the new beginning of human culture according to Froebel's idea, and the fitting of the female sex to work out this idea as mothers and teachers.

Froebel could not therefore befriend the one-sided experiment, on account of his deep conviction that the first principles of the science of motherhood taught by him must lie at the foundation of the elevation of the female sex, conformably with truth and its own nature.

Already in the fall of the last year he had spoken to me with disapproval of the Hamburg project of the high school as running counter to his endeavors. It followed, therefore, that on my arriving at Liebenstein this year it became the first subject of our conversations.

After I had expressed to Froebel that I thought the age unquestionably demanded arrangements for the higher education of women, and that if the first attempts made might not be all that could be desired they would pave the way for better things and things more adapted to the end, he burst out, not without vehemence:

"But what good will come out of this knowledge, stamped and cemented upon the outside, which is, indeed, no knowledge at all, for it conceals and defaces the real human nature like a parti-colored patch? All that does not grow out of one's inner being, all that is not one's own original feeling and thought, or at least awakens that, oppresses and defaces the individuality of man instead of calling it forth, and nature becomes thereby a caricature. Shall we never cease to stamp human nature, even in childhood, like coins? to overlay it with foreign images and foreign superscriptions, instead of letting it develop itself and grow into form according to the law of life planted in it by God, the Father, so that it may be able to bear the stamp of the divine, and become an image of God? For hundreds of years we Germans especially, through imitation of foreign nations, have worn these fetters, which do not allow the deepest nature of the people or of individuals to move and unfold freely. But shall we, therefore, never make a beginning of allowing a tree of life to germinate in each one's own heart, and a tree of knowledge in each one's own mind, taking care for its beautiful unfolding, that it may bring forth fresh and healthy flowers and ripe fruits, which shall take root in this world and shall germinate again in the other? Shall we never banish the fear that minds ripened through their own observation, their own experience, and their own thinking, will be able to overthrow those universal truths which, in the course of history, have been unfolded and sanctioned by revelation? Can what is true ever be overthrown? Can this individual mind, in its original power, find other truth than the universal mind? And are not the errors of one and of another always, in the progress of development, turned again into the right path? Does not God's providence always again send guides who lead back into this right path and illuminate it?

"But I will protect childhood, that it may not, as in earlier generations, be pinioned, as in a strait-jacket, in garments of custom and ancient prescription that have become too narrow for the new time. I shall show the way and shape the means, that every human soul may grow of itself out of its own individuality. But where shall I find allies and helpers if not in women, who, as mothers and teachers, may put my idea in execution? Only intellectually active women can and will do it. But if these are to be loaded with the ballast of dead knowledge that can take no root in the unprepared ground, if the fountains of their own original life are to be choked up with it, they will not follow my direction nor understand the call of the time for the new task of their sex, but will seek satisfaction in empty superficiality.

"To learn, to comprehend nature in the child, is not that to comprehend one's own nature and the nature of mankind? And in this comprehension is there not involved a certain degree of comprehension of all things else? Women cannot learn and take into themselves anything higher and more comprehensive. It should therefore at least be the beginning, and the love of childhood should be awakened in the mind (and, in a wider sense, this is the love of humanity), so that a new, free generation of men can grow up by right care.

"Instead of diffusing, before all other things, the knowledge necessary for the welfare of future generations—that is, that the human mind is already choked in the germ by the burdensome crowd of notions heaped up and patched on foreign to it, rooted in nothing within, we foolishly strive to increase them still more!

"And what else will these high schools do with their surfeit of the mere culture of the understanding, and superficial word-cramming, which they call philosophy? They ruin everything for me, and shall I lift a finger to support such things? It is impossible! I cannot and never will consent. I know my way which God himself has pointed out to me, and I must remain in it even were all the world against me."

Froebel expressed this his deepest conviction with great excitement. I had for the most part entire sympathy with him, and I answered:

"I most certainly share your opinion that we shall never be able to remedy the evils of our system of education by the mere accumulation of knowledge. The originality of human nature must be rescued; the real, inner self of each individuality allowed to appear freely, in order that at least the more gifted and stronger souls may not be stamped with the impress of mediocrity, or wear themselves out in pain because they are not suited to live in a conventional manner among men of wood (*schablonen-menschen*). If anyone knows this pain of not being able to give out his best, most individual self, without being misunderstood and branded as a heretic by the common superficiality of even intelligent people, he will become your ally in preserving and unfolding the originating power of mankind.

"That your mode of education by creating and producing from the earliest childhood, through one's own experience and knowledge of things and objects, is one of the first and principal conditions for this, I am fully convinced, and on that account chiefly I shall be compelled to help the work. At least let it be asked *how* we are to educate, instead of everlastingly repeating what is to be attained.

"Woman's nature has unquestionably retained the stamp of its originality and spontaneity better than that of man. She owes this largely to the smaller measure of mere knowledge that has been forced upon her, and this is at least one advantage of the ignorance in which the sex has been left. But the most original element of the woman's soul is maternal love, which at no stage of development and in no decline of the human race can belie the stamp of the holiest nature. This love, the strongest of all human love, assures victory to your educational work, for it will understand and learn to apply your idea with the heart, however long it may wait for the full recognition of it.

"But why are you opposed to the founding of such institutions as this high school, when you yourself recognize experience as the best master? Let the matter take its course, and the reasonable persons among its founders will change and improve many things, and gradually find the right way. Until the children of the kindergarten grow up, we shall not have those originally growing natures that can stand on their own feet, and will know how to work out and make their own that which is enjoined by authority. The mass of the men of the present day understand only the old accustomed way of teaching, and need leading-strings and acquired wisdom. While for this reason there are not yet original men, we must let them follow the impulse of their time in their own way. They will produce much that is useful and healthy, and provide for the necessities and enjoyments of the moment sufficiently. Must we not always have with us men of the future, men of the present, and even men of the past, so that that connection in time may not be wanting, the recognition of which you consider the first condition of right education and unity of view?

"Those women who have defective or scanty intellectual natures we shall not win to our cause; they must go their own way. They will be attracted externally to the great and brilliant incidents of the time, but they will not work for the little ones or for the humble cause which will only become great after they have left the stage. You say yourself that every one has his own—and a different—problem to solve. The present movement draws women in another direction than the one in which you would have them go. They are striving to free themselves from the narrowness of their home life, and they think the educational office required by you would condemn them to the greater limitation of the nursery. I have had some experience in this matter within the last few months. A universal enthusiasm of women for their mission as educators of humanity is unattainable in our time. The majority of women will take advantage of the more elevated and independent positions opened to the sex, and enjoy having their influence and making it felt, and they will not give themselves up to work for future generations.

"How can you expect women to look at things from an elevated standpoint, when their previous education and position have tended almost exclusively to folly and externality, if they have not been forced to labor like beasts of burden? Only those who have suffered deeply and severely, who have learned under the heavy pressure of a life's experience to overcome and sacrifice personal ease, will undertake such a duty as to labor for future times. It is only the few who live and work with a conscious aim. But the instinct of motherly love will impel many among the mass of average women to offer you the hand of fellowship, and further your work for the sake of their own children. We can count most securely on them for the support of the necessary outward arrangements, but not for a deep comprehension of the spiritual meaning of our cause."

"That may be true," said Froebel. "Everything that happens in the world is far more the result of unconscious impulse than of clear thought. But the time has come—a new stage of life—when the buds on the tree of humanity must open, whence will come a new impelling force which will not rest, but will awaken the intellect and spirits of men in different degrees. Whether in the heart as faith or in the mind as sight, it matters not if it only awakes. But you, will you continue in this work which is to renew and rejuvenate human life through the right nurture of children?"

"Certainly I will, as far as in me lies," was my answer. "It has often seemed to me as if I saw the genius of humanity struggling desperately in many children's souls, as well as in those of maturer youth, to live out externally the divine ideas it has brought into the world, to bring its ideal to the light in deeds, and to evolve its undeveloped, fermenting, creative force. In vain it stretches out its arms for a leader, in vain lifts its wings to rise into the heaven of the beautiful, the good, and the true; the earthly weight draws it down, the fetters laid on it from birth hinder and circumscribe its flight, and the dust of the surrounding atmosphere conceals the forms of light which had allured it. Then comes more and more the desire of enjoyment, which should seek something higher, and which takes the senses into its pay, and genius sinks extinguished in ordinary men, or becomes a Lucifer separated from its own ideal, turning itself away from God, its source.

"So have all human souls, devoted to the ideal, struggled in all time hitherto, always in the minority, the exceptions in the world whose careers have been ordered by the majority, according to its own needs and wishes. Supposing it to be true that the mass of people are necessary to the earth *as ballast*, and will never be extinct in spite of all culture, then progress can only be conceived of in this way, namely, that the time must come when those inspired by genius, the nobler souls of humanity, will be the majority and direct and govern life according to *its* needs and wishes.

"And if it should soon be that those who are now the exceptions shall no longer need to live as pariahs and martyrs, forced to submit to the vulgarity and arrogance of the masses, a complete transformation would have been effected! The law by which the higher must dominate and absorb the lower, or at least transform it, will lead necessarily to this result in the intellectual world. From the carrying out of your method of education, I expect immediately the awakening and unfolding of the creative powers in the souls of children to be the counterpoise to the perverse influence of generations of men bound into solidarity by the errors and sins of ancestors, and also to get rid of numberless roundabout and indirect ways in the labor and efforts which are necessary for reaching the general as well as the individual aims of everyone.

"If it should demand centuries in order fully to reach this end, to which the cooperation of very many other things besides is necessary, the object is so great and so beautiful that it is worthy of every effort. If we shall succeed in awakening countless divine sparks in humanity, then single ones will cease to shine preeminently.

"The more I understand your idea of education, the more I see the important influence women may exert upon the development of human society. If they are fitted by your science of motherhood to do for families in general, by means of an education consciously understood and adapted to the child's nature, what hitherto a few distinguished women only have been able to do, the foundation of at least universal morality will be laid. As the kindergarten and that which follows it in your method furnishes the elements of knowledge for all, by opening the outer and inner eye, preparing the way for original thinking, and already in childhood vanquishing aversion to labor by freely exercised powers and habits of continuous activity, there is a degree of culture attainable by everyone, and at the same time the way is opened for the more gifted to cultivate themselves further according to their powers and talents, and to rise to higher planes. More than this cannot be attained on account of the great differences of natural endowment, nor can more be reasonably demanded for the universal culture of the people. By it also the foundation will be laid for women to cultivate themselves more generally, according to their talents, and the exceptions to this rule can be of use in solving higher problems than the ordinary ones. Only when their own thoughts and modes of observation are allowed, or made possible, to the intellect of women, can it develop its own individuality to the fullest extent, and can the feminine genius really show what it can accomplish. This goal lies yet in the far distance, and great impediments will make it difficult of attainment, but it must be attained if there is to be any progress."

After we had discussed this subject still further, and had found ourselves generally in accordance, Froebel said: "Yes, women are my natural allies, and they ought to help me, for I bring to them what shall relieve them of their inner and outer fetters, terminate their tutelage, and restore their dignity with that of still undervalued childhood. But whoever will work with me must undertake a great deal, must suffer ridicule and blame, and let themselves be burnt or torn in pieces. Can you do that?"

"I hope I could do it; but if I should be burnt up I cannot do anything more for the cause," I said, laughing. At that time I knew nothing of the moral funeral pyres which awaited me because I defended the idea and method of Froebel against those who abused it for personal ends, or I should not have laughed.

6

Visit of Dr. Gustav Kühne

In the course of the summer many visitors, among them some well-known and distinguished men, came to Liebenstein, who sought out the "old friend" of children in Marienthal. Of this number was Dr. Gustav Kühne, the well-known poet and author, and at that time editor of the *Europa*. He entered into our small circle with true warmth of heart, and often brightened it with his sparkling humor.

Froebel and his efforts were known to him at that time only by hearsay, and in response to my first invitation to him to go to Marienthal, he said he had come to Liebenstein not to study new methods, but to give himself up to *dolce far niente* and the enjoyment of nature.

It was difficult at all times to induce the visitors at Liebenstein baths to go to Marienthal for the serious purpose of being converted to a new method, for the other walks were more attractive to the majority, and at a watering place people gladly avoid all intellectual exertion.

But one afternoon a few ladies and gentlemen made the plan of visiting the "Morgenthor" on the Altenstein, and calling at Marienthal on their return. Dr. Kühne joined the party without knowing of this last intention, and when, during the walk, I alluded to the projected visit to Froebel, he began to banter me about my enthusiasm for "panaceas for the redemption of the world," adding that every possible advantage which Froebel's method could include had its real basis in the idea and method of Pestalozzi, who had already uttered the word of our time for educational reform, and there was nothing to be done but to build further on that foundation.

"What more can Froebel desire," said he, "than an education conformed to nature from the cradle up, the grounding of all instruction upon observation, the union of physical labor with learning, the exclusion of all artificial support or the forcing of matters foreign and contradictory to child-nature? Pestalozzi has offered all this already."

"Froebel's method," I replied, "not only harmonizes with that of Pestalozzi, but receives into itself whatever is good and right in it, and not this only, but it has something new and different to offer. Moreover, I will add that I look neither upon Froebel's nor Pestalozzi's system as a 'panacea for the redemption of the world,' for I see very well that as it has been in former times, so it is now. Many various levers are needed to bring about the reforms demanded of the times. Therefore no irony.

"In my opinion, Pestalozzi and Froebel are laboring for the improvement of mankind in different fields, one of which is as important as the other. The general principles enunciated by them both were already set forth by their predecessors and recognized by all thinkers as just. But the main point is still the complete application of these principles. The practical means necessary and sufficient for this will be found only by degrees and through experience, by means of new prophets.

"Froebel's ideas with respect to the earliest education from the cradle up are quite different from those of Pestalozzi. They are founded on a new theory of the child's nature, even if they do not contradict Pestalozzi's, but the practical means to carry out his ideas are offered by Froebel, not by Pestalozzi; for by Froebel the instinct and educational intuition of the mother are first elevated to an intelligent mode of action, and the right means for this are presented to them.

"And that is an important factor if the earliest education is, in truth, to lay the foundation for all succeeding stages. There can be no such thing as education in the cradle, unless the object of it and the means for it are intelligently recognized and applied by mothers and teachers. Otherwise there will be as heretofore merely physical care; but education has also to do with the soul. Froebel teaches the right way to deal with the child's soul as it gradually awakes from unconsciousness, and he can do it because he understands clearly the relation between the unconscious condition of childhood and the consciousness of the mature mind.

"That is one thing; but in another direction he goes beyond Pestalozzi. Instead of the principle of observation on which Pestalozzi rests, Froebel combines doing with observing. Then he lets children represent their observations objectively and certainly, not only by imitation but freely by remembrance, which thereby prepares for *inventive* activity. In this way only is Pestalozzi's demand, that of combining power of action (*können*) with knowledge, fully realized.

"The using of labor as a means of education was limited by Pestalozzi to mechanical work and cultivation of the ground. Froebel's method proposes to banish all that is merely mechanical, and offers the means of methodically exercising the limbs and senses in every productive work, and also of uniting with this gymnastics of the intellectual powers and capacities; children are thereby elevated to productive activity in the full sense of the word, and artistic conception will be prepared for wherever the inborn capacity for it exists.

"Has not the intellectual consciousness that stamps the productive works of an author, and makes it his own spiritual property, great importance for the education of the people where the position of the working class is daily becoming higher and higher, on which the solution of the social question in a great part depends?"

"The peculiarities of Froebel's method are not yet sufficiently known to me," said Dr. Kühne, "to enable me to judge of their worth in this respect; but what you say impels me to a closer examination of it. But let us have no methods that are to bring universal salvation. The world has already seen many new methods and ideas, and yet on the whole remains very much what it was."

"That I dispute," I answered. "The world and the men in it are always changing, and have changed from the earliest barbarism to the present stage of culture, although it moves slowly, and this is the consequence, in part, at least, of new methods and new ideas."

"Yes," said Kühne, "but the civilized barbarism still remains; meanwhile I am very far, as you know, from denying progress. And you shall be satisfied; I also will interest myself in Froebel."

"If we weigh the value of Froebel and Pestalozzi for educational reform," I remarked, "it may be said that we chiefly owe to Pestalozzi the transformation in the nature of instruction, and thereby progress in the cultivation of the understanding, while Froebel preeminently takes up education as a whole, including moral culture and the development of character. Froebel's educational thought rests on one vital point not very easy to be discovered, and which will be entirely understood and valued only in the course of time.

"But what is the use of putting these men into the scales? To each his own. They were both noble and excellent men, true to nature, and original as few men are, and they had this in common, that the doctrine grew out of the ground of *immediateness*, of intuition, and was nothing artificial or reflected, and that is one of the guaranties of truth."

We had now arrived at the gate of Marienthal, and heard the voices of the children singing in the kindergarten, whom Froebel often led himself in the afternoon, in order to give to his pupils instruction in the manner of conducting the movement plays. He was in the midst of the troop of little ones when we entered.

"This, then, is the house of the prophet," said someone in our party, as we entered the great courtyard of the Marienthal house, which stood back, two stories high, with a front of eleven windows, looking more like the dwelling-house of a farm than like a castle, but pleasant and homelike in the midst of the old green trees that surrounded it.

In a large square before the house door, to which stone steps led up, was a grass plot upon which was planted some shrubbery, and on one side were very beautiful old lindens, which in flowering-time spread their fragrance far and wide. In their shade were some benches and tables on which, in good weather in summer, Froebel was accustomed to give his morning lessons.

At the moment when we entered, he stood in the midst of the courtyard surrounded by his pupils and a troop of little children, who had wound themselves round him as their central point in the play "Little thread, little thread, like a little wheel," and were just beginning to unwind their skein again. With glowing face and eyes beaming with happiness, Froebel greeted the company, immediately asking whether they would like to see some of the movement plays before going up into the hall. The guests were quite willing. With truly childish delight he again conducted some of those ingenious plays, the first gymnastics of the childish limbs. These he had copied from the traditional plays of children and the people, leaving out their rougher features in order to make them serve his educational idea; partly to make children represent, somewhat dramatically, facts out of the life of nature and man.

Froebel said, while he explained the plays to the bystanders, "All these plays, in their elements, have originated from childish instincts; but they must be consciously understood in their meaning and aim, in order to reach their educational end. People think the child is only seeking amusement when it plays. That is a great error. Play is the first means of development of the human mind, its first effort to make acquaintance with the outward world, to collect original experiences from things and facts, and to exercise the powers of body and mind. The child, indeed, recognizes no purpose in it and knows nothing, in the beginning, of any end which is to be reached when it imitates the play it sees around it, but it expresses its own nature, and that is human nature, in its playful activity. The further its development proceeds the more significant are the various movements which we know as the movements of the human being, from which all human culture has originated.

"But this is only the case when these movements can express

themselves unhindered and unfalsified, and the child's nature has not been perverted and led into false paths. The human instinct needs guidance by free movements, while the brute instinct finds its goal without guidance. This guidance can only be given by one who knows the goal which is to be reached by the manifold activity of the blind, natural feeling of the child. Without rational, conscious guidance, childish activity degenerates into aimless play instead of preparing for those tasks of life for which it is destined."

"It seems to me," said one friend, "that such continuous guidance on the part of the adult must take away from the childish play its artlessness."

"A continuous guidance is not practised," said Froebel; "the children have the larger part of the day to play freely among themselves. There must be no irritating oversight over them; but in the kindergarten they are guided to bring out their plays in such a manner as really to reach the aim desired by nature, that is, to serve for their development. Does it disturb the plant in its growth when the gardener protects it, prunes it, waters it, takes the best care he can of it? Do not the higher order of animals teach their young those activities which they need for self-preservation? For example, don't we see how the parent birds help their young in their first flight? The younger and more undeveloped the little creatures are, the more they need care and support. The weak instinct of the human child makes it the most needy of all creatures. Do we follow and remain true to nature only when we let its products shoot up without care? Without care even plants grow rank and wild. All nature is destined for culture in all its stages and in all its kingdoms. But culture must never go against nature. On the contrary, it must follow its order, take into account its ground and its goal, acknowledge its law, and recognize it as its standard, or it will be a false creature.

"Human culture has not always been nature becoming conscious to itself, as it should be; human education needs a guide, which I think I have found in a general law of development that rules both in nature and in the intellectual world. Without law-abiding guidance there is no really free development. You see what national life becomes when misunderstood ideas of freedom proscribe law."

At this moment, outside the gate, the rude cry of some peasants who were passing was heard, and Froebel turned smiling to the gentleman who had made that remark, asking, "How do you like that? Is not our children's song better? Singing must be learned in order to have agreeable sounds. Where the people sing well, they are seldom rude."

"The children's singing is charming," said one of the ladies present. "The plays are so touching to look upon, that I can scarcely keep back my tears. No one who ever sees children play like this can believe they are constrained, or deprived of their freedom. I have never seen anything so artlessly gay, so entirely unconstrained."

"Yes," said Froebel, "the kindergarten is the free republic* of childhood, from which everything dangerous to its morality is removed, as its lack of development requires. Childhood must be taken care of and protected, for it cannot protect itself, and the more tender the age, the more it needs guidance, that the body as well as the soul may not be crippled."

The children had ended their play and had sung the closing song, and were led to the door by the young ladies who were playing with them.

Froebel now invited the company to follow him into the upper story of the house, where he resided. He crossed the great hall, situated in the midst of the rooms, from whose four windows we looked out upon the lovely landscape as far as to the distant blue mountains of the Rhone.

In the midst of the hall stood a long table covered with Froebel's "gifts for play," and a multitude of little productions of children from various kindergartens.

*The word *republic* is here substituted for *state* by the translator, on account of the double meaning of the latter. In this place it does not mean *condition*.—Tr.

The same gentleman, a privy councillor from Berlin, who had made some objections to the playing of the children, and had also repeatedly opposed my statements, expressed the wish to learn the art and manner in which Froebel prepared for mathematical ideas by his plays and occupations, of which so much had been said. This hitherto very cold and reserved gentleman became quite animated when Froebel formed various figures with his little sticks, and then explained by these embodied lines the areas enclosed in the different surfaces and angles, and especially the relations of size and number of the geometrical figures, and then still further the simple representation of the numbers, beginning with the unit, and showed also the representations of form and numbers with other materials.

The figures made with the little sticks were only loosely laid together, without being fastened, but broad slats being united crosswise and interlaced formed permanent figures. Paper, cut in squares and folded, showed the relations of surfaces, and also geometrical forms. The perception of mathematical relations, as matters of fact, needs no explanation. The child understands, by manipulation of various materials, and by easily comprehended directions, the relations of size and number, as simple facts, without any abstraction, through mere observation of the forms brought out from them, without reasoning upon it, for which they are too young.

The councillor thought these demonstrations were remarkably clear in their simplicity. Only he doubted, in a measure, whether this embodiment of abstractions could lead later to mathematical conceptions, which are of purely intellectual nature, whose analogies are only found in the human mind.

"But are not all abstractions derived from something actual and physical, and does not the whole material world rest upon mathematical relations—indeed, does not all and everything imply relations of size and number?" I ventured to ask. "With my small knowledge of mathematics, for example, it would be quite impossible for me to understand mathematical truths, if I could not perceive them by means of a visible representation. Therefore it seems to me quite undoubted that if these truths are to be taught and conceived by means of words, the preceding perception of physical relations is needed to explain them completely. According to Froebel's method, the child, like the uncultivated artisan, makes progressive experiments which teach it by experience, and by this way of experience men arrived originally at knowledge; can mathematical knowledge be any exception to this? Mathematics remain the same whether expressed in the human mind or in the physical world, and the logic of both, therefore, has only one source—the Divine mind."

The councillor smiled, and said: "Much may be said upon that, but we must not mix up the intellectual with the physical too much."

"A dualistic theory of the world," whispered my neighbor on the other side; and a young painter sitting opposite turned and asked Froebel, somewhat impatiently whether the contemplation of the beautiful, at the child-age, would not be more conducive to the awakening of the imagination than occupation with mathematical figures, which are not beautiful.

"You are quite right," answered Froebel; "the beautiful is the best means of education for childhood, as it has been the best means for the education of the human race. Look, here are my forms of beauty." And he unrolled a long strip of paper on which was lithographed a series of figures, quite simple and symmetrical, copies of the forms laid by the children with delight, with Froebel's eight cubes. "These forms, in spite of their regularity, are called forms of beauty. The mathematical forms, which I designate forms of knowledge, give only the skeleton from which the beautiful form develops itself. Look at the figures on the old Egyptian buildings; they are always straight lines which show mathematical relations. Not until you get to the curve line, which came forth later in the development of art, do you have beauty of form. I take the same course in my educational method. Symmetry of the parts which make up these simple figures gives the impression of beauty as harmony to the childish eye. It must have the elements of the beautiful before it is in a condition to comprehend it in its whole extent. Only what is simple gives light to the child at first. He can only operate with a small number of materials when he is beginning to make forms, therefore I give only eight cubes for this object. But the material for making forms increases by degrees, progressing according to law, as nature prescribes. The simple wild rose existed before the double one was formed by careful culture. Children are too often overwhelmed with quantity and variety of material, that makes formation impossible to them. And where shall we take the rule, if not from nature? We mortals can only imitate what the dear God has created, therefore we must make use of the same law according to which he creates.

"With this law I give children a guide for creating, and because it is the law according to which they, as creatures of God, have themselves been created, they can easily apply it. It is born with them, and it also guides the animal instinct in its activity.

"You see," he went on, turning with shining eyes to the company, "the time has now arrived when men are coming to the consciousness of their own being and of the law which rules them, and according to which they are active, therefore the earliest childhood must be guided according to this law, and at first in the activity of play. Consciousness of the law is only prepared for by action and the application of the law. Unconsciousness is raised to consciousness chiefly by action."

Froebel illustrated these remarks by some examples, showing how the law, which he named "connection of opposites," was applied in the childish occupations, but nevertheless he was not completely intelligible to most of those present.

New views can break their way only gradually, after the general theory out of which they have sprung has been well diffused. Froebel's theory rested upon a profound intuition, which will be looked upon as hypothesis until its law, or rather the application of it (for the recognition of the law in general is as old as philosophic thinking), is scientifically established, and that by the empirical method of investigation.

A question of Dr. Kühne's about the teaching of language according to his method, plunged Froebel into explanations about the origin of letters, their significance in relation to ideas, and the like, a matter which involved him in inquiries of a scientific nature too deep to have an educational importance at present, but interesting as the original beginning of all and every side of human nature.*

By such digressions from his subject, in which Froebel often pursued his own thoughts without respect to his hearers, though revealing new relations of his idea, he often greatly confused his statements and gave room for the criticism that they were incomprehensible.

Dr. Kühne was led to the remark, "Froebel reminds me of that wise man of antiquity who discovered a natural law while in the bath, and ran naked through the streets, dripping from the tub, shouting, 'Eureka! Eureka!'"

In spite of these confusing digressions, Froebel's statements always called forth warm commendations from receptive minds, as a real strong conviction of *truth* alone can do.

Some of the ladies present, wearied with the dissertations of the men upon the origin of letters, were examining the various productions of the kindergarten, and could scarcely believe that very young children could produce such.

"It is all very charming," said one of the ladies, "but it seems to me the effort must be too great for the tender age of children. In the first years of life, I think children should only play undisturbed as they can and will."

"Certainly," I replied; "but if the child is to find satisfaction in

*Before the date of this conversation Dr. Kraitsir, the Hungarian philologist, had published in Boston his *Significance of the Alphabet*, and endeavored to show its value for the education of the present. It was ably reviewed by one of our greatest scholars in the *North American Review* of the spring of 1848, and in 1851 Dr. Howard Crosby, of the New York University, succeeded in publishing by subscription in New York Dr. Kraitsur's fuller work, *The Nature of Language and the Language of Nature*, G. P. Putnam, 1851.—Tr.

his play, the aim of nature must be reached, and this aim is bodily and mental development. Play—that is, the first childish activity—is now left to chance, therefore it reaches its aim but imperfectly; it needs guidance, and this guidance every genuine mother and educator naturally gives when the child desires it, as is always the case. 'Play with me!' is the cry of every child who has not playmates of its own age.* A child can play only for a time by itself, and with dolls, or prattle to the creations of its own imagination; then it comes with its never-ceasing questions to the grown-up—a living note of interrogation, which it must be in order to develop its mind. Even when these questions are answered suitably to the requirement (and how often does this happen with the otherwise busy mother or nurse?) it is only in *words*, rarely understood well by the child. It is necessary first to know the things that words describe—that is, matter and its properties. Froebel's gifts and occupations offer just this knowledge.

"The material prepared for this end furnishes opportunity to make experiments on material things, and it is that which the child seeks in the blind gropings of his undeveloped impulses. The effort of his little powers is increased by giving him the requisite material, and showing him the right use of it; or rather is not the thing made easier for him thereby?

"For example, the child tries to make a form out of a piece of paper—a box, a little bird, or something else. He does not succeed, because the paper has not the right form, and he does not know the requisite manipulations. In the kindergarten he receives paper of a square form, and is shown how he can bring out the desired thing from it. Besides that, he is instructed in an easy manner how to invent new forms at pleasure, in endless variety, by application of Froebel's law of formation. The forms and figures thus brought out, which, going from the simplest, proceed step by step easily to the most complex, only *appear* difficult and

*They always prefer mamma, if they can have her, for a playmate, and is not this because they enjoy the guidance?—Tr.

beyond the child's powers when we do not know how they have proceeded from each other."

I showed the ladies the beginning of Froebel's cutting occupation, by which, with two or three cuts in squares of paper, folded in a certain way, the most varied forms are obtained, and it called forth general surprise and astonishment.

"That is remarkable, truly splendid!" said the lady, who had raised the objection. "Now I understand the thing, and I take back my remark."

"In such ways," I added, "the child learns by playing the most important mechanical manipulations, and his sense of form and beauty is cultivated. The important thing is that he becomes accustomed to consecutive action, and by productive occupation, which gives him real pleasure, is made capable very early of useful little acts, and is prepared for later work. Moral gain is attained in the highest degree, and how necessary is this in our time!

"All that the development of human culture has gradually found and practised by experiment, discovery, and invention in the course of thousands of years is recognized by Froebel in his principle of LAW; and the technical skill thereby gained he has reduced to the simplest and most original manipulations, in order to attain the universal elements of proper work for childhood.

"These occupations, however, like everything else, can be misused if unintelligent kindergartners occupy the children too long, or give them too difficult tasks."

"A remarkable discovery!"

"Truly, full of significance for our time!"

"Who could have looked for such genius in this plain and unprepossessing man?"

"How touchingly childlike in his whole manner!"

"To devote his whole life to the welfare of mankind in childhood!"

Such were the various exclamations concerning Froebel, and his method of education, by the several individuals of the company during our half-hour's walk back from Marienthal to

Liebenstein. They all expressed themselves greatly satisfied with the visit, and with Froebel's method of education. Even the Berlin councillor thought "the use of Froebel's method, especially for mathematics, might bring about a very important reform in schools."

Dr. Kühne said: "The thing is really of great importance, and supplements Pestalozzi's method. This Froebel is an exceptional, a rare man; so much poetical elevation in his simple, homely way of acting, and such joy in self-sacrifice as his are necessary if a universal, humane work is to succeed."

"And now, will you set your pen in motion in favor of the subject?" I asked.

"I will seek for some way in which I can further it," said Dr. Kühne. And he kept his word; for in the very next number of the *Europa* he described his "Thuringian Wanderings," which in novel form gave the visit to Marienthal, mingling truth and poetry; and, later, a biographical sketch of "Froebel and his Efforts." This was republished in a fuller form in the book entitled "German Men and Women," and after Froebel's death appeared a pamphlet entitled "Froebel's Death, and the Success of his Teaching." For this last great thanks are due to Dr. Kühne, for he was the first well-known writer, not pedagogical, who turned his attention to Froebel's cause, and by his pen introduced him into circles which otherwise never would have known him.

Whether the warmly expressed recognition given by other members of this little walking party ever brought any practical support to the cause is not known to me.

7

Visit of Dr. Hiecke

When Froebel came, on one of the following afternoons, to the "private hour" that had been agreed upon between us, I informed him that the gymnasium director, Hiecke of Merseburg, had just been with me, and that he was desirous of making Froebel's acquaintance, and would come to Marienthal with me on the following day.

"Ah! the gentleman who asked me those peculiar questions, which you sent to me last winter from Merseburg?" asked Froebel.

"The same," I answered; "one of the most learned and distinguished of our contemporary school-directors, who can be of great use to us if he will take up the subject."

During a sojourn of several weeks in Merseburg, in February of this year, where I had given almost daily lectures on Froebel's educational method, some of my most zealous auditors—besides my friends School-councillor Karo and his charming wife—were Professors Hiecke and Wieck, the old blind privy councillor Weisse, brother of Froebel's former superior at the Berlin Museum, and the School-director Lüben, who had just entered upon his duties there.

Whoever saw these men, and others, especially teachers of the town-school there, and saw how enthusiastically they received Froebel's idea, and undertook to study it, and to further its extension, would hardly understand, in view of this example, which was followed by others without number, why the cause advanced so slowly and painfully to recognition. Those here mentioned have, however, favored it honestly, and even in the public press. At that time Director Lüben had some articles in recommendation of it printed in the Merseburg weekly paper.

The letters sent to Froebel from there (which, among my letters returned to me by Madame Froebel, lie before me) contain expressions of the highest and deepest acknowledgment from my auditors of that time. It is there said, among other things: "Hiecke, a philosophically cultivated mind, has talked much and profoundly with me about your idea and method. He said the subject was one of the most far-reaching importance, incalculable in its consequences," etc. He was especially interested in the fundamental idea of "sphere, cube, and cylinder," and he said, when I explained it to him, "Had Froebel expressed this idea alone, it could be called a great deed. It is possible for Froebel's cause to advance so suddenly into general acceptance that within a year his judgment may have authority in all Germany. But for that there must be able cooperation through the press, and its relations to present politics must not be forgotten."

I said to Froebel, "When I spoke to Hiecke and Wieck on the following day, they said that they had been occupied day and night in thinking of your educational idea, and would like to know how you stood with Krause and Herbart. These questions I was not able to answer sufficiently. But the idea has struck a spark in these minds, and you will be convinced of this, if these men come to you in Marienthal, as Hiecke and Lüben propose to do.

"Hiecke desires to know your answers to the questions noted on the accompanying sheet. He has commissioned me to express to you his regards, and his wish to make your acquaintance. At my request he sends you herewith two copies of the *Educational Monthly*, which contain two essays of his. He will request his friend Gude to make himself acquainted with your cause, and, as much as possible, from your own lips. The other schoolmen also have had communication with their colleagues on the subject.

"You see, then, Merseburg if favorable to us, and our cause has gained here a real triumph, although it was before entirely unknown. The higher circles of society, indeed, are here, as everywhere, lethargic and indifferent about *important* things."

So far the extracts from my letter to Froebel. The questions asked Froebel by Hiecke (which also lie before me) are as follows:

"1. What is the course of development under your system up to the age of 18–20 years?

"2. What use do you make of foreign languages; and the order and distribution of these over the different ages?

"3. The choice, order, and ages for the epoch-making achievements in the various arts, e.g., the use of the Odyssey?

"4. What German poets, and in what order, would you use chiefly?

"5. How far and in what way should *Tradition* be regarded?"

Froebel had never answered these questions—which, indeed, lay very far from the educational field in which he was working—and had written to me on a former occasion, when I reminded him of them, "that they could be answered in his sense only after a better understanding of his educational cause, which rested on a different foundation from those questions, the details of which had scarcely been considered by him," etc.

Froebel said the same thing at this time, and added, with childish *naiveté*, "I wish these learned men would not always ask me about things that they understand much better than I do!"

"The schoolmen will want the connection of your educational method with school-instruction to be fully explained if they are to give it—or, perhaps, indeed, take away from it—their interest," I replied. "The earliest childhood is too far distant from them, even if they are fathers of families, and the majority reject any plan of methodically influencing the early years.

"They have no idea that you have to do with the principle of the development of the human being, and not with methods of instruction in the school. To questions asked with this view I continually make answer that you agree with Pestalozzi's method, that you desire only to supplement it and to add some things to it, and to bring the school into nearer relation with real life."

"Very well," said Froebel; "but for this purpose I propose to take, in one way and another, many hours from school-lessons, to devote to educational *work*. And this will not be listened to by the learned men, who see salvation in the amount of knowledge which the school gives to its pupils for their life-journey, as if *all* must or even could be learned men! You know what M. and S. said about that, and how they made the strongest opposition to your painstaking for the kindergartens, and how they turned the mind of Minister W., who was already half won over."

"The minister is coming here, nevertheless, to acquaint himself with the subject and with yourself," I answered, "and, indeed, very soon. But you must not class Hiecke with these people; he is not so one-sided. On the contrary, he takes a broad view, and is capable of enthusiasm. And you must not forget when you talk with him that he is a philologist and a philosopher, and not a natural philosopher in your sense."

Much as Froebel liked visits, and especially those of educators, which gave him an opportunity to explain his educational method, yet he was somewhat afraid of them on account of the frequent experience of not being able to make himself understood, at least completely. Moreover, he felt that he was not a "learned man," inasmuch as he lacked much positive knowledge in this department of science. And very naturally every one of these men desired a special reference to the relations of the method with his own particular department of science. The result was, that some left Froebel ill satisfied, and admitted that he was a "good man," who was working very usefully for the improvement of children's games, and for adapting them to the preparation for school—but nothing more! Others, philosophically educated men, had some fixed philosophical system by which to level their judgment, and if Froebel's theories would not adapt themselves to these they were rejected.

How often did Froebel's brow contract into painful folds,

when in such discussions he could not extort any understanding, and knew that on the other hand he possessed little authority.

The obstacle to arriving at a mutual understanding was, in most cases, that he took his point of departure from the things of the concrete world, i.e. from the thoughts made objective, and from the laws of the *Divine* mind expressed therein, while his opponents would admit no other starting-point than their own *Ego* or their subjective *inner* experience.

And this could not in truth be otherwise, since the struggle after new knowledge for the solution of the old question—the connection of the material world, or unconscious nature, with the intellectual world, or the conscious mind of man—was just opening new paths in which new problems presented themselves, which would require centuries for their complete solution, so far as this is vouchsafed at all to the human mind on earth.

Froebel's idea, the "connection of contrasts" in the course of the process of development—since in the world of phenomena no absolute contrasts, but only relative ones exist, and the absolute only exists as a principle—was almost always misunderstood, especially by those minds who considered the dualistic theory of the world as the only correct one. These generally rejected the Froebelian theory before they had examined its point of departure closely. They would easily have learnt that Froebel did not deny the truth of dualism, but recognized it as a part only and not as the whole truth, which he found rather in the repeated resolution of it, and in the final harmony or connection of contrasts, i.e., in the *principle*, and not at all in the finite things and relations and their development.

If by some of these denying spirits, penetrated with the *praxis* of Froebel's method, Froebel's *thoughts* could be better understood, their deep concurrence with the ideas of the time would be recognized, and they would be welcomed as *one* of the means of preparing minds for the higher theories of the world which are forming. But, indeed, what a request, to ask highly educated men to plunge into children's plays!

And if these doubters were referred to Froebel's writings—

these fragments and aphorisms of philosophy and pedagogics, as they undoubtedly are—then it was to these one-sidedly developed minds very bad indeed. Then it was said, "There is nothing here of *system*!" "These theories of unity are untenable from the standpoint of philosophical science." "The style is intolerable." "The principles are Pestalozzi's." "The method is not carried out to the higher ages, up to the school." "There are some good and even striking things there, but confused, and on the whole unintelligible," etc.

Only a few penetrated into it to find its deep meaning, in spite of the faulty manner of expression, the lack of system, and the merely aphoristical views of a mind living entirely under the power of intuition. These few were sometimes seized hold of by the truth lying at the foundation of them, so that they *must* follow them whether they would or not. But for the great majority the interest was a transient one, that was soon obliterated by some other subject of thought lying closer.

So it has resulted that, notwithstanding all recognition on the part of individuals, even of authorities, the cause in its great whole and in its deeper significance remained unknown, and its spread has progressed almost alone through the—mainly not understood—*praxis* in the kindergarten.

It was not until the following day that I spoke with Hiecke after his first interview with Froebel, since I had been prevented from accompanying him to Marienthal. As I feared, the two men, standing on entirely different grounds, had only partially understood each other. Hiecke was a little disappointed, although, like everyone who had a heart, he was impressed by Froebel's devotion and joyful sacrifice to the cause of human welfare.

"He has Pestalozzi's love, and a great power of persuasion," he said. He admitted also the usefulness of a preparation conformable to nature for children before and for the school, but the great significance of a methodical educational influence during the earliest instructive life of the child, *before* the awakening of personal consciousness, was not obvious to him. This appeared to him almost fantastical. The school was for him the chief factor in education, and in it languages and aesthetic culture, which especially interested him, could, in his view, only be gained by instruction.

"But there is other instruction than that given by *words*," I replied; "practice, action, is a self-instruction which the school cannot give sufficiently. All musical theory does not teach one how to play an instrument without practical exercise at the same time. And all morality learned with words and out of books does not lead to a moral life, to moral power of action. Knowledge and goodwill are not sufficient to enable one to rescue a fellow-creature who has fallen into the water; one must have learned to swim. Here are the defects of the church and of the school!"

Hiecke said, "I do not deny that something must be done in this direction, and I think that Froebel has come just at the right time to help in the work begun, of simplifying the work of teachers and scholars in the school, and of cutting down the time for it, in a certain degree, in order to use it for bodily exercises and for gaining practical power. This is especially true of the people's schools. Froebel's *school-gardens* can be of great use—if Froebel will only create for us the necessary situation for them in the great cities," he added, laughing.

"The cause will be wrecked first on this want. Such thoroughgoing changes of the whole school-organism involve great difficulties, which it will require the work of long years to overcome. Moreover, the classical schools and the gymnasia could take but a small share in a reform of that kind."

I answered: "As to the question about land, some fields in the neighborhood of the cities could easily be obtained for cultivation by the school youth. By this means labor would be saved on the one side, while on the other the powers of the youth would be increased, and public economy would make a real gain."

At that time—twenty-five years ago—it seemed almost Utopian to wish to carry the kindergarten on in such a manner to *school-*

gardens, and quite so to hope to bring about workshops, art studios, playgrounds, great excursions, etc., for the school-youth.*

Today we see the Austrian government assisting in every way the labors of Professor Dr. E. Schwab, in Vienna, in founding school-gardens; and since 1872 an order of the Minister of Instruction requires the school-inspectors to join a kindergarten with every school where it is possible to do so, makes the knowledge of Froebel's method obligatory upon elementary teachers, and prescribes it as a branch of the teaching at the seminaries.

Within the last two years a great number of school-gardens have been established, in Austrian Silesia, in Lower Austria, in Moravia, in Tyrol, etc. In St. Poelten and Neustadt, near Vienna, large school-gardens have been made, likewise in Brunn, Laibach, Krems, etc., and also in many villages, under the initiative of the community. The "Agricultural Society," the "Trade-Union," and other associations in Vienna have aided the work successfully begun by Dr. Schwab, who has worked unceasingly and with the greatest energy. The Minister of Agriculture, also, has given his assistance by the assignment of land, and invites proposals for the management of the matter, from all parts of the country, as far as Bukowina. Schwab's efforts for the foundation of school-workshops, in which the first experiments have been made, meet with a like sympathy.

To this is to be added the activity of the Dekans, Dr. Hoerfarter, in Kufstein, in Tyrol, who, besides a kindergarten and a training institution for kindergartners, has founded a school-garden for the schoolchildren of the place, and labors for the cause in every way with devotion worthy of great praise.

Such successful practical beginnings in one country cannot but have speedy results in other lands, of which I hope one of the first will be Germany, where single beginnings on the part of private individuals have already been made.

*See further on this subject, *Education by Work*, by B. von Marenholtz-Bülow.

An educational reform of this sort is so pressingly demanded by the present condition of culture, entirely apart from its being a consequence of Froebel's educational method, that its realization cannot be very far distant.

At the time of which I am speaking (1851) but a few believing ears were found in our Liebenstein circle for Froebel's cause, and the schoolmen at that period seldom went into anything that was not immediately practical. Therefore the views of Hiecke were the more encouraging.

Women were far more urgent than men for the reform, perhaps because they did not so well understand the difficulties that lay in the way of it. If the Duchess of Weimar had not died so soon, a first attempt might possibly have been made with her assistance, since she not only felt a warm interest in Froebel's cause, but also cherished a lively wish to see it carried into execution.

On the occasion of a visit to her when the Countess of Hessen-Phillipsstahl was present, and the conversation turned upon the kindergarten and the furthering of it, the interest of the Countess was so warmly excited that she determined to bring Froebel's method into the educational work of her own family.

A little grandson of hers, son of the reigning Count, four years old, sickly and almost weak-minded, was so backward in his development that he did not even incline to the usual play of children, and was almost always in an apathetic and sluggish condition of intellect. On the next day after our conversation the Countess visited Froebel, and after nearer acquaintance with the practical occupations of the kindergarten, and learning the principle on which they were founded, she made an agreement with him that one of the pupils then taking the lessons should, at the end of her course, come to Phillipsstahl as the educator of the little prince.*

*Fraulein Marie Kramer undertook this with much zeal, so that the parents, as well as his grandmother, acknowledged the advantage of the method very warmly.

Froebel was exceedingly pleased with the judgment of the Princess, and hoped from it a wider recognition of his method in the higher circles of society.

On the day when Hiecke went with me to Marienthal, in the afternoon, after long discussions on the subject, Froebel's very anxiety, or his fatigue, rendered him less capable than usual of clear expression. His explanations, however, of the practical bearings of the method were recognized by Hiecke entirely, though it lay far away from his own pedagogic domain. But as soon as the fundamental principle came into view, the mutual understanding was in a measure destroyed, and Hiecke was not quite satisfied with what Froebel said, and at the moment Froebel was unable to explain it well.

On our way back to Liebenstein, Hiecke said that the philosophic foundation of the thing was unsatisfactory to him; he must especially disagree on one point, namely, the supposition Froebel seemed to go upon, that children had by nature exclusively good dispositions.

I denied that decidedly, but I had to admit that such a misinterpretation was natural from the statements that Froebel had made. I undertook to give him Froebel's theory myself, somewhat in the following form:

"The dispositions of the human being are destined by God's will to develop themselves on all sides into the good and the perfect—the image of God. Therefore these dispositions cannot in the end be sinful or evil, so far as they are given by God in order to realize this destiny.

"Froebel says, in his 'Education of Man,' 'Qualities evil in themselves cannot be found in man unless we understand the finite, bodily, and transient as evil in their nature and consequences; these have their necessary basis in the destination of man to conscious reason and freedom. Man must be able to err, in order to become good, honest, and virtuous. Whoever would enact the divine and eternal with self-determination and freedom must be permitted to do finite and earthly things. Since God has willed to make himself known in the finite, this must be done in the finite. Whoever calls whatever is temporal, individual, and bodily evil in itself, despises nature itself, creation, that which is; in short, he blasphemes God in a special sense.'"

I added, "The freedom of the will, necessarily given to man in order that he shall develop himself as a reasonable being, having prevented the normal development of his powers by capriciousness and error, he has by these been led into unlawful paths contrary to the laws of God, and brought on the *fall of man*."

How far Froebel considered this fact in education can be seen from an example in his *Mother and Cosset Songs*, where he refers to the fall of the child as an unavoidable fact, and points to its application as a wholesome experience.

Froebel denies by no means that the deviation from the lawful and normal way of development must have changed and affected the nature of human dispositions, and still must continue to do so. One sees these consequences, even in the animal and plant world, where deficiency of care and culture, even in the higher races of the domestic animals, for instance in the horse, causes deteriorated posterity, or when poorly cultivated plants bear imperfect seeds, leading to the degradation of the species. But, on the contrary, we also see that proper care and culture improve and ennoble species of the animal and vegetable world, and overcome the deterioration which has taken place.

Froebel desires that the educator should treat the child as good and pure until an instance of the opposite nature appears, since no one can know when the moment of the first failing or individual fall takes place in the child who has inherited different qualities from parents and ancestors, and in different combinations, out of which arise this or that form of error which we call sinful. No less are the inborn dispositions modified and shaped by the influences surrounding the child which act favorably or unfavorably upon its nurture and education. The dispositions themselves, before they are developed in either direction, are neither good nor bad—they are the seeds out of which, according to circumstances, good or evil may proceed. There are dispositions destined by God for goodness that, in a measure, are perverted to evil by the parents and ancestors of all children, and which are inherited by posterity with a thousand modifications, as are the tendencies to bodily weakness and malady. Inherited weaknesses are of mental as well as of bodily nature, but together with these weaknesses and faults are also found good and healthy qualities; with inherited tendency to sin is also found in the human being inherited tendency to virtue.

But if criminal families show an inheritance of misused powers and dispositions, it should not be inferred that every criminal's child must certainly walk in the footsteps of his parent. Let him be brought into a good moral atmosphere; give him a good education, and he will perhaps become a noble and useful man. Let one only look into the eyes of children of even the worst families, and one will not doubt the ever-regenerating power of the human being. If it were not so, the Christian idea of redemption would have no significance.

The progressive culture acknowledged by all generations, and therefore by every individual in each generation, must by degrees lead to the victory over evil in man, notwithstanding the thousand backward steps of individuals, and even of individual nations; and the dispositions that have been injured by sin must be ennobled and reinstated in their original purity. To what degree this is possible upon earth, what special historical acts and revelations of Divine Providence have been at work for it hitherto and will work for it in the future, in order that the final practical redemption from evil, determined by God, and the possible perfection of the human being on earth shall be reached, is another question, whose solution is not denied or doubted in the Christian point of view. The superficial views of our time, which deny every deep idea, Froebel did not share in any degree. If anyone has ever seized the innermost kernel of the Christian idea, and recognized its eternal truth, it was he. In one of his treatises he says: "The relation of man to God has been determined conclusively and exhaustively, for all time, by the Christian religion."

Because this eternal truth of the Christian religion is yet really known to but very few; because it has been hidden by the innumerable misconceptions of centuries; and because God wills that the contents of our faith shall be brought to light, new means of help must come into the world for that end. A better education, really corresponding to the nature of the human being, belongs undeniably to these means of help, and particularly if—as in the case of Froebel—the law of the development of the human being is recognized and applied. Just because Froebel recognizes the danger of departure from the right way, and the possibility of the perversion of human qualities in their first building, he considered the education of the earliest childhood the most important. If the child had come into the world with only perfectly good and pure disposition, the early educational influence would not have been necessary; education would have been superfluous, because human dispositions and powers would then have developed themselves aright spontaneously, according to their nature.

But the good disposition of the child will be in danger, according to Froebel, of being turned contrary to good by nothing more easily than by supposing evil and sin to exist where it has not appeared; for example, to suppose untruth where this has been far from the child's soul. Thereby a child is robbed of its innocence, as it were, before it is time, before the opposite has manifested itself definitely. Froebel requires the educator to take for granted the good and the pure in the child, to proceed tentatively, and not to look upon the child as a little devil. Without in any way denying the significance and importance of theological and philosophical studies and investigations for deeper knowledge of the truth, it must be granted that in reference to the immediate practical education of children and the masses little has been gained hitherto. The truth expressed in words alone is not enough to form the moral man. Moral *practices* are needed to insure subsequent free moral action. These moral practices are insufficiently brought into action in the present mode of education. Froebel wishes to introduce them, and to put *doing* and *creating* in the place of word instruction.

The striving of our time to find reason ruling even in the unconscious being, and to discover and establish the relations of the human being to nature and to the organisms subordinated to him, exhibits certainly a point of development willed by God, and will serve to compensate humanity for the long-continued estrangement of man from nature.

Insofar as Froebel took his starting-point in the knowledge of real things (the works of God), he also goes in the same direction, and he does so in the conviction that truth in the word, and through the word (doctrine), can only be set in clearer light, and be more deeply understood thereby, so far as one revelation confirms the other, which they must do, since they have their common origin in God. The deeper knowledge of human beings as "children of nature" (as Froebel says) is the best means by which to discover and combat budding evil, since that evil is in the natural and not in the spiritual being of man.

Froebel has certainly not established any philosophical system, at least not in words, but a deep philosophic and religious view of the world lies at the foundation of his "Education of Man," and is embodied, in a measure, in his means of education, which carry back the ideas of the human mind to their origin in the material world (God's world), and furnish symbols of it.

In spite of his different point of departure from that of the existing philosophic systems, Froebel is not on that account antagonistic to them, at least not so far as they stand on the ground of theism. He particularly agrees, on many sides, with the views of the philosopher Krause, notwithstanding the difference of their standpoints.

Through the knowledge of pure human nature, in spite of its actual degeneracy and obscuration, he wishes to establish the right goal for practical education quite in unison with the representation of this pure human nature in Christianity, and wishes thus to preserve it, if possible, from mistakes in the period of unconsciousness, or during the human life of instinct in childhood.

These ground principles for a new system of education, and the practical means corresponding to it, are given by Froebel. Upon these grounds his intellectual descendants can build further to meet the present wants; the life of man does not suffice to do more. This problem will not be fully solved till the present intellectual struggle for a broader general theory of the universe shall have brought a satisfactory result. Meanwhile it is of the greatest importance that the significance of Froebel's idea be sought in itself and its further development, and not in the commentaries of his followers.

After exchanging much conversation with Hiecke, he promised to suspend his judgment till he had studied Froebel's "Education of Man," and had learned to understand the cause better; expressing, meantime, his full concurrence with the practical means.

The shortness of his Liebenstein residence prevented his entering into it any further at the moment. The acceptance of his new place as director of the gymnasium in Griefswald called him away, and claimed his whole activity for a long time. Besides that, the shortness of his life may have prevented him from studying into the cause any further; it would otherwise be inconceivable that that profound mind, after having received so favorable an impression of the cause, should not have left behind him a well-founded judgment for publication, although there are not wanting examples of the loss of a lively and enthusiastic sympathy when the occupations of one's calling, and interests attracting one in opposite directions, prevent a comprehensive survey of a subject.

A corresponding elaboration of Froebel's writings would at any rate have in a great measure made the study of his educational method easy to the specialists who were overburdened with occupations, and been a great help towards its acceptance on their part.

8

Educational Value of Festivals

Froebel and Middendorff had already in the preceding summer often spoken of the plan of a play-festival, which was to be celebrated at some beautiful place in the neighborhood, with the cooperation of the children and teachers of the neighboring districts. This plan had frequently been discussed between us, in connection with Froebel's ideas of the educational use of festivals for childhood and youth, and also for the mass of the people.

The misuse of political liberty, which in our day is becoming more and more marked and extreme, is occasioned in part, in Froebel's opinion, by the rareness of the opportunity which youth and children find to act freely in a lawful and orderly sociableness, between the extremes of the imposed restraint of schools and the irresponsible freedom outside of them. The present degree of liberty granted to all classes requires a thorough education for liberty that does not yet exist in a corresponding degree. This education ought to begin before the school years begin, in a wider social intercourse of children, in which each under an established order may act freely, as in the kindergarten.

The narrow circle of the family cannot fulfill all the conditions for this end, because children surrounded by love at home rarely find occasion to learn to check and deny themselves for the sake of others. In the social life of the school, on the other hand, passive obedience is requisite for giving to all an adequate opportunity for freedom of action. Abuse of freedom granted rarely occurs under the regulated activity of schools for youth, or in the hard work of adults. Experience sufficiently shows that excesses generally occur in the hours of recreation. It is coarse and rough enjoyments which lead to this danger. Youth must be educated to nobler pleasures and enjoyments, if freer institutions are not to be misused. Those who are shut out from the pleasures derived from nature and the arts cannot easily be restrained from excessive rudeness.

General morality, according to Froebel, depends in great measure on having this ideal side of the human being awakened and gratified from the *very beginning of life*, in order to afford a counterpoise to sensual desires, and to prevent as far as possible the awakening of the lower appetites. The development of the sense of beauty, while the reflective powers are still slumbering in the child's soul, offers the best means for this. Therefore the eyes of the child are to be opened in its earliest years to forms, colors, etc., and the ear to music, and the weak, childish powers are to be prepared and used in the formation of beautiful objects.

Froebel looks upon this formation of beautiful objects as the best means of making the soul susceptible to the ideal on every side, and the cultivation of the creative powers he considers one of the most important means for overcoming coarseness and immorality.

The necessity of elevating one's self above everyday difficulties and of placing one's self in ideal circumstances, even if only by dreaming, or at times giving one's self up unconstrainedly to childlike, innocent amusement, is gratified by festivals, which at the same time serve to give expression to special sentiments, such as gratitude, admiration of great and good deeds, commemorations of the services of distinguished patriots and public benefactors, great minds and inventors, etc.

Play, or rather art in the garment of play, constitutes the chief ingredient of such festivities, if they are to rise above a merely sensuous enjoyment. In order to ennoble and idealize children's festivals, the children's bodies and minds must first be prepared for enjoyment.

It is a great educational error (which Froebel wishes to combat) to deprive childhood and youth of its legitimate joys, for nature has planted the need and craving for them in their hearts. As bodily development is interrupted and even injured when the lawful wants of nature are not satisfied, the soul and its natural development are cramped if the craving for joy is not met.

The youth who grow up in too great restraint and privation show the justice of this view by their excessive pleasure seeking as soon as freedom and opportunity are given to them. On the other hand, it is rare that youth who have grown up in innocent, happy childhood rush into any excess of pleasures.

Natural gratification, when permitted, prevents excesses, while one extreme always calls forth the opposite. Moderation in everything, indeed, is the first educational rule, and a right limitation of the pleasures of youth should not be wanting.

Froebel found the right way when he made the correct estimate of those childish joys which ennoble the mind, satisfy the desire for the beautiful and the ideal, and above all things prevent every merely idle pleasure by giving that activity to the powers which precludes destructive desires.

Enjoyment, as a means of unity for men, resembles in its highest and finest expression true religion, which binds together in the worship of God all ages, all the different social ranks, and all the different grades of culture. Enjoyment delivers from all dissension; all enmity, and all separation during the season of the enjoyment.

In the drawing of men's souls together sentiment is one and the same for one and the same end. Froebel saw the beginning of the final and highest destiny of mankind upon earth, which he designated by the expression "unity of life," and which with him had a manifold significance, according to its various relations and the various steps of its realization.

In reference to individuals, this "unity of life" or harmony brings about as a last consequence that resolution of discords between the sensual and spiritual nature which in reality is only *thinkable* for moments. Taken absolutely, it would be that lifting out of sin that is the last and highest destiny of man, and the final goal of all education as of all religion.

In nature, or the material world, Froebel saw an image of this "unity of life" in every organism, so far as its conditions require that all parts serve the end of the whole as a connected unity. The circle, with its radii running from the centre to the circumference, was to him a symbol of this idea; for a circle is the representation of the general law, "the connection of opposites," since the periphery and centre stand in contrast to each other, and are connected by the radii; this law was with him the indispensable condition of all harmony, and therefore of all "unity of life."

The organic life in nature, as the first beginning of the harmony which rules in the universe, and imitating this last as *microcosm* (world in miniature), offers the first rudiments of "unity of life" in human society, whose organization has to represent that spiritually which nature presents materially.

The recognition of the analogy between spirit and phenomena, and the deeper understanding of the above-mentioned law, which governs equally in both, must lead to the view that national organization and civic arrangements also require for the stability of the whole the concurrence of the parts, and this view impels individuals to the conscientious and voluntary fulfilment of their civic duties and the maintenance of national order, and thus the conditions would be fulfilled for reaching national unity.

Therefore nationalities must recognize themselves also as individual organisms in the great whole of humanity, which create "unity of life" for themselves by the conscious community of their parts, and lead the way through their association with each other to the condition of the highest community, the unity of all nations upon the earth.

Through the fulfilment of these conditions, humanity is made into a conscious or spiritual whole, and thereby is the "unity of life" established fully and completely in the world. This theory of Froebel's agrees in its general features, in many respects, with those of some other philosophers, especially with Krause's. Not less is it in unison with the Christian theory and its idea of redemption, taken in its deepest meaning.

To the realism of our time this would be nothing more than a useless hypothesis, if it did not lead in its consequences to a practical educational result. The immediate practical application which Froebel makes possible stands as it were in contrast, if not in opposition, to those philosophical systems, and is of the greatest importance.

Our time will hear nothing of mere speculations which have no practical results for the bettering of human society, as has been the case for centuries. Science, today, moves in the service of practical life, without, however, on the account giving up its own aim. Froebel's method of education is the practical result of a philosophical theory by which, for the first time, a complete embodiment of abstract ideas, and their immediate realization in deeds, is brought forth; and thus this practical philosophy of Froebel's is separated completely and fully from all other philosophical systems.

In the association movements which prevail at present in all classes, Froebel saw a sign of the idea of that unity which governs the times, and whose ultimate goal he designates as the "unity of life." This unity, at first making itself felt for outward and material aims, was to him the precursor of the coming spiritual unity which hovered before him as his highest ideal, and whose final aim is a universal sense of religion, or divine unity.

For the realization of the pure humanity in it, the full and complete development of every individuality is needed. The more independently human nature shows itself as peculiarity in individuals, the more unfettered and freely they can act, physically and intellectually, the more capable they become of union into a whole and of voluntary self-renunciation to its law. The larger wholes and communities can in their turn only have vitality when they proceed from the narrowest circle, the bosom of the family, which is the earliest community of life. Only the most moral and the most holy family life can lead the wider circles of life to conscious community, and bring them near to the highest ideal of a perfected humanity.

But a truly noble family life springs out of the first and most original union of two mortals—marriage. According to Froebel, the counterparts, man and woman, united, form "the most sublime and divine of all earthly objects, exalting man to the likeness of God. It is the fundamental condition, the highest law for the continuance of mankind, and therefore for the progressive existence of the divine in humanity." The eternal law of connection is love divine, all-penetrating love, which streams through the world out of its source in God like a magnetic power, from the most insignificant organism up to the highest spirits that have conquered the human and risen up to likeness with God.

This theory of love is to serve as the highest goal and polestar of human education, and must be attended to in the germ of humanity, the child, and truly in his very fist impulses. The conquest of self-seeking EGOISM is the most important task of education, for selfishness isolates the individual from all communion and kills the life-giving principle of love. Therefore the first object of education is to teach to love, to break up the egoism of the individual, and to lead him from the first stage of communion in the family through all the following stages of social life to the love of humanity, or to the highest self-conquest through which man rises to divine unity.

This is the same thing that Christianity designates as the "following of Christ," and expresses in the words, "Love one another"; "He who loves not his brother whom he has seen, how can he love God whom he has not seen?" etc.

9

Child-Festival at Altenstein

Insofar as Froebel holds fast to the connection of the greatest with the least, and wishes to have it considered in education, this theory finds its application to child's play, which mirrors human nature in its universality, and shows the germ of human culture in its condition of unconsciousness. Therefore it is of the greatest importance that the understanding of the grown-up should come to the help of the dark striving of the young child, in order to point out to the blind impulses that are endeavoring to express themselves the right way of reaching their aim, and also to bring out the right meaning of the symbolism expressed in the childish utterance, in order to give direction to the later conscious life in the most suitable form.

The undeveloped mind needs sensuous perceptions, the visible signs, in order to arrive at an understanding of truth. As the savage needs his fetish, as the people of antiquity in a higher stage of culture personified their ideas in the form of their gods and in various allegories, as even the Christian church cannot make itself understood without symbols, without the cross and the host, so the deepest need of childhood is to make the intellectual its own through symbols or sensuous forms.

Therefore symbolic representations are in the first place necessary for this, representations which the children enact in their own persons, that is, plays, in which a company of children are the representatives of an idea lying at the foundation, and whose meaning they bring out in their action.

Froebel's movement-plays have this aim, for they are in a certain sense *dramas*, and make the ideas of the children objective by means of natural and human action. The child's soul unconsciously seeks for the meaning of the phenomena of life around it, but needs guidance to be able to find it truly; and this understanding cannot be gained merely by words, but only by actions connected with words, and above all by *their own* action.

The religious exhibitions that prevailed in Greece, in the form of games like the Olympian, etc., satisfied this want for that people, to whom religious ideas were thereby brought into view. The theory of the world that prevailed at the time was chiefly made intelligible by dramatic action, in the form of games. In the flowering-time of the Greeks, the harmony between the intellectual and the sensuous world is expressed as with no other people, and is therefore the right representative of the ideal season of youth in humanity. The formation of the beautiful was the deepest need of that people cultivated in all their senses, and with all their senses alive, therefore it shows more than any other the needs of youth still living in the world of the senses. The intellectual or higher contents of life, the ideas of the true and the beautiful, must be symbolized if they are to be understood and are to drive out the vulgarity of lower sensual pleasures.

The capacity for belief, or sense of truth, is killed out in the childish heart when the truth is presented to it only in the form of abstract language, and offered unclothed. More than one aspect of history teaches this, and yet people persist in it and offer religion and philosophy to youth distinctly as doctrine. Froebel, on the contrary, wishes to awaken original conviction and original insight by religious acts and by philosophical knowledge of concrete things, and thereby to prepare for religious doctrine and for philosophic instruction. Rousseau shows his concurrence with this plan of procedure in these words: "Every truth given too early by words plants the seeds of vice in the childish soul."

The symbolic plays of the kindergarten will cultivate youth to repeat the symbolic plays of the Greeks. But of course they are not to mirror the views of the Grecian world, but of our own time, and thereby to prepare for the nearest future. And out of the newly formed children's festivals shall grow the newly formed people's festivals.

The play-exercises which succeed those of the kindergarten must have their practical results, that is, to teach the government of life in some form and to assist cultivation, intellectually as well as materially. The chief domains of life must be taken into consideration, so that the first acquaintance with the world may connect the ideal side with the living reality. Every child learns more indirectly than directly, that is, rather by his own experience than by instruction. The organized playground, the school-garden, the workshop, artistic exercises of every kind, and excursions into the country, offer means for this in connection with the literary school. Most of these opportunities are already in existence. Singly, none would avail. There must be an organizing idea in order to connect them into one whole.

The proposed play-festival could not be complete without Middendorff, so he was obliged to come to it. He arrived at Marienthal towards evening on the 2d of August. Wearied with the journey, the last portion of which he had taken on foot, heated and dusty, but with a countenance beaming with joy, he gayly entered Froebel's house. I had been making with him some preparations for the festival. Froebel had already arranged everything he could; had had communications with the teachers of surrounding districts, had chosen the playground in the park that environs the castle of Altenstein, had drawn up the plan of the games, and had also practised many of the songs and plays with the scholars of his institution, and the children of the Liebenstein kindergarten.

It was arranged with Middendorff on that same evening that the next day the two friends should together determine the details of the festival on the spot. They were to send for the teachers of the different villages and their troops of children, that they might come to their appointed places and at the time designated. I was desputed to invite the Duke's family, then at the castle of

Altenstein, to the festival, for which they had already given kindly permission. The invitation was not only cordially accepted, but the Duchess promised to have the children provided with milk and rolls.

On the day before the festival, which was arranged for the 4th of August, Froebel and Middendorff scarcely had a moment in which to sit down, so eager were they in making their preparations. The joy of their souls was visible in their faces, like that of mothers the day before Christmas. To make children happy blesses all human hearts.

With the penetrating glance of the weather-wise, Froebel contemplated the evening sky, to see whether the next day would be favorable for the festival. All signs gave the best promise, and this promise was fulfilled, for a warm summer day, not too hot, shone in the blue sky, on the beautiful festival of love, the first child's festival of this land.

On the 4th of August, at two o'clock in the afternoon, more than three hundred children in five different columns, four abreast, came from the little city of Salzung and the surrounding villages, Liebenstein, Marienthal, Schweina, and Steinbach. The teachers and kindergartners at their side, decked with garlands, came singing into the great square, the Altenstein plateau, which had been chosen for the playground. At the entrance, upheld by oak-wreaths, was placed a large crown of flowers, in the midst of which were to be read the words of Schiller:

Deep meaning often lies in childish play.

The troops of children with their teachers from the various districts, distinguished by different-colored bows of ribbon, had assembled in the village of Schweina that lies below Altenstein, in the place designated for them. Those coming from the more distant Salzung were brought in wagons decked with green festoons, in order to go up from here together to the playground, where they were received by Froebel and Middendorff.

These columns, coming from various directions, the variety of ages, including adults and old people, the difference of rank and degrees of culture to which the children belonged (especially marked by the children of the guests at Liebenstein), all this manifoldness had its special significance for Froebel. It was necessary, in order to represent his idea of the "unity of life." Play and its joys were to unite the different spheres of life, the inhabitants of different regions, and various callings and grades of culture, in a common elevation, through ennobled enjoyment in play, just as public worship unites all individuals in religious devotion.

An order went out immediately for arranging the children in eight different circles, which surrounded the centre of the great sphere. Each of the circles was led by its teacher or one of the kindergartners belonging to Froebel's school.

The spectators were arranged outside of the square, in the shadow of the surrounding woods. There was a beautiful intermingling of the people of the surrounding villages, in their different peasant costumes; most of them were the parents and brothers and sisters of the children, the inhabitants of the city of Salzung, and the bathing guests of Liebenstein. In most of the faces beamed that love which is to be seen in the countenance of the roughest man, when his highest feeling—paternal love—is stirred; and this love shone especially in the eyes of the old white-haired peasants who accompanied their grandchildren. The love of grandparents seems specially lively in country people. Perhaps their narrow lives and the rest from heavy work, which old age insures, lead them to concentrate all their feelings upon the children of their families, whom old age easily understands.

When the three hundred clear children's voices sounded in the opening song,

See us here united,

it was accompanied by a kind of marching play, consisting of various evolutions of the different circles. Then the eyes of all sparkled with joy, and none turned their gaze from the players, who, like all simple children, entered into the play with unmistakable joy and hilarity, indeed, with earnestness and devotion.

To children their play is life, activity, work, and enjoyment at the same time, therefore they plunge into it with all earnestness, at least till the ecstasy of play carries them away and impels the livelier temperaments even to extravagance. This extravagance seldom appears in the large assembly of grown-up players, and even the joy of the wildest child restrains itself within certain limits, suggested by the feeling of fitness.

This was the case here. All followed the voices of the leaders of the play, who in their turn obeyed the signs of Froebel and Middendorff.

Every one of the plays that succeeded the opening song was indicated in an intelligent manner to the children less by the words of the song than by the action itself. The predominant idea was always an interchange of the action of individuals with the action of the whole of the circle (making a unit), to which all belonged. Soon one of the company was chosen to do something in the midst of the inner circle, as, for instance, to make some one systematic motion at some individual's suggestion, which all the rest imitated, or some one determined and directed what the rest should do.

For instance, the different circles formed garlands, each one of which represented a different flower, celebrated in the song as the emblem of a different virtue. At the close they all united in a single circle, representing the German oak-wreath, which, as a symbol of German nationality, united them in one whole.

In the game of the pigeon-house, the flying out of the birds into the distance and their return were represented, and the doves that had flown out were required, on their return, to tell the rest what they had seen or heard.

SONG

We open the pigeon-house again
And set all the happy flutterers free;
They fly o'er field and grassy plain,

Delighted with joyous liberty.
And when they return from their merry flight,
We shut up the house and bid them good night.
And now you are safe and happy here,
Tell us what you have seen, little pigeon dear.
The bird tells his story, and then says, "Coo, coo,
I'm so glad, dear mother, to get home to you."

Then the children represented hedges with green twigs, which they held in their hands, under which the youngest children, as little birds, slipped through, singing "Little Bird in the Wood."

Similar plays, leading the children's thoughts into nature and the life of animals, are very numerous in the kindergarten.

The Salzungen children, who were, generally speaking, larger than the other children, practised gymnastics intermixed with many well-known plays of the children of the people, whose text was changed to suit the kindergarten. Generally, the peculiar kindergarten plays were the most pleasing, as being most suitable to children.

The meaning or point lying at the foundation of each play, which comes out in some jocose way in the popular plays, is unintelligible to the young child, or at least unsuitable. The present condition of culture requires these plays to be reformed to suit the times. Froebel's clothing of his ideas of play, which are to awaken determinate ideas in the child's soul, is not always happily chosen, but it generally hits the right vein in the sense of the child, crystallizing itself around what springs from the childish impulse of the moment, or from the people's wit, which is the original source of all games.

Froebel has succeeded with true genius in interpreting and giving expression to the sensuous part of the child's nature, even if the verses which express it are often very defective, and here and there are, on reflection, to be condemned.

And the music of the songs, which were the popular melodies, was not always the best. Froebel took what was at hand, for he was neither a musician nor a poet, and he only aimed at embodying his intellectual ideas. These faults, with other imperfections incident to every work, are easily to be improved upon. But because people have as yet penetrated so little into the deep grounds of Froebel's educational system, criticism, so far as it exists on this subject, speaks of these external things alone, the poor verses and songs, the versified reflections, etc., not separating what is designed for the children from what is addressed to the mother, as for example the mottoes to the "Mother and Cosset Songs." Such superficial and nonsensical judgments have, however, done injury by giving occasion for the so-called advocates who take up the method for their own personal ends, to make use of them in order to give themselves the appearance of impartial judgment in their own pitiful, bungling work, in which they often make use of Froebel's thoughts as their own, while they are criticising and blaming him. These superficial judges are not capable of entering into the child's nature, to which their standard of literary worth does not apply. The lisping babe on the mother's breast, and the little child of five years old, do not understand Goethe and Schiller. But surely the little child can understand when it is allowed to look at the animals in the yard, and to sing Froebel's little song about their language:

The doves fly, and the little colts jump,
The little geese gabble, and "Quack" says the duck!
The little bees hum, and moolly cow moos;
The little calf frisks, and the peacock struts,
The little lamb baas, and the old sheep bleats.

These indeed are neither beautiful thoughts nor beautiful verses, but the right language for the young child, whose attention we wish to call to the various motions and sounds of the beasts, putting them into the measured language which attracts at this age and awakens the sense of rhythm. What can be more suitable to the child's understanding than the following song?

White snow comes down in gentle flakes;
The field is covered, the seeds are safe;

All snug the green grass lies there too;
By and by it will peep out at me and you;
When the snow is gone, up jumps the seed,
Its sleep is over,—grass covers the mead;
The stalk grows high, the corn waves in the air;—
So my darling will grow all lovely and fair.

In the close hedge mother bird makes her home;
In the pretty nest two eggs will come;
When the little birdies peep from the shell,
The mother spreads her wings to keep them well;
Soon they grow strong to fly with mamma,
And listen to songs from dear, kind papa.

The circle of children make the pantomime of this with their arms and fingers: first the falling snow, then the snowy cover spreading wide; afterward the seed sprouting up, the rising of the cornstalk and the bowing of the full ears, for which the children bow their heads. Joyfully the little ones listen to the homely songs that accompany the finger-plays, the gymnastic exercises of the child's hands.

Then the mother shows the child a bird's-nest by interlacing his little hands, and sings,

On the tender green bough
Mother bird builds her nest,
And drops within it two eggs.

When the young ones are born
She spreads out her wings
To keep them all snug and warm.

By and by the birdies call,
"Mother dear, peep, peep,
And now will you teach us to sing?"

Then they sing on the tree
While the sun shines warm,
And Willy shall listen with me.

Such childish songs as these accompanying the child's observation of nature are quite in their place. To the uncomprehending critic we must quote Jean Paul's words: "Stand far away from the tender flower of childhood, and brush not off the flower-dust with your rough fist."

The best proof that most of Froebel's plays are suited to the childish mind is the never-failing joy of the children, great and small, in playing them again and again. Even grown-up young girls, whether kindergartners or not, indeed, many still older people who retain their susceptibility to the pleasures of childhood, practise them with children or among themselves with great delight. Every institution for the culture of kindergartners affords proof of this.

Whoever could contemplate this great troop of children at the Altenstein festival without the deepest emotion, could have his feelings stirred by nothing purely human. Even the country people who had grown gray with rough work expressed deep sympathy, with tears of happy emotion.

"That is a sight for the heart!" said one. "How beautifully playful the children are!"

"Yes, Mr. Froebel understands how to exercise children; no doubt of that!" said another.

"This is delightful!" said others.

A stout, robust peasant who had accompanied his grandchild, said, "See one of those sacramental child-people who knows how to make all that is beautiful!"

A stiff military captain said: "If all children had gymnastic plays of this kind, the drilling of recruits would be a real pleasure!"

A lady from among the Liebenstein guests said to Froebel, with tears in her eyes, "I never saw anything that struck me like this child's play. It seems as if I were in a church; it sounds so devotional."

"Yes," replied Froebel, "that is the uniting power of play which blesses and exalts children, and even grown-up people. Real human joy is only a divine worship, for it is ordered by God."

There was a pause for rest, and the children spread themselves on the turf-covered banks of the grove in order to partake of the refreshments provided for them. The grown-up people took part in this, and enjoyed it hardly less than the children. When this pause for rest was over, and they were making arrangements for new plays, the family of the Duke came to look on. I called Froebel and Middendorff to receive them, and they both approached, glowing with heat, and their faces beaming with happiness.

The Duchess said, "What a beautiful sight is this troop of happy children! But you work too hard in guiding the plays. Won't you take seats with us?" pointing to the places prepared for the princes.

Froebel answered, almost with irritation, "No, your Highness, that will not do; I must go back to the children; I am never wearied; playing animates me and makes me young again."

"It is not so easy at your years," said the Duke.

"Froebel has discovered the secret of remaining forever young," said Middendorff. "Among children one keeps fresh, and does not grow old."

And both these youthful old men returned to the circle of the playing children, of which they had not lost the least motion, as the sharp glance of both had been directed over the whole.

The young nine-year-old princess looked upon the playing with the liveliest interest, and, as it appeared to me, with longing eyes, as if she would gladly have taken part in it. This little one was not wholly unacquainted with Froebel's occupations, for she had been taught some of them, especially the weaving, by Fraulein Levin.

The children of the great in this world must, early in life, learn to do without that which makes children most happy—association with companions of their own age, and the cordial intimacies of childhood. Rarely can they take part in these. The unrestrained freedom of children standing on the lower steps of the social ladder is always wanting to them. The advantages which they usually have in their education hardly outweigh this disadvantage connected with it. In the conventional world the full happiness of childhood is scarcely ever enjoyed.

After the playing was ended, and the princely family had conversed with amiable courtesy with many of the company, they left the playground.

The troop of children now rested again to get strength for returning home, which some of the youngest had to do mostly in the arms of their parents. When the columns were arranged anew, they were first led before the ducal castle, in order to sing a song of thanks for the favors they had received, and the place granted for the festival. They then proceeded to a spot under some beautiful old lindens, below Altenstein, from whence the road parted to the different districts. The garlanded wagons of the Salzungers were waiting here to take home the young guests.

But the children were again obliged to rest before proceeding on their way, and Middendorff used these moments to speak a few words of consecration before parting. He stepped upon a stone table that stood under the lindens, in order to gain a hearing, and then out of his full heart, with the inward earnestness peculiar to himself, spoke to the children and their parents. After he had reminded the children (the older of whom could fully understand his words) that they were to thank their parents for the day of pleasure, and their Father in heaven for his goodness, and must deserve a repetition of it by their future industry in school and by obedience and love at home, he cried out to the parents Froebel's motto, "Come, let us live with our children, that all things may be better here on earth," and explained to them its meaning.

Among other things, he said: "The time is now come in which

the human race, according to God's decree, is to rise to a higher stage of life. At such a time there is already a great movement in all minds, and also in outer life, as is the case at present, when everything evil which has been concealed comes into view, and hinders the good and the progress which should come. Hence it is now fitting that everyone should help to conquer the evil and make a free path for the good. The first thing to be done is to make better men by a good education of the children. Therefore Froebel calls upon his contemporaries to live with the children in order through them to solve the great problems of the time for the future.

"Froebel has regained the lost paradise in his kindergartens, in which little children are guarded as much as possible from sin, and are trained to become virtuous men and women by the harmonious development of their powers and dispositions. Childish innocence belongs only to the first years of life. Hence they are to be protected and guarded at the beginning, and that is the task of the mother; but all mothers and maidens should help to build up and take care of the kindergarten, in order that pure human life may prosper.

"The child-festival of today has given one aspect of the paradise of childhood. Let all hold it fast in remembrance, and follow the call of the time, which is God's call, and be, as Froebel says, true guardians and gardeners of children."

The assembly had listened to Middendorff's words in profound stillness, interrupted only here and there by the low sobbing of some of the mothers. When he had ended, the whole company pressed up to him and to Froebel, to take their hands and express their warm thanks. All the hands were grasped, and nothing was heard but concurrence and good wishes.

An old woman of one of the villages said, "How beautifully Herr Middendorff speaks. It seems as if our Saviour himself was speaking."

"How happy I am to have been at this festival!" said one of the Liebenstein guests from a great distance.

"I only wish we could have such among us," said another.

"God's blessing rests upon such a day," said an old peasant, and, deeply moved, pressed Froebel's hand, who stood with glorified features looking at the children himself—"the new buds on the tree of humanity," as he called them, whose blooming he felt he had furthered by the day's festival, the exemplar of a custom to be universal.

We now broke up, while all repeated once more the children's closing songs: "Friends, let us part," etc., and "Farewell, to meet again."

The description Froebel wrote of the festival ends in these words: "Yes, it was a festival of the union of nature, man, and God, and God's blessing rests on such a day, as the old peasant expressed it. How easily might such a child and youth festivals be exalted to a universal people's festival! Should we not do everything to call such festivals into life, that so we may at least reach what the hearts of all desire, an all-sided 'unity of life?'"*

The troops of children had gone forth; on every side sounded the clear childish voices, repeating the last strophes of the parting song. The sun was going down, a crystal-clear, glorious sunset, as Froebel said when the grown-up of the Marienthal circle broke up to go home. All were rejoicing in the soft moonlight of the summer evening, which was exceptionally beautiful in our climate. In Froebel's and Middendorff's faces was a high, holy content, as they now walked silently away, inwardly happy in having brought a long-cherished thought into fulfilment in such a beautiful manner.

Froebel said, at last: "O, other child-festivals will follow ours! Since one has been realized, why may they not be nationalized, for they have a true and beautiful meaning? People's festivals for a higher, nobler humanity will follow, and contribute their part to the final attainment of the complete 'unity of life.'"

"It has often occurred to me during our festival today," I said, "what is expressed by Goethe in his 'School Regions' (*Pedagog-*

*The description is printed in the third volume of Froebel's work, *Pedagogics of the Kindergarten*.

ischen Provinzen) in the *Wanderjahre*, which coincides in many ways with your views, particularly the symbolic form which is there given."

"Yes, and to think," answered Froebel, "that I have never yet read Goethe's *Wanderjahre*. My intention to do so was always baffled, so I only know the *Lehrjahre* and its sequel from hearsay."

"O, then we must immediately take the *Wanderjahre* in hand!" I exclaimed. "I will bring it to you, and also a book upon Egyptian antiquities, in which I have lately found some passages proving the truth of your educational views."

We separated here, and took leave of Middendorff, who unfortunately could not remain away from Keilhau more than a few days, but he promised to make another visit in the autumn.

"It was beautiful!" were his last spoken words.

When I went, on the afternoon of the next day, to see Froebel, in order to read to him Goethe's "School Regions," he was already busy with his description of the festival. But he gave me a willing hearing, and was truly in transport at Goethe's educational views and their expression in the *Wanderjahre*. He often interrupted me with such childlike exclamations as: "How well Goethe understands the nature of man in childhood!" "He has also found that the connection of human history must be held fast if a new development is to be attained. We must look upon our children as a product of the past if we would lead them into the future!" "Childhood can only be led through symbols to the understanding of truth and the understanding of itself. It needs symbolic action." "Gestures have the greatest significance for childhood."

Goethe also recognized this when he spoke of the manner of greeting of children of different ages in the "School Regions."

Goethe, truly, with his seer's glance into the future human development, could not but concur in Froebel's view, which also embraced humanity in its past, present, and future. What does his expression in Faust (Second Part), "Everything is a parable," mean, but that everything is the symbol of an idea? He maintained, like Froebel, that a symbol of the truth must go before the word, to aid the human mind in its development.

Froebel busied himself especially with the beginning of human culture, and with what the earliest childhood of man betokens, therefore everything particularly interested him which had reference to it. I called his attention to the fact stated in the above-mentioned volume upon Egypt, that in the beginning of the culture of that country the three graces, or goddesses of beauty, were represented by three cubes leaning upon each other—by which he was made happy as if he had discovered a treasure.

"You see, now, how correct is my choice of the cube as the first regular form, for the child's inspection, next after the sphere. The Egyptians did not know that it was the first regular form of solid bodies in nature or crystallization. But the regular symmetrical forms of nature, because they are the fundamental forms (types) of all phenomena, are only to be found in nature. Man carries in his mind natural forms and their law as an inward testimony of his origin; so far he is a child of nature. The ancients had this presentiment of the truth. We moderns shall come to a consciousness of it."

"This peculiar fact in regard to the cube form, mentioned in my writings, has been frequently repeated in the writings of others."

I also quoted to Froebel out of *Kreuizer's Symbolik*, that "golden balls were given to the young Bacchus to play with, by his educator, and also that the young princes of Persia played with such, and alone had this privilege." This plunged Froebel into deep thought, and he said: "What a power of presentiment! Yes, the presentiment of truth always goes before recognition of it. To show unity in the sphere is the greatest privilege, for God is unity, and the undeveloped man can behold unity only in a symbol."

At such moments the seer in Froebel came forth. It was as if he looked far back into the past of humanity, and there sought the thread which from the beginning connects all times and leads to the farthest future, even to the goal.

10

Herr Von Wydenbrugk

Froebel had built hopes on the visit of Von Wydenbrugk, the minister, who superintended educational matters in Weimar, and believed that his support of the cause would insure its firm establishment in that part of Germany at least. To judge from the lively interest that Von Wydenbrugk, as well as the minister-president, Watzdorff, had expressed in my communications concerning Froebel's educational idea (during my stay in Weimar the preceding winter of 1850) and in connection with the sympathy of the princely family, this expectation of their official support and assistance in the introduction of the cause were justified. Too much, however, is always expected from influential people, and in most cases more than they are in a condition to give with their best will; for the thousand obstacles they have to conquer are not always perceived. The greatest of these obstacles generally come from subalterns through whose agency only can innovations be brought about. The power of a minister seldom reaches to carrying reforms immediately into operation, if their necessity or the beneficial effect of the means necessary for their accomplishment is undervalued by the subordinates, or perhaps not wished for by them on some other grounds. How little could even great minds, like Stein's and Hardenberg's, carry through in their own lifetime the reforms which they strove for! Indeed, even rulers upon thrones cannot always do what they would. Joseph II died of a broken heart because his great ideas were neither appreciated nor could be carried out. Contemporaries are never ripe for understanding the ideas of minds in advance of their time. Posterity only can understand and carry them out to their full extent.

To these advanced ideas belongs Froebel's educational principle. We should have spared ourselves many a painful disappointment at the time, if we had always remembered this universal historical experience. But painful experiences are spared to none who strive for those improvements for which everything must be attempted that promises any good consequences.

So we attempted, during the several days' stay of the minister Von Wydenbrugk in Liebenstein, to gain him over to our plans. He was my table neighbor at the Kruhaus, which gave me many opportunities of speaking with him on the subject. I saw at once that many objections occurred to his mind in consequence of consultations with two prominent schoolmen of the district, who had influence on account of their knowledge, but who had shown neither goodwill to Froebel nor real acquaintance with his idea, and Froebel already looked upon them as opponents. Then came the well-known hesitation at every reform and innovation, which makes all good things so difficult of accomplishment.

"Caution must be used at present in regard to the pursuit of novelties, and the foolish plans everywhere prevailing would lead to abuse. The idea of connecting practical work with the school has already proved to be unattainable; the requisite improvement of the school has been gained through Pestalozzi's method, whose universal adoption is first to be striven for. In Froebel's method so much is found that is obscure and impracticable that we must not lavish public money upon it before it has been tested by private investigations. Children and youth should not be given up to experiments whose success has not been proved," etc.—and other objections not applicable in themselves to a definite thing, but true in general.

The most useful and important reforms are often dismissed and their advocates shoved aside, instead of being granted a thorough trial of the subject, which a practical experiment would often justify. We owe to this rejecting caution of Philistines that some reforms have been adopted too late to be of any use to the present generation. Extreme necessity often first opens the eyes to means of help that have long been at hand, whose timely application would have averted great evils.

This ever-recurring experience is fully applicable to Froebel's educational method, which will only be universally appreciated when the evil consequences of a popular education *not* in consonance with the wants of the time, and laden with crying faults, shall open the most purblind eyes.

Herr Von Wydenbrugk had incontestably the most thorough interest and the best will for all the improvements which the time demands, especially for those which promised the right education for the people. He did not, like many other dignitaries, look down superciliously upon Froebel's strivings, which embrace for the first time the care of the germs of human power and their correct nurture in early childhood. The great use of an early development of the working powers, in view of its economical as well as moral influence, was perfectly plain to him; and, personally, he was quite ready to further the cause as far as possible, "when the right moment should come," as he often said.

And truly at that time it seemed, on the side of the magistrates, that the right moment had not come, because among the adherents of the Froebel cause were found many who were comprised politically, and who interpreted it in their own sense, giving their countenance to it precisely because it belonged to the novelties of the time, and laid great stress upon the free development of the human being.

But Froebel's views on education for freedom were certainly very different from those of the youthful fanatics and agitators, who thought to teach freedom by the overthrow of national order.

When I spoke of *education for freedom,* Herr Von Wydenbrugk warned me not to use that expression, for it would always give rise to misapprehensions. "It is indeed not clear to me," he said, "how far you think this mode of designation is correct yourself."

"Certainly," said I, "it is correct, inasmuch as men can be

made capable of outward or political freedom only when they have been educated to the requisite degree of inward freedom. Only a correct education from the beginning can teach to individuals the necessary self-government and self-restraint, and the necessity of their submission to natural laws. All the teaching at universities upon national rights and national law are inadequate to spread universally the right view that the state, as such, with its arrangements, is the necessary condition of the freedom of the whole, and therewith the freedom of individuals. It is only for the most part a vanishing minority which frequents the universities, and even of this minority only a part comes away with a correct view, as is sufficiently proved by many of the leaders of the present revolutionary movement, the majority of whom are scholarly men.

"Besides this, mere knowledge, or rather knowledge gained only through literary instruction, without contemporaneous personal experience, does not suffice to make men capable of the self-government and self-restraint necessary for true freedom. Students who almost daily hear lectures upon national and natural law are not prevented thereby from occasionally committing the greatest misdemeanors, and from speaking with contempt of all law and order. Undoubtedly it would be timely to make arrangements through some schools for advanced culture to instruct the mass of the people in their civic duties and rights and the laws of the land. But that would not be sufficient to protect the freedom gained from abuse; the early habits of life are the main things that later decide the issue. So long as the children of the masses remain without education, before and with the school, and are left to the lawlessness of street life, so long they cannot be ripe and fitted for free national institutions.

"Let us only look upon the little vagabonds who have grown up in asylums, and see how hard it has been to win them to a well-ordered life. They had rather suffer hunger and thirst, and bear all the possible privations of their free robber life, than give themselves up to the constraint and order of even those institutions which are conducted with love and gentleness! In fact, the public notices of the asylums founded in New York for homeless children testify that, in spite of all the amenities offered in these institutions, a considerable number of the children always prefer, even in rough weather, to find their usual sleeping-places in the open air, in sheds, on steps, under bridges, rather than be subjected to the domestic arrangements of the asylums designed for their good. So much for the power of habit and the desire for rude freedom, when the restraints of morals and of the habits of orderly life do not exercise their influence early. The storm-spirit breaks loose, or an unconstrained and lawless life gets the upper hand when room and opportunity offer."

"Even the best education cannot prevent that," said Herr Von Wydenbrugk. "Men always remain men, that is, imperfect beings."

"But the progressive development of men under all circumstances," was my answer, "has to combat the evil of every time, and circumstances are always different according to the change of epoch. Should we not in our time, therefore, seek for the causes why children do not obey their parents any better, and why the great mass of the citizens will not obey the magistrates and their ordinances? You grant that general revolutionary movements have some historic ground to justify them, and that a great measure of general freedom must be granted at the present time?"

"Yes," interrupted the minister, "but it can only be granted when preservation of the state and its order are guaranteed."

"Certainly," said I, "that is obvious; the granting of the demand for a more extended political freedom, which is not to be put off, involves a condition at the same time of providing for its right use, and for a protection from its abuse. In the emancipated slave, or the rough masses, the capacity for this is completely wanting. The very knowledge of the necessity of law is wanting to them. They will always transgress it whenever and wherever they have freedom. Therefore power must always be arrayed against power.

"The obedience of individuals, in the interest of the whole human race, has been and will continue to be necessary. In the lower stages of development, blind obedience to parents and superiors, like servile submission under national authority, was necessary to the existence of social order. The further historical development of men and circumstances has given more value to the *personality* of individuals in reference to the whole, and therefore individual right has come into conflict with national right.

"That blind obedience and servile subjection of earlier times have now become an impossibility, and will become more so the further the consciousness of personal right is cultivated and impressed upon the masses. Nothing is left, then, but to set free obedience in the place of blind obedience, and to render the rough masses, through cultivation, capable of seeing that only the self-restraint of individuals and their voluntary subjection to law make greater freedom in society possible. That mode of education which can solve this problem may justly be called 'education for freedom.' Only he who does not know the whole power and importance of the first impressions and earliest habits of life can laugh at Froebel for placing in the earliest childhood the foundation for the later life of the citizen, and for making the mind of the child receptive of legitimate order before wilfulness and lawlessness have become fixed conditions in it.

"The Spartans took the nurslings from their mothers in order to educate them for a national end. It would have been better if they had taken care of the correct education of the mothers for their educational office. And if the Jesuits, in spite of their opposition to an advanced culture, are yet always able to bring about the blindest subjection to the decrees of the church and its dominion, then education to free obedience, which is in harmony with the demands of the time, will also be possible."

"Shall we not, then," said Von Wydenbrugk, laughing, "like the Spartans, according to the views of our great Fichte, withdraw all children from the family, to educate them in national institutions?"

"That neither you nor anyone else who is acquainted with Froebel's method can really believe, since the education of the female sex for its maternal duties is his first requisition. But can it hinder or disturb family education in any way, if, by means of kindergartens, a place of education is created which represents a *miniature state* for children, in which the young citizen can learn to move freely, but with consideration for his little fellows? That cannot be done, at least in the family; it needs a larger social circle, for in the family the mother or the nurse is already accustomed to foster in the nursling wilfulness and the spirit of opposition. Family education, even under circumstances still so bad, must remain; but a corrective and complement must be given to it, and this before school.

"This pressing want has been met for the children of the working and poorer classes in a certain way by asylums. If it were not for their salutary influence, the present savagery would doubtless be greater than it is. How many children, who receive only demoralizing influences in their homes, and are almost constrained to lawlessness and obstinacy, have had the only moral nourishment of their whole lives in these institutions! This is acknowledged, yet the old method of exacting passive obedience still prevails in them. Many conditions wanting in them must be fulfilled, in order to educate the right citizens of the future.

"The people's kindergartens, or the asylums that have been reformed in conformity to the times, fulfil these conditions.

"Besides the greater freedom of movement of the pupils in what one may call, from its analogy to the state, an orderly, lawful community of life, something is added which constitutes the chief lever for order and the chief means against all misuse of freedom. This is the use of powers adapted to the age of children. All unused power seeks some outlet. If it is restrained, it explodes. This is also the case with human powers. What are revolutions but the explosions of the unregulated, unused powers of men, whose way to make them manifest in a lawful and appropriate manner has been effectively blocked? This is the case, more or less, even with noble men when they oppose existing national evils for the ideal of better conditions.

"No one, neither the adult nor the child, finds well-being and content without the use, that is to say without the development, of his powers.

"If this just demand is not fulfilled, the lower or animal side of the human being seeks its welfare in the gratification of its coarse impulses.

"There is no need of any constraint or any command for that activity which is in harmony with the being of man in general, and at the same time with his individual disposition, and it will act freely and with love, and not overstep the measure of the powers at different ages.

"This free activity is one of the chief conditions of an education for freedom, but it is only possible when the law of free creativeness is known and applied; for that a free creativeness only can be a lawful one, we are taught by the smallest blade of grass, whose development takes place only according to immutable laws.

"Insofar as Froebel has learned from nature (or from the Creator) the law of creation, he can apply it to the productions of human, and therefore of childish, powers, and make really free creation possible to them.

"This sounds mysterious and mystical. It is a riddle before we see *how* the egg is made to stand on its end. Only he who arrives at the knowledge of its solution can understand Froebel's method, which, *without that*, is wholly wanting in significance. But it is a very difficult task to give such knowledge to others by words, without their own observation and experience."

"The word 'mystical' does not recommend anything in our day," said the minister. "More than ever men desire clearness and understanding in all things."

"Every new theory that comes into the world," I replied, "seems more or less mystical, because it is not quite understood; and it is not quite understood because it has not yet found its place among the generally received views, and the right formula and expression are yet wanting to it. Therefore it happens that every new thing comes first into the hands of the rapacious, who have no understanding for ideas, and only take hold of their outer rind to make them serviceable for their own ends. That all formation in the material as in the intellectual world proceeds according to law, we know; but the *how* of this proceeding we know not. This law, which lies at the foundation of every process of development, must be recognized by the human mind as that law according to which all formation proceeds. It is the law by which God creates all things. And man, whose destiny it is to imitate what God has created, can only produce his own works according to the same law, since the human mind of itself can discover no law—that is, no original law—but everything is fixed and determined by God. Man only creates relatively by ever new combinations of existing things, while God alone is an absolute creator—creates all things out of himself. The unconscious creativeness of instinct in the animal world as in the human world proceeds according to this same law of formation. The childish instinct hears the same law within itself as that by which the spider weaves and the silkworm spins and the bee makes its cell. Therefore the mind of the child, living still in the twilight of unconsciousness, can easily apply this lawful procedure as soon as it is brought before his eyes in an elementary manner, in concrete things, and he is shown the mode of applying it. It is only because Froebel recognized this law of all formation, and found the method of its application, that his educational method is truly conformable to nature, since it leaves the natural process of development partly to self-activity, and guides and supports it according to that law. Therefore on this side, that is, for the activity that exercises all the powers and tendencies, free obedience is secured; for every being strives, *must* strive, for his own development, how unconscious soever this striving may be.

"This free production or creative activity shows the stamp of originality in the human being yet undimmed, however it may be obscured through deviation from God's law, in consequence of the freedom granted to him, and the inheritance of the sin and guilt of his ancestors. Formative activity brings to light the individual tendencies and peculiarities, makes each individual know himself, and creates that satisfaction and sense of dignity which is inseparably connected with it.

"In early childhood the outward form of this activity can only be that of play. To convert this play into creative action, in the smallest measure, offers to the development of the whole being, from the very beginning, a support and a guide as counterpoise to all wilfulness, which leads astray from the right. At the same time, through this free action of the individual tendencies, a counterpoise is gained to the levelling tendencies (*Gleichmacherei*) of our present conventional mode of education, which in the school and in the family proceeds only in a formal way, according to traditional prescriptions or demands, without respect to the measure of the powers of the pupils and the new demands of our time. The consequence is, that a too early excitement and overstraining reduces and weakens the sum of the powers, deadens and turns into machines the great majority who thus are incapable of living out in an original way the divine ideas dwelling in every being.

"All progress, all culture, is the result of the original creativeness of the minds of every age, which have been able to increase the sum of existing intellectual and material wealth by producing something new.

"The imitators in a generation who allow themselves to be satisfied with what they have found at hand, and live and do only as they have been accustomed to do, can never bring about such an enrichment of civilization. Through them no advance, nothing new, has come into the world.

"The creative power of every generation of living geniuses which leads to a higher state of culture is nothing else than that original power which, according to the indwelling law of God, can freely form and even organize. A generation is rich in power and influence in proportion as it possesses such original vigor. Therefore, of what immense importance is a method which can awaken and cultivate original creative power!"

"Are all men to be made geniuses by this method?" said Herr von Wydenbrugk, with an incredulous smile.

"Certainly not," I answered. "Genius must first be born before it can be educated for its task. There will be plenty of ballast. The method proposes only to increase the sum of creative power so far as it is according to God's will the task of each generation, and as is significantly expressed by all the demands of the present time. In the meantime, not the remotest pretension is made that the salvation of our time is to be secured by this educational method alone. Much must be done, many things must concur, in order that this slow transition in which we live shall give way to a new and better time. But one of the means for this end is the new education. We shall not have new men without a new education. And that can only be a new education which shall free human nature from the crushing fetters of a perverted education, and shall remedy the entire want of a true method for the masses. But indeed the new education can only reach the result indicated when its complete and universal application shall proceed with real method; and we are as yet very far from the point. The dangers which threaten national order should require, it seems to me, of those whose duty it is to guard it, that they support with all their powers a cause which strives to oppose the bulwark of educational influence to the present perversion and demoralization, and smooth the path for the future free and conscious obedience to law, and thereby lead at the same time to the highest possible degree of freedom."

"If national support were so easily to be gained, I think," said Herr von Wydenbrugk, "it would not be found wanting in us. During the storm-flood the earth cannot be cultivated. We must first become masters again of the political situation before we can take in hand such necessary improvements. In the meantime, little as I deny the importance of a national education adapted to the time, and well as I see the advantages that may grow out of Froebel's method, yet I cannot believe so confidently as you do in the success, at least in the immediate success, of such improvements, which often pour but a drop into the sea! The rough masses—do you know what that means?—*there* is the Rubicon in which for centuries numberless reforms have foundered."

"On that very account," I replied, "by means of a better and more general education, those rough masses must vanish out of society. This may indeed proceed slowly. When we look at long periods of time, the progress of humanity and its culture are undeniable. All higher activity that reaches beyond the span of a life or a generation would cease if we could not have faith in an eternal progressive development of earthly things. We know not when the seed we sow shall ripen, but we must sow it if we would do our duty to posterity. But everyone who sows his seed must leave its growth to higher powers."

"That we will do," said Herr von Wydenbrugk, "and enter upon the work as soon as the moment has come, and there is rest in the land; only do not expect too much, and do not forget that we small States cannot act quite independently, but must yield in everything to the Great Powers. Advise Froebel to exercise caution in the interest of his cause, in regard to connections, and in the choice of his *representatives*. There seem to be some among them who, because they are in danger themselves, endanger his work. These unripe political minds bring upon Froebel the reputation of adhering to the destructive tendencies which they proclaim."

"I thought," I replied, "that even a superficial knowledge of Froebel and his teaching might have protected him from such a suspicion. The motto of the revolution is *overthrow*, while Froebel's motto is *development*—development of men and things. And the means by which Froebel would strive for the renewing of society and of the state are just the opposite of those of the revolutionary storm-birds, who, however, as well as real reformers, have by their alarm-cry undoubtedly their part to fulfil for historical progress.

"In order to be able to build up anew, there must always be destruction and removal of rubbish. Among these destroying hordes are also idealists who strive for the noble and the good, and are only led astray in regard to their means; but all idealists and minds striving for progress and reform have undeniably their points of contact, and feel sympathy for each other, however far their views on the ways and means of reaching their goal may differ. These sympathies may lead Froebel astray in regard to persons; and his own self-sacrificing spirit exposes him, perhaps, to be deceived by men following only the impulse of self-seeking. Caution and criticism are not his affair; and who can see but with bleeding heart how the noblest and best must fall a sacrifice in political strifes! Froebel feels this also, but he has nevertheless separated from his nephews, who formerly, in their youth, shared very naturally the dominant revolutionary views, as is widely known."

"These sacrifices to politics are unfortunately unavoidable in times like ours," said the minister, "however much many individuals may claim our sympathy and even our admiration. Where the preservation of the state and order are involved, the law can make no discrimination nor exercise forbearance in reference to individuals."*

When Froebel, toward the evening of the day on which this conversation passed, came into Liebenstein, and I introduced him to the minister, the latter took up anew our last conversation, which I had related to Froebel.

Addressing Froebel, he said: "You do not, then, concur in the axiom of the revolutionists, which is, 'Everyone is born free, and brings the right of personal freedom into the world with him'?"

"No," said Froebel, "not in their sense. Man, on the contrary, is born entirely fettered on all sides, and truly for this reason, that he can and must obtain freedom only by his own striving. Freedom cannot be bestowed upon us. God himself cannot bestow it upon us, since it must be the product of our moral and intellectual unfettering, which it is possible to attain only by self-activity. Every individual has to free himself from the narrow fetters of his undeveloped condition of childhood by the help of

*These extracts from my conversations with the minister Von Wydenbrugk are given here especially for the sake of contradicting some statements which were made afterwards in the Froebel circle, as if the minister had failed in promises given. He made no definite promises at that time.

educational influences. Nations, and the human race also, which in the course of ages, taking its departure from the extreme condition of slavery, has risen, step by step, to the degree of freedom that has now been reached, have the same task. As soon as we apply the idea of organic development to human history, we recognize clearly and significantly that every kind of real freedom is the result of culture, which excludes as contradictory to it the caprice of the individual. But this culture of individuals and of nations cannot be forced, and cannot be gained at a blow. It is the result of consecutive development. Hence the rude masses can never be free; on the contrary, it is they who hinder all freedom, even for those who possess the requisite degree of culture for it. This our heroes of freedom forget when they expect universal freedom from merely outward national and political changes and innovations. The freedom of nations depends on the degree of culture of the majority of their members, and, like all good things—like man himself—is at once the work of *nature*, *man*, and *God*, which depends not on the arbitrariness of individuals, not even upon the greatest possessors of power. The human race needed many centuries, a long and strong school of experience, before it was ripe for the present stage of development, which demands of renewing of human life in all its departments. But people misunderstand the call of the time, which is 'unity of life,' or the equilibrium of existing contrasts in the human world, the abrogation of the two great differences in culture, the elevation of those unjustly oppressed and neglected."

"If you mean that diversities in human society are to be abolished, a levelling and equalizing of men to take place, you do agree with the innovators and their ideas," said the minister, interrupting him.

"Certainly I do not," rejoined Froebel, "for then the manifoldness of human relations would cease, upon which depend all unanimity and all equilibrium in the human world as well as in God's world—the universe in which the infinite variety is the means of order and harmony. This variety in the world is ordained by God; it is the law of the universe, which cannot be abolished by the caprice of individuals; it is the united work of *nature*, *man*, and *God*. The motto of the revolution cited by you ought to be, 'All have a claim to culture, to the development of the powers and dispositions with which they are endowed, but this within the limits which his earthly relations point out to each one, and which is enjoined upon the whole through the duty of individuals.

"But there are two classes of oppressed people who cannot enjoy the proper degree of culture in the existing state of things, and to whom more freedom—I mean more freedom of development—must be granted, to make it possible for all to reach a higher degree of culture."

"And they are?" said Herr von Wydenbrugk.

"Women and children," answered Froebel. "These are the most oppressed and neglected of all. They have not yet been fully recognized in their dignity as parts of human society. If progress and a greater degree of freedom depend largely upon the degree of universal culture, then it is woman, to whom God and nature have pointed out the first educational office in the family, upon whom this progress especially depends. And if childhood in its whole importance, in its lofty dignity as the germ of mankind, was sufficiently respected and honored, recognized in its nature and its claims for education, means and opportunities would be offered to all classes of society and to every individual to develop their God-given powers and dispositions, and to enable them to use them for the benefit of society within the limits set by their circumstances and talents.

"I know that this is the work of centuries. The present time demands that the foundation be laid for it by an education corresponding to its demands, and worthy of human dignity. And to lay this foundation is the aim of my kindergarten, which is to prevent the children of the masses from growing up like little savages, and also to save the schools from a lawlessness which is miscalled liberty.

"This earliest age is the most important one for education, because the beginning decides the manner of progress and the end. If national order is to be recognized in later years as a benefit, childhood must first be accustomed to law and order, and therein find the means of freedom. Lawlessness and caprice must rule in no period of life, not even in that of the nursling.

"The kindergarten life, according to its ideal, is a micrometric human life in the past, present, and future. Kindergartens inherit the acquired riches of inward and outward experiences, and the knowledge of the human race of all times in its collective result; they carry man as child back into the original relations to the family, to nature, and to himself, in order to fit him for living his life both in and out of himself with conscious perception; I say perception, not knowledge, for which his age is yet unsuitable. Perception is the beginning and the preliminary condition for thinking. One's own perceptions awaken one's own conceptions, and these awaken one's own thinking in later stages of development. Let us have no precocity, but natural, that is consecutive, organic development.

"This process of going through all the stages of development that the human race has traversed from the past up to the present can alone lead man to a clear consciousness of himself and his life, as is demanded by the present stage of knowledge. From this knowledge will be gained how the action of mankind, indeed, of the smallest child, depends upon willing. But the will is determined by the mind. The mind is the thinking power, and thinking develops according to laws. The mind works only according to the laws of thinking, and the laws of thinking determine the intelligent action of man. The cultivated action of thoroughly cultivated men depends, then, not upon arbitrary will, but upon laws as sure as the phenomena in the life of nature. As motion in the universe depends upon the law of gravitation, so human life depends upon the law of the 'unity of life.' The laws of the 'unity of life' are the elevated laws of the solar systems, consequently those of the universe, in which man is the highest blossom and fruit. Thus the laws of spiritual development need to be comprehended as distinctly as the laws of the formation of the world.

"*The laws of the universe are the same as the laws of human education.* Kindergartens form a stage of development in the culture of man, out of which the succeeding stages will follow according to a determined law, as is the case in organic life. Every noble friend of man should help to make the first stage of culture such as to insure the right conditions for the following stages—let him belong to what party he may.

"By establishing kindergartens that nearly approach the ideal, men would learn whether or not it is a work of God, and would see what practical, all-sided, and deeply grounded development, as a creative being, man is capable of.

"My object now is to bring such a model institution into operation at Marienthal as will at the same time include the educating of kindergartners. But not merely shall women learn to be conductors of kindergartens, that is, to understand the nature of children, and to be able to take care of and to educate them, physically and spiritually, but the whole female sex, in all classes and conditions of life, shall take up the new education of man, and learn to apply it, as God appointed nurses and guardians of children. If the female sex, as a whole, shall be made capable of administering this holy office as the present general stage of development of civilized humanity requires, then it will itself be liberated from its own ignorance and oppression. For this office involves all culture and all elevation which the female sex needs in order to show to the other half of humanity the place befitting itself in the community and in humanity.

"Support us in making the beginning of this education, without which the demands of the present time, and still less those of the future, can never be fulfilled, and without which the new springtime which will open, by God's will, will be arrested in its opening. What must come, according to eternal laws must come, and cannot be prevented by man's work—it is the work of God and nature; but it can be delayed and interrupted by the freedom granted to man when caprice rules instead of law."

Herr von Wydenbrugk, who had listened with evident attention and interest to Froebel's exposition, pressed his hand warmly, and promised for his part to do the best he could for the support of the work as soon as outward circumstances would permit;

adding that "too extravagant bounds should not be given to this possibility."

None of us, including the minister, had at that moment even a distant presentiment of what the next year would bring to our holy cause, which still stood so inconspicuous and defenceless, but upheld by the unshakable faith of its immediate representative, who knew himself to be the bearer of a divine idea.

"Our cause now stands firm," said Froebel one day soon after the visit of the minister, "even if the enemies of all popular education and every kind of advance should come out against it ever so violently."

"Yes, I think so too," I replied; "at least, with respect to the introduction of the kindergarten, and in general the external and practical part of the cause. But the idea lying at the foundation is understood hardly at all. I see more and more how the statement of it in short public lectures is insufficient to create the right understanding, even in the best minds, unless earnest study follows. You must write something which shall state briefly the fundamental idea and the principles of method growing out of it."

"Briefly!" repeated Froebel; "then people will misunderstand me more than they already do in my 'Education of Man,' which I should think expresses clearly my fundamental thoughts, at least. The generally received ideas upon the being of man are so vague, the child's nature in its first springs of motive and in its expression is so little understood, that but very little can be done by written statements.

"See how the votaries of different philosophical systems quarrel with each other, without being able to make themselves mutually understood. Not the word alone, but, above all, action must guarantee the truth of my cause. At present, if the practical results of the kindergartens and the maternal feeling is favorable, then, later, writings will appear that will recognize my idea in all its depth, show its necessity for the present stage of human development, and put it in its right place in the new views of things now forming.

"Yes, even should my idea be lost for the want of a correct understanding of it, it will surely awaken anew in some other mind, since it is a need of the time, and God sends nothing into the world which does not bring forth its fruit in due season.

"Go on quietly. Nothing happens without God's permission, and however much men may interfere with the good and true by their caprice and destructiveness, man's work cannot prevail against the work of God and nature; either of the latter is stronger than the former. Men can interfere obstructively and destructively for moments only with what is ordained by God, but they can never really prevent it. That is my trust, even if I am neither understood nor supported—indeed, even if I am persecuted.

"Once, in a moment of doubt whether I should have the power to persevere with my cause, the thought came to me: What could you do to save your idea if you should be thrown into a dark dungeon where you could not write or express yourself in any way? But I soon found what I should do in order that the truth of which God made me the bearer should not be lost even to the present generation. If human tongues are silenced, the stones will speak, in order to testify to the truth, I thought—"

Froebel here interrupted himself to look at the clock, which pointed to the beginning of the hour when he was accustomed to go to his school of kindergartners, and he requested me to go with him and take part. In vain I endeavored afterwards to come back to the subject; the time for it never came. How much, indeed, has remained unexplained, which would have made me understand many obscurities in his views and ideas! But it was impossible to hold him for a long time to one train of thought, or to turn him from his thought of the moment into any other direction. If he was occupied with one subject it was difficult to move him from it to enter upon any other.

The increasing number of visitors to Marienthal who wished to understand his education claimed almost entirely the time of his leisure hours, and he exhausted his powers by statements of his views more than was good for his health. Besides, the plan was often considered of summoning a teachers' convention at

Liebenstein for the next summer (1851), in which his educational principles should be discussed. A great domestic festival was also in view for the spring—Froebel's nuptials with Fraulein Levin, who had for several months been betrothed to him.

Froebel longed for a real family life. He wished his pupils to be able to take part in one, according to his principle that the education of girls for the family must take place in the family circle.

When he imparted to Diesterweg and myself his intention to give his hand to Fraulein Levin, who superintended the household with so much discretion and conscientiousness, and was already such a motherly friend and teacher to his pupils, we could only sympathize with it, and rejoice that he was thus secure of a faithful and tender nurse for his old age. His vigor, which his constant activity still insured him, made the thought of his second marriage appear less strange. No one who did not know it could believe that his age was sixty-eight. The youth and freshness of intellect, which were so remarkable in him, prevented one from thinking of his actual age, whose infirmities had not yet appeared. Those minds which live only for the service of mankind, and have a universal human work to carry out, begin their eternal life upon earth.

Froebel possessed in an extraordinary degree the sense of family life—domesticity—which he hoped to animate and exalt by his education. The communications he had made to me at times concerning his profoundly honored first wife, and her letters, from which he had often read to me, showed how he had striven to realize his high ideal of marriage in his own life.

11

Dr. R. Benfey and Teacher Hermann Pösche

Among the visitors to Marienthal in the summer of 1850 were Dr. Rudolph Benfey and Teacher Hermann Pösche, afterward zealous promoters of Froebel's cause, both of whom are now full of enthusiasm for his doctrine, and are to be counted in the small number of those who have worked for it from free conviction, without personal views, and with enduring zeal.

The comprehensive learning of Dr. Benfey gave much opportunity for conversation on themes lying apparently quite far from our circle of thought. With great courtesy he yielded to our request to illustrate in short discourses historical epochs and personalities, by which occasion was afforded almost always to compare Froebel's views with those of others, and particularly with the pedagogic views of Greek antiquity, especially with the ideas of Plato on the education of children, which in manifold ways concurred with Froebel's.

On a social walk to Altenstein, where I had invited the company to sup at the little inn at that place, some remarks of Dr. Benfey's upon the Greek manner of viewing things were fully discussed in a lively manner by Froebel.

Upon my saying how history, particularly the history of culture, demonstrated the uninterrupted connection between the past and present, the consideration of which Froebel always pointed out to us as one of the most important principles of education, Froebel said: "In human development, unity and connection show themselves everywhere; the past, present, and future form a chain whose links are joined inseparably. Human history shows the same uninterrupted development as the universe, and all development in the spiritual, as in the material world, proceeds according to the same law. The height of culture in the Greek world could not possibly have been reached without the preceding stages of development of that and other nations. Beauty of body, suppleness of limb, power of muscle, and gracefulness of movement in the Greek were the result of the physical exertions and exercises of their forefathers, and the inheritance of a culture measured by centuries. But the higher development always has the task of influencing and elevating the steps of culture below it.

"Thus the Greek, afterward the Roman culture and civilization have acted upon other uncultivated races and made them capable of higher cultivation. Indeed, even at the present time that cultivating influence is indirectly at work on ourselves, as well as directly through the classical literature of time.

"As the life of the human race moves on through all epochs, in living connection, like a single life, so the life and development of every individual proceeds in uninterrupted connection.

"The peculiar character whose germ even the nursling shows to him who contemplates the child's nature understandingly is found again in the older child, still further on in the youth, again in the adult, and at last in the graybeard. No one stage of life can be separated from the others. So each generation of men is connected with the preceding, and at the same time determines the character of the following.

"What use shall we now make of this fact of an inseparable connection of all things and all times for the education of our children?

"This use: that we look upon them and treat them as individual spiritual beings, and then that we teach them to perceive things in this connection."

One of the company present interrupted Froebel with the question: "How is this practicable in the first years of life? The child may be treated in this manner by the grown-up educators, but how to effect the object of making the child perceive things in their connection is inconceivable to me."

Froebel replied: "Every child brings with him into the world the natural disposition to see correctly what is before him, or, in other words, the truth. If things are shown to him in their connection, his soul perceives them thus, as a conception. But if, as often happens, things are brought before his mind singly, or piecemeal and in fragments, the natural disposition to see correctly is perverted to the opposite, and the healthy mind is perplexed.

"How one shall begin practically to make for the child the first representation of things in their constant connection, in a correct and clear manner, I have shown plainly in my 'Mother and Cosset Songs,' and still further in my play-gifts.

"Look upon these last; how they proceed from the ball as a symbol of unity, and then pass over from this in a consecutive manner to the manifoldness of form in the cube; how the cube is then divided according to the law of the connection of opposites; how each succeeding form (in the play) goes forth from the preceding, and how not only the connection according to a law of all the parts of the play-material exhibits clearly the union into one whole, but the child perceives through his own action that he only obtains his building (or other figures) when he unites into a whole, in a regular and lawful manner, the parts which he is handling. In such ways he is to perceive that all connection implies opposites which can be joined together, and again that no opposites are to be seen in the properties of things which cannot be connected.

"The linking together that is everywhere found, and which holds the universe in its wholeness and unity, the eye receives, and thereby receives the representation, but *without understanding it*, except as an impression and an image; but these first impressions are the root fibres for the understanding that is developed later. The correct perception is a preparation for correct knowing and thinking. What the child perceives by the material and by the handling of it must be and is supported by the plays and songs of the 'mother' book, because what the child is pleasantly occupied with, and gives its whole attention to, leads to the proximate cause of the effect perceived, and this leads later to recognition of the ultimate cause—God.

"This seems to us impossible and strange only so long as we do not know the *how*, which is perfectly simple, like all truth.

"Look now at the book, and you will learn to know the how. For example, when the child drinks his milk, what is more natural than to show him the cow or point to its picture, then to the cow's food, the grass, whose growth does not depend upon man, and so gradually come to the invisible Creator of visible things?

"Another example shows in picture, in word, and in reality the bread which serves for the child's nourishment, from the grain to the flour, till it leads back to its source. Thus we put the sequence together for the child in a childlike manner, so as to be easily apprehended by him.

"Does any other connection rule in philosophical deduction than this which I call the child to perceive when I play with him at bread-baking [pat-a-cake]? The logic is and remains a consecutive thinking and conclusion, whether applied to the things themselves or to the abstract conceptions of things."

"That is perfectly evident," I answered; "the child before whose eyes sensible objects are brought, in the correct order of parts to the whole, and in the logical connection of things, will, when reflective power is developed, perceive this order and logical connection clearly and definitely in the intellectual world also, and be constrained in a measure to refer back the visible objects to their invisible causes, to the ultimate cause of all phenomena. It is just as evident that no order and no connection can exist without a rule or a determining law at the foundation, and it is impossible that there should be two different laws of logic in the world of sense and in the world of mind, since both are inseparably connected.

"The thought that forms anything whatever can perfect it strictly only according to the law of its thinking (logic), and therefore all harmony between the material formation in the conception of the mind and in the representation rests upon law, and, indeed, it must be one and the same law. That is as clear as the sun.

"You have recognized the law of harmony or equilibrium which rules in the universe, and you have made it the regulator of the child's action. Therein lies the significance of your method. Its practical exercises spring out of this idea, and are only important so far as they bring the law lying at the foundation into application. When only used mechanically they are nothing but technical exercises. But how difficult it is to make this generally apprehended!"

Froebel thought that would be effected hereafter through the pupils who were growing up from the kindergarten. He went on with his explanations.

"Every age of life has its own peculiar claims and needs in respect of nurture and educational assistance, appropriate to it alone; what is lost to the nursling cannot be made good in later childhood, and so on. The child, and afterward the youth, have other needs and make other demands than the nursling, which must be met at their proper ages, not earlier, not later. Losses which have taken place in the first stage of life, in which the heart-leaves—the germ-leaves of the whole being—unfold, are never made up. If I pierce the young leaf of the shoot of a plant with the finest needle, the prick forms a knot which grows with the leaf, becomes harder and harder, and prevents it from obtaining its perfectly complete form. Something similar takes place after wounds which touch the tender germ of the human soul and injure the heart-leaves of its being.

"Therefore you," here Froebel turned to his pupils, "must keep holy the being of the child; protect it from every rough and rude impression, from every touch of the vulgar. A gesture, a look, a sound, is often sufficient to inflict such wounds. The child's soul is more tender and vulnerable than the finest or tenderest plant. It would have been far different with humanity, if every individual in it had been protected in that tenderest age as befitted the human soul which holds within itself the divine spark.

"The first impressions which a young child receives are stronger and more lasting than those in later life, because that power of resistance is then wanting which its later consciousness brings. As the thriving of the child's body depends in a great measure upon its breathing pure air, so the purity and morality of the soul depend partly on the impressions which the nursling and child receive. The careful nursing of the inner spiritual life must begin much earlier than the expression of it is possible, before its tender susceptibility is disturbed by outward influences. This tender susceptibility requires a tender handling, or it is in a certain sense choked, as if I should cover the growing roots of this little plant I have here with sand. No development can be forced—not in nature, still less in the human mind. With right care, everything blossoms in its own time. If I forcibly tear open this poppy-bud, its fine folded leaves may be seen, but the flower will not unfold; it withers within. In the same manner many a child's soul, artificially and violently broken into, will wither within, be despoiled, and at least not bear the fruit it was destined to bring forth.

"Now, what can we do for the unfolding of these heart-leaves of the life, which contain the whole future man, with all his finest tendencies?

"We must launch the child from its birth into the free and all-sided use of its powers. That is just the aim of these plays and occupations which exercise they yet unseen powers of the nursling on every side. But we must not, as is often erroneously done, take care only of the bodily powers by exercising merely the senses and limbs, and then later, when the school-period arrives, make the intellectual powers alone act; but steadily, and during the whole era of childhood, body and mind should be exercised and cultivated together. The mind develops itself in and with the organs that are inseparably connected with it in the earthly life. Child's play strengthens the powers both of the soul and the body, provided we know how to make the first self-occupation of a child a freely active, that is, a creative or a productive one.

"The will is strengthened only by voluntary activity. By striving to create and produce the beautiful and good, the feelings are developed, and by all lawful, thoughtful, free activity the mind is cultivated. But such activity sets aside all extraneous education, and that outside indoctrinating that is not in unison either with the nature of the child or with his actual state of development; and its puts self-education and self-indoctrinating in their place.

"In our public instruction we generally begin with the abstract, with which we should close. This is in the highest degree ruinous, particularly for the mass of the people, whose task in their later life is work that should be productive.

"The first educational task is to make the child acquainted with the things of the material world, which constitute the basis of the abstract. Knowledge of material things can only be had by handling them, and the formation and transformation of material is therefore the best mode of gaining this knowledge for childhood.

"My plays and occupations show the possibility of doing this. Even if I have brought no new thoughts to the subject, as some will maintain, even if the goal and aim of this education has long been known, I have given something new in my childish plays, for they show how we must begin to give activity to the powers of childhood, in order that they shall neither rust and be lost for want of use, nor overstrained by too early study, the capacity of which at that age is still wanting.

"When we ask for artistic industry, that our dignity may not be lost by the substitution of machine-work, we find stiff and awkward fingers; we ask for a sense of beautiful form, harmony of colors, etc., in the workman, and find only dull eyes and senses, which cannot tell the crooked from the straight, and know not how to put light and shadow in the right places. Indeed, when professional and art schools are opened for grown-up youth *only*, they cannot repair what was lost in childhood, let ever so much teaching be furnished.

"Technical skill must be given in early childhood if the human hand is not to be outdone by the machine, and the sense of beauty must be awakened in the soul in childhood if in later life he is to create the beautiful.

"But the life of the unconscious being—reason and the principle of law which govern in it, and express themselves in childish action—is not yet recognized, and on that account it is thought we must wait for a higher degree of consciousness before we point out their aim to be blindly groping powers, and furnish them the means of reaching it, else the unconscious action which instinctively and correctly feels its aim will be turned aside from it and peremptorily forced into other paths. It is not seen that reason is on the side of unconsciousness, and the want of reason on the side of consciousness, but we must discriminate between what is legitimate and what is arbitrary in that instinct in which God rules with iron necessity. Nature is God's work, not God himself, who rules it but never violates its laws which he himself established.

"Even in the child nature does not allow itself to be forced, but only checked or disturbed. Therefore education must follow nature gently and protectingly, not forcibly or violently. Education smooths the way and creates the material which serves the forming instinct; protects and leads the feeble powers, and offers to the investigating senses the types of the beautiful, the good, and the true; then the bud of being will unfold as surely as the bud of the tree, to bring forth its fruit. It is true that many a young bud conceals the worm that destroys it, and in spite of every care makes the fruit fall off before the time, or allows evil fruit to ripen, but that is not the rule. An education true to nature conquers many a bad tendency, removes the mildew from many a flower, and brings to shame the worm that is gnawing upon it.

"Do you know how you can awaken the divine spark in your child? Let him behold the beautiful in form and color, in tone and gesture, whenever the spiritual element in him threatens to sink away in the satisfaction of bodily wants, or desires threaten to draw him into the animal sphere. Then awaken to him the impulse of activity, and exercise it to a degree of effort which will steel the will, even in the nursling, while he is playing with his limbs, exercising his lisping organs of speech, and while his ear is taking the cradle-song into his soul.

"Only by the mediation of the agreeable do the germs of the spiritual awake in the child. He must be knit to what is pleasant, and that in his own action; he must be gained over through his own effort; this will not satisfy coarse wants, but will awaken that slumbering ideal which waits for the incentive from without to burst forth. But the sense of the ideal dwells in every child's soul, even if not in equal strength at all. If it were not so, human life would never be enlightened by rays of the ideal. Nothing can come forth from the *conscious* human being that did not lie germinating in the *unconscious* soul of the child.

"From unity—God—everything goes out unconscious to return back conscious. In consciousness ripens personality (relative in man, absolute in God), which is eternal in its particularity and peculiarity—one note in the great harmony of the universe, never passing away, continuing into infinity.

"The stage of personal consciousness once reached can never retrograde, even as nothing that has once been done can be undone; no personal consciousness can pass away, it is eternal; no grain of sand can perish, it can only enter into new connections, be transformed as everything else is; for everything must go on developing—that is the universal law."

Thus Froebel often talked at length upon his personal views, and forgot the time it occupied, and even the persons to whom he was speaking. Those who listened to him were often obliged to supplement his aphoristic precepts, in order to hold fast the logical thread which was apparently often broken.

The thought of the "unison" between nature and man as sprung from one and the same Creator always reappeared in various forms and relations. The unity of man with nature must be recognized. This has hitherto been prevented by the separation in the human soul brought to consciousness through guilt and sin. Froebel saw fully expressed in Christianity the recognition of the unity of humanity with God (as the child of God). As he has said in one of his essays: "The Christian religion entirely completes the mutual relation between God and man; all education which is not founded on the Christian religion is one-sided, defective, and fruitless."

But the knowledge of the method of that union and unity with nature, to which the present stage of human development is leading, is still wanting. This would bring about a deeper understanding of the eternal truths of Christianity which has been lost up to the present time by empty word-teaching, without awakening religious feeling and man's inborn sense of truth. This recognition of truth begins in the real, visible world in the phenomena of nature, in which the laws of God are to be found, learned, and known as unchanged and unchangeable. This knowledge forms the firm foundation and underpinning for the recognition of supersensuous truths which, speaking from all things, are by the sense of analogy bound up with the visible, material world of God, in which all and every development proceeds, from the lowest to the highest, from the least to the greatest. The unity of the human mind with the Divine mind shall find its confirmation through the easily acquired knowledge of God's mind (Reason) in creation and the sensuous world, and the life of man in it must be immediately knit with the supersensuous spiritual world, in order to abolish the separation between these two poles of human knowledge and human life, and bridge over the abyss which is created by a too far-reaching dualism.

But Froebel was far from wishing to abolish the distinction which separates the sensuous and spiritual world, and gives to dualism its partial justification. And he was still more distant from the coarse or the refined materialistic theories at present in vogue, which deny everything spiritual in order to lift unconscious matter to the throne and make all spirit subject to it. The idea of unity of life, in his sense, is a much more complete contradiction of materialism, and better fitted to abolish that error than anything else, and to lead us into the right path for the further advancement of the idea of the accordance between the laws of nature and those of the mind.

Froebel now stayed the stream of his speech, which had been poured forth with a certain youthful ardor; for it was growing dark, and the coolness of the autumnal evening warned us to go in and take the supper which was ready.

After the most earnest disquisition, Froebel was wont to change with perfect case into a gay and cheerful mood, but I had hardly ever seen him so childlike and animated as on that evening at our simple omelette supper. He was full of jokes with his pupils, bantering Fraulein Levin with doubts of her power to make omelettes equal to those, and disputing with Herr Benfey on the events of the time, which they did not view quite alike. At last he said to me that I ought to arrange such suppers more frequently.

On our way home, I put to him the question, whether he was not of the opinion that by and by, after the fullest introduction and application of his method of education, every one of those so educated would be able to think philosophically, because independently; since ideas indwelling in things and going forth from them with the conceptions thereby conditioned would gradually come to be understood, adding, "It appears to me that through this connection of the intellectual and concrete worlds there must be given a concrete foundation to the philosophical systems resting upon abstractions, which the least thinking power would suffice to understand."

Froebel smiled, agreeably surprised by these suppositions, and said: "A correct and sound perception of things, even a certain degree of capacity to form conceptions proceeding from them, must undoubtedly, in the course of time, lead to a natural and completely satisfactory education of the human being, notwithstanding the differences that will exist in the gift of recognizing the supersenuous and intellectual.

"As the true poet must be born, so must the true philosopher. But it is my deepest conviction that the time must come when the chasm between things and the more or less abstract conception of things will be filled up. You are right in saying that hitherto philosophy has been without the true foundation which natural science alone can afford it. It is just this foundation which my method of education is to supply. The understanding of the unconscious is the germ and beginning of the conscious, and so surely as they stand in connection with each other, so surely the one as well as the other has its origin in unity—God.

"How does all the world's wisdom help us, so long as it remains only a thought in the mind, and is not LIVED OUT, and does not pass over into the human world? Everyone must act, therefore there must be a universal wisdom comprehensible by all, and everyone must learn its application (that is, be practised in it) from childhood up. This wisdom is contained in Christianity—in *pure* Christianity; but it is buried deep for most men. Men learn to teach it indeed, but only in words, which least of all things lead to actual understanding.

"But whatever is to be applied in actual life must be understood, while everything else belongs only to the domain of belief. Acting and producing, moreover, cannot be taught by words alone; they require practical exercise from the beginning.

"We wish to create for children a practical school in which they shall learn to act according to the descriptions of pure Christianity, that is, according to the commands of God, before they learn these prescriptions and commands as dogmas. Such exercise in doing will bring them that experience which Jesus required, when he said, 'If any man will do his will he shall know of the doctrine, whether it be of God, or whether I speak of myself.'

"And when the stones speak, and nature confirms the written revelation by its laws, who will then be able to doubt its truth? Religion is union with God, and man can be united with God only by seeing, believing, and acting with God, and not by either one of these three things alone. Expressions of this truth are not wanting in Holy Writ. But we only take a note of that which theology has taken out for its most important dogmas. We have not yet come nearly to the full understanding of the Holy Writ; its truths always require new vouchers; ever new and deeper recognition on other sides, in order to be placed in their right light. Jesus himself by many of his expressions has pointed out that the human mind is to rise to ever higher knowledge of Divine things; that under God's leading it shall go on from faith to sight. Hence the expression, 'I cannot tell you all things now,' said Jesus, 'but the Comforter will come, who will lead you to all truth,' etc."

Whoever doubts Froebel's deep understanding of the Bible and the Christian idea, should see a Bible which he possessed from childhood, whose leaves are worn quite thin by constant use, and all whose margins are written over with remarks testifying to his earnestness and deep spirit of inquiry. Some communications which he made to me from these commentaries, and his partial inspection of manuscripts in which my own religious views were expressed, gave many occasions for discussion of his religious opinions. But time was wanting to return often to this subject, and I was obliged on this, as on other points, to fill many a gap by later study of his writings.

At that time I could not possibly have given the above *résumé* of his clearly expressed views of the spirit and the reason in the unconscious, for which he sought types and symbols in the concrete world, in order thereby to awaken and enlighten the unconscious mind of childhood.

In spite of Froebel's defective mode of expression, and the frequently aphoristic way in which he suggested his views, the present investigators of the conscious might reach many an explanation through his idea, and would arrive at other and more satisfactory results than have heretofore been brought to light by that "philosophy of the unconscious" which heats the heads of today.

12

Dr. Wichard Lange

To my question who among his scholars he considered the best able to illustrate and work out the philosophical and psychological side of his teaching, he answered that Dr. Wichard Lange (just at that time betrothed to Middendorff's daughter) would certainly be capable of it, if he would give himself wholly up to the subject, but that unfortunately he had already decided on another direction for his practical activity, and wished to continue in the school department of education, so that he would be prevented from giving all his time and powers to this cause, as would be indispensable to his success.

I saw, however, that he did not give up all hope of making Dr. Lange favorable to his wish, which was that he should instruct kindergartners and other teachers in the method, and subsequently spread it by his word and pen. He hoped that a proposed visit of Dr. Lange to Liebenstein would lead to a decision. This visit took place later, but without leading to the hoped-for result.

When I went to Marienthal one stormy autumnal evening, I was told that Dr. Lange had arrived. After all that Froebel as well as Diesterweg—whose favorite pupil Lange was—had said to me in praise of him, I was desirous of a personal acquaintance. When, on entering, I heard loud and eager talking in Froebel's apartment, I waited in the adjoining lecture-room, in order not to interrupt the conversation. They soon came out to greet me, however.

At that time Lange's whole manner expressed the same energetic character which he afterward showed in his action; and no less did his remarkable thinking power and great natural gifts appear on his high, broad brow. His open, free, natural character infused trust and sympathy immediately; and, therefore, I regretted the more not having opportunity at once for the more intimate exchange of thought which I have enjoyed in later years.

The contests that occurred between him and Froebel, in consequence of the demand of the latter that Lange should devote himself entirely to the cause, and give up the school career that he had chosen, took away time and disposition for sympathetic conversation.

Lange's refusal, supported by sufficient and intelligible reasons, to comply with Froebel's demand to give up the career he had already chosen, with all its consequences, threw Froebel into great excitement, for he wished to win in Lange a prominent advocate of his idea.

Lange, on the contrary, felt his inner calling to be a schoolman, for which he had been inspired by Diesterweg, of whom he strikingly reminded me in his whole nature. He was of the opinion that the practice of the Froebelian method must in the first place be advocated and organized by women, before men should interpose with their help, and before the method, as such, should be taken in hand by men of science. To the instruction of the female sex, which was desired from him, he felt neither inclination nor calling; he wished to go his own way independently, especially not to follow exclusively in the footsteps of another, even of Froebel, in spite of his full concurrence with him in his idea, and his recognition of the greatness of his work.* His support of Froebel, and the application of the principles recognized as the correct ones, he promised to undertake with his best powers, so far as his chosen calling permitted.

Such nearly were the views of Lange, the justice of which was not to be contested; but Froebel inconsiderately required his full surrender, and every sacrifice for the working out of his idea.

*In his pamphlet entitled "The Understanding of Friedrich Froebel," Dr. Lange had already advocated Froebel's cause with profound recognition and enthusiasm.

"Cast everything behind you and follow me," he thought he also ought to require from his disciples. So, of course, it came to a violent conflict between these two energetic characters and impassioned minds, without either, from his own point view, being in the wrong. It pained my heart that they could come to no agreement, and must separate without it.

My later friendly relations with Dr. Lange have made me understand that he could not allow himself at that time to be bound completely, when his individuality and circumstances drew him in another direction.

It is known how he has nevertheless given his weighty support to Froebel's cause, and how he has done the most important service by editing his works. His relation to Froebel and his cause is explained by himself in the preface to that edition, therefore I need say no more about it than the course of these remarks inevitably involves.

Dr. Lange has lent double significance to his advocacy of Froebel's cause, and served as a protecting shield to it in the time of its persecution, and will, I hope, contribute yet further to fix attention and gain recognition from a world generally ignorant of this weighty reform.

When Middendorff came for a short time to Marienthal, in the middle of November, this subject was often spoken of, and Middendorff endeavored to console and tranquilize Froebel in his disappointment. He repeated again and again:

"Lange is still true; he does not desert the cause, you may rely upon it. He must make for himself a firm place in which to work out his own views and bring them fully into unison with yours, and then he will also be active for your idea and advocate it with full power. You certainly wish that everyone should follow out his own convictions, and independently determine for himself and reach his own place in life? Lange's probity is the guaranty that he will not desert our cause."

Such assurances from Middendorff, expressed as his innermost conviction, contributed to cheer Froebel, although he seldom made reference to the matter, but silently withdrew within himself, as was his wont at every downfall of his hopes and at every pain.

As the cause stood without sufficient permanent support by good and scientifically cultivated men, I shared Froebel's wish only too warmly to secure Lange completely and practically to our cause; and at the time, in the midst of my fresh enthusiasm for the idea, I sometimes felt much solicitude as to how the important work should be adequately accomplished while it found so little solid, intelligent furtherance.

One evening when we were talking in Froebel's room, Middendorff said: "You must found a society, Madame von Marenholz, which shall consider the holy cause of human education as it apostolate, and undertake the great task that falls to women in our time. There is no greater one than the perfecting of the human race by an education truly worthy of man."

Froebel added: "Women are to recognize that childhood and womanliness (the care of childhood and the life of women) are inseparably connected, that they form a unit, and that God and nature have placed the protection of the human plant in their hands. Hitherto the female sex could take only a more or less passive part in human history, because great battles and the political organization of nations were not suited to their powers. But at the present stage of culture nothing is more pressingly required than the cultivation of every human power for the arts of peace and work of higher civilization. The culture of individuals, and therefore of the whole nation, depends in great part upon the earliest care of childhood. On that account women, as one half of mankind, have to undertake the most important part of the problems of the time, problems that men are not able to solve. If but one half of the work be accomplished, then our epoch, like all others, will fail to reach the appointed goal. As educators of mankind, the women of the present time have the highest duty to perform, while hitherto they have been scarcely more than the *beloved* mothers of human beings.

"Make them understand (particularly the young women) that the sex takes on itself a heavy responsibility if it refuses its cooperation in the work of the new education. Tell women to take part immediately, by their educational activity, in the destiny of nations; tell that the recognition of the dignity of the female sex depends upon this. The sex must be torn, not only from its instinctive and passive, but from its merely personal life, in order to live as a conscious member of humanity. The consciousness of its elevated lifework, and the capacity truly to accomplish it, will do more to bring on the kingdom of God than all other means. For childhood leads to nature and to God, protects and awakens the sense of Divine unity, and will make the whole human race capable of a higher unity with God. What higher work can there be?

"Even the great work in the domain of practical life, which falls especially to the male sex, needs the indirect cooperation of women; for they alone can, by their education of men, make them capable of their calling. Repeat to your sex the saying of Herder: 'Meditate upon and educate (for you alone can do it) a happy posterity.'"

"Will you tell me some means," was my answer, "that will change domestic dullness into true, warm enthusiasm, and rapturous eccentricity into logical thinking? Then I will undertake to form a league of women who will battle and work, sacrifice and live, for your educational cause. Without that, it is difficult to do much in these days.

"The endeavors I have already made have convinced me that only through the cooperation of men can women be set in motion persistently for work of universal utility. I hope, therefore, that the idea will kindle in the minds of some virtuous men who are capable of undertaking its further development. Passive obedience and mechanical activity for universal welfare, as Catholic and Protestant nuns now practise them, need not exist any longer among the women of the present time, if the female sex can be awakened to the consciousness of its higher and highest life-tasks, and be active, like men, in the service of humanity. But the present day-dreaming, pleasure-seeking, and frivolity are increasing, instead of a strong sense of duty; empty superficiality takes the place of sound knowledge, so that women are not fitted, by their care of childhood, to forming men anew for self-sacrifice and self-surrender.

"Let us also be just. The great majority of women are not sufficiently cultivated to understand the idea lying at the foundation of your method of education. The mere practical carrying-out of the work without the idea is not calculated to satisfy the exceptionally superior intellects and lively imaginations among women. Women must understand beforehand in how far, even for themselves, an education corresponding to nature and their being is an emancipation from the fetters of centuries; and it will make female genius capable of miracles in future of which we have now no conception. Where this misapprehended genius flutters its wings at present it brings only heavy sorrow to the individuals whom it affects, while the mass dance through life like gnats.

"Now the question is, how to make your teachings comprehensible by individuals; and I presume you believe that I will do all in my power especially to warm up youthful feelings for the cause, which is now my cause as well as yours.

"I will interpret your doctrine, and endeavor to make it intelligible, which I can now do better than yourself in some respects, for you always set before your hearers depths of thought not familiar to them. But, if I am to succeed, you must teach me further, hold back nothing, and not desert me if I fall to the ground."

"Good!" said Froebel, laughing. "I will spare no trouble to be intelligible, and you know how willingly I hold converse with you; but time is always wanting."

It was now almost midnight, and high time to break up. It was the blackest of nights; the November storm was howling, and making the windows rattle. Middendorff brought the not cheering information that the peasant who was accustomed to accompany me from Marienthal to Liebenstein with his lantern, when I remained there to a late hour, was not there, and he wished to accompany me himself. The way led through a thick wood, against whose trees I had often struck my head in the dark. The little footpath led to a ploughed field, in which one often sank to the ankles after a long rain. The better way back by the road was quite long. For these reasons I was very unwilling to allow Middendorff to be my guide. But he persisted.

When I had prepared myself for the walk by covering my head with cloths, as was necessary, and had hitched up my skirts and stepped back into the room to bid Froebel good night, Middendorff led me up to him with these words: "Now look at our Lady von Marenholz in this masquerade. Does she not resemble a Schwarzburger peasant-woman?" And with that, both the old friends shook with laughter.

A delightful intimacy existed between us all in Marienthal at that time, so that insignificant scenes remain strongly impressed upon the memory.

That summer of 1850 was the last that passed freely and serenely in our circle. The next year was to end with the great disturbance of the prohibition of kindergartens.

13

The Last Summer in Liebenstein

The second Whitsuntide day of this year (1851) was fixed upon for Froebel's nuptials; and all the friends and pupils who found it possible to do so hastened to Marienthal to take part in them. Scarcely risen from severe illness, I arrived a few days before at Liebenstein.

Everything was already in gay movement at Marienthal, in preparation for the impending festival. The pupils were arranging various costumes for the masquerade that was to take place the evening before the marriage ceremony, and were learning their parts for some poetical representations and charades. Fraulein Levin, who was already housewife and teacher, was occupied with arrangements in the house; and I found Froebel at his writing-table in his study. He greeted me with an expression of the profoundest satisfaction.

It was clear how truly happy and pleased he was made by the newfound home, which had already formed a cultivated family circle of young, bright pupils, in quiet, undisturbed domesticity. The battle of life lay behind him; he had parted with the world, which did not understand him, and whose applause he had never sought. He now found himself in rural surroundings, which he had always desired, and could give himself up, unmolested by opposition and obstacles, to the further development of his idea, and to the improvement of the practical means for it, and could sow the seeds of his doctrine in the receptive minds of his female pupils. He was assisted and well taken care of by her whom he had chosen as the companion of his last days. After a life of labor and cares, trouble and combat, he could, to all appearances, reckon upon a beautiful, peaceful evening of life, which would allow him to look with increasing clearness upon the development of his cause, and fill up the gaps still existing in it.

But rarely in the life of man are such promises of lasting rest, and happy, peaceful existence fulfilled, most rarely for those who have devoted themselves to the service of mankind and to the realization of an idea. This was to prove true with Froebel.

Middendorff soon arrived, the never-failing aid in Froebel's life, and the sole representative of the family circle of Keilhau, whose members, for various reasons, were not in accord with Froebel's second marriage. And here, also, Middendorff had again undertaken the office he had filled on previous occasions—that of soother and peacemaker. In order to spare Froebel as far as possible from any discord on the impending days of festivity, he besought of me, on our first interview, to stand by him and to withstand these things wherever they might appear.

Among the arrangements for the festival, it was decided that Middendorff should be the groomsman and that I should be the bridesmaid, offices that we both undertook joyfully.

On the evening before the festival, the pupils brought in their presents with all kinds of play, with poetic effusions, songs, and allegorical representations. The apartments gayly decked with garlands of flowers furnished the necessary stage, and joyous gaiety inspired young and old, and above all Froebel himself, who at the close led off in some of the kindergarten plays, in which all present took part.

On the following day, Pastor Rückert (brother of the well-known poet Rückert), from the neighboring village of Schweina, blessed the marriage union in one of the halls of Marienthal, at a flower-decked altar, and spoke with deep recognition of Froebel's blessed work. Whoever saw Froebel at this moment of inmost concentration, when with the deepest devotion he rose in prayer to God, could surely never doubt his religion, and must have received the fullest impression of his true and lofty piety. At that moment one could see his heart overflow in thanks and praise to

Him who "had always guided him like a father," as he frequently expressed it.

He met our congratulations with streaming eyes, and after the seriousness of the ceremony had passed was as gay and happy as a child, thanking us all most heartily for the assistance we had afforded to his cause. Till late in the evening the playing and dancing continued, in which both Froebel and Middendorff joined in spite of their sixty-eight and sixty-nine years.

No one could have looked upon their participation in the youthful amusements with censure or ridicule, so touching was its childlike artlessness and genuine dignity. Only in the absence of personal pretensions, when every one gives himself up wholly to the moment, and every individual in the whole circle in which he finds himself feels in harmony with all—only there can true happiness and noble enjoyment rule the hour, whatever may be the outward surroundings. The simplest surroundings, or the most incomplete in respect to space, beauty, and glitter, will not disturb genuine joy.

The earnest, heartfelt conference under a garret roof, lighted by a tallow-candle, is often counted amongst the most beautiful memories!

The guests at Froebel's nuptial felt nothing of that oppressive feeling of tedium which has become proverbial at such festivals. Everyone went away with the feeling that they had spent some hours in childlike gaiety.

On parting, Froebel said to me, "Now we will go to work again with new power." And on the next day he resumed the instruction of his pupils.

14

Second Visit of Diesterweg

Some days after this came Diesterweg, who had been prevented from taking part in the nuptials.

Froebel listened most earnestly to our report of what we had done for his cause during the last winter in Berlin.

I had formed a society of women, chiefly belonging to an already existing society for the improvement of domestic service, to which I gave lectures every week upon Froebel's educational doctrine, and to which Diesterweg belonged as our aide and counsellor. Froebel was particularly delighted when I informed him how specially his *Mother and Cosset Songs* had awakened the interest of the young girls, and excited the earnest desire in some of them to become his pupils.

To accomplish these purposes, often prevented by the want of pecuniary means, we agreed to collect a fund for kindergarten scholarships, in order to make it possible for those who were without means, to attend the institution at Marienthal, and at the same time to insure a future calling and livelihood. Numerous letters of the earlier pupils of Froebel proved how suitable to the female mind is the calling of the kindergartner—as a rule decidedly more suitable than any other. From these communications it appeared plainly how many stunted existences had recovered themselves in this occupation by intercourse with innocent, happy groups of children, which had enabled them to look serenely again upon life and hopefully into the future. The expression, "I can scarcely describe how happy I feel in the midst of my children," was repeated again and again in the majority of these letters.

In after years I received similar expressions from my own pupils, many of whom had occupied themselves with the education of young children before they had studied Froebel's method. But they had gained an insight through that, which made their calling a different one after they had spoken the "open, sesame" to child-nature, and at the same time learned the means of occupying their pupils in the right way.

"How difficult I found it to be skilful with children, to make them obedient and tractable," said one of them, "while now, with the greatest ease, by the help of Froebel's occupations, and following out his educational instructions, I succeed in this and can very soon win over and improve the most spoiled and refractory children."

Another kindergartner said, "If the *mothers* could only learn to understand Froebel's method, and would cooperate with us in following it out, how they would develop themselves, and how much trouble, care, and conflict would be saved on both sides!"

Such remarks pleased Froebel more than anything else, and also the proposed foundation of the first kindergarten in Berlin, which we had prepared the way for by means of our society. He recommended one of his earlier pupils, Fraulein Erdmann,* to be the directress of it.

But we could not conceal from him the great difficulties which the cause had to overcome, especially in Berlin, where, in that time of reaction, everything new and all activity in the direction of progress were looked upon with distrustful eyes as destructive.

Diesterweg said: "As long as the rabble rules in Berlin, the cause will go miserably there. Frau von Marenholz will not see that, and therefore takes much useless trouble with people who are not to be made of any use to us."

*Fraulein Erdmann conducted our first institution for three years.

"I care very little for the direction which men take, either politically or religiously," I replied, "if they act from conviction, and have honorable souls; and such men are found in every party and even among the *rabble*, as you call them. We can count among these many a one who is neither a bigot, nor a hypocrite, nor a blockhead, but truly and sensibly has connected his religious faith with the letter of orthodoxy. Those in the liberal party who acknowledge no religion, and allow themselves to be satisfied with the present earthly life, are seldom inclined to work for better circumstances in the future. The crude materialists we can use least of all; and the scientific who work for the solution of the problems of our time with conviction and noble love of truth, striving to reconcile and unite spirit and matter, after the long disunion of centuries under the dualistic theory, are too much taken up with their own problems to offer us assistance in solving ours.

"This growth of our time, which has appeared both in the rabble and among the priests, will fall to the ground by its own unsoundness, and those who make use of it as a lever for their own selfish designs will forsake and betray their party when the influence from above them shall flow in another direction. But if by means of the new education we should smooth the way for real and true religion, sound and seasonable theories, we must think of the children who either grow up in families without any religious culture, or are forced into extreme directions which do not stand against the knowledge of our time, and generally lead either to looseness of religion or to one-sidedness and fanaticism. The children who grow up under either extreme, need special guidance to true religious thinking, and correct knowledge of God. Therefore I seek to win over the parents of every party to the kindergarten, or at least to conquer their false prejudices against it.

"The religious foundation which the kindergarten gives can only be a general one, because of the age of the pupils. It prepares the ground for the later seeds of doctrine which are to be sown. The good ground will then improve many bad seeds and prevent the growing of mischief."

"You are quite right there," said Froebel; "we must receive the children of all parties, of every religious tendency, and not ask where the parents stand or to whom they belong. Every child is a new man, and brings with him into the world the possibility of a virtuous man. We must combat by our education the perversities of parents, and the false, unsound atmosphere of life. If we gain in this generation but a small number of children for the right and the good, the next generation will double the number, and so on in each succeeding generation till all are drawn up to the new stage of development, and there will be still new steps to climb. In times which are specially fitted to lead into higher views of truth, extremes and caricatures of earlier views will always appear.

"The understanding of the old truth is lost, that is, the form in which it was first recognized corresponds no longer to the point of view now gained. But what is true always remains true.

"Before, however, the new, higher form of knowledge is gained, such perversions appear either as the most crass superstition, or as unbelief. But a new revelation of truth can appear only if the old one is understood, or understood in a higher sense, for God can only unfold to us so much of truth as we are in a condition to accept. And therefore religious revelations have come into the world by degrees and in fragments, as it were, and this must go on continuously till we have become sufficiently ripe to seize the whole truth. In every portion of truth the whole is contained in a certain sense, as the macrocosm shows itself in the microcosm, but only to the spiritual eye that can perceive it.

"One side of truth without taking the other side into consideration is *one-sided*; as if I let a child see only one side of a cube, and conceal the other three by my hand. The human mind, in course of time, has thus ever developed every truth that has come to its recognition in *one-sidedness*, and thereby manifold perversions of it have occurred. The perception that there is another side places the one first seen in the right light, and thus leads to new knowledge.

"In general, the human mind can seize upon the aspects of truth only one after the other, as it can perceive things only in succession. One age must bring one knowledge, another another, so that the next truth can be seized; and the last seen always changes the form and expression of the preceding one.

"This takes place in all the domains of human knowledge and practical power, and even of faith—faith, which is the seizing of truth by the feelings, while *seeing* belongs to the intellect. Should the knowledge of God and of divine things develop in the human mind otherwise than knowledge in other domains? That cannot be, for the mind of man is one, and in unity—mind out of God's mind.

"Knowledge of God, like all knowledge, enters the human mind by degrees, from the first presentiment up to faith, and then on to sight, till the spirit comes up into highest unity or consciousness of God. And it can only become conscious of God because the tendency to the knowledge of truth is inborn, because the consciousness of God is immanent in every human soul, or is, as it were, a disposition native to it.

"Every new stage of human development which occurs in its own time as surely as the time itself comes, and like the time brings in cyclical consequence its own peculiarities, increases the capacity for the understanding of truth, and thus broadens the knowledge of God. But in each generation also the most various degrees of this capacity are found in individuals. The undeveloped peasant receives the divine truths of Christianity in a different manner from the learned theologian, or the thinker standing upon the height of culture, although these truths are precisely the same in themselves and everyone receives them in the same statements. The truth cannot change, for it is one and eternal, though the degrees in which it is comprehended vary from each other. But that manner of viewing things which conceives the development of humanity as completed, and, as it were, repeating itself anew or in greater universality, is partial beyond expression. Every succeeding generation, according to that view, is only a bad imitation, an external dead copy, a cast, as it were, of the earlier image, instead of a living one for the new stage of development.

"Humanity, looked at externally, is not seen to be an already perfected thing, not an already established, lasting thing, but a continually progressive, growing thing, rising from one stage of culture to another, striding toward the goal that touches upon infinity.

"The educator of man can only fulfil his task truly when he clearly recognizes the whole of the man and of mankind, and knows how to separate the universal, the eternal in his being, from the particular form that belongs but to one time or person—or the casual.

"The church, our Christian church, would not have failed so often in its educational task if it had been mindful of this irrefragable truth, had taken more into consideration the tide of development that is always rising.

"The Absolute alone remains unalterably the same, but the Absolute is not to be comprehended by the human mind. The Absolute in earthly phenomena is only a manner of relation, or relative. Therefore the moral model of an epoch may carry within itself the absolutely moral or divine, while the outward phenomena belong to the men and to the time in which they appear. If in reference to Jesus there had not always been this confusion between what is absolute and divine and what is relative and human, which latter belongs to the time and to the capacity of comprehension in the actual generation, the efficiency and influence of the church would not have sunk so low as is at present the case.

"The orthodox will hold fast to the antiquated form of expression, to the letter which kills; and the living, productive truth which is thus lost for the time is paralyzed to them, for it really is not understood. They have the idea, but do not know that they do not understand it. And the children are the sufferers. Both our present rationalists and the religious liberals do away with the fundamental idea of Christianity while they think they free themselves only from useless accessories to it."

"I do not agree in that opinion," said Diesterweg; "it is high time to clear away the old rubbish in the church. If we wish to preserve a sound view of religious things for our children, if all religion is not to be overthrown, we must throw overboard the theological future of our times. Jesus indeed never dreamed of what the preachers would make out of his great, childlike, simple teaching. I am entirely in agreement with his original, simple teaching; it was addressed to man out of the soul—but away with all that has overlaid it, or the high-sounding exegesis! Religion must be—it *is*—the deepest need of the human soul; I feel this as much as those who call me infidel or atheist. The church must be—it *is*—the expression of reverence for God; but every religion and every church must answer to the actual stage of the people's culture, and not contradict reason. All that is actually, historically handed down to us must, from one century to another, be purified again and again from the rust and dross which time and the errors of individuals have left upon it. Such a work of purification the Reformation accomplished through Luther, and shall our time be refused a renewed and necessary purification of the church from antiquated dogmas and false interpretations of the idea?"

"No, not that," answered Froebel; "but we must not, in this work of purification and refining, throw aside the peculiar, fundamental idea, as the rationalists really do in the free-religious societies. God in humanity, humanity from God—that is and will be the eternal, true, Christian idea, which Jesus, living and teaching, revealed. Judaism, as the beginning of the monotheistic view, was the means of bringing the knowledge of God into the universe, or gave rise to the truth of the single divine Mind in nature, which is from God. This truth Christianity did not annul: we have, on the contrary, retained the traditions of the Old Testament in our Holy Scripture. We may designate the Mosaic dispensation as the *history of creation*, while Christianity is rightly named the *history of redemption*.

"If the present stage of development is destined to infuse the knowledge that man and his being is one with nature, and to call upon spirit and nature to be reconciled by spiritualizing the nature of man, this is no denial of Christian truth—*God in humanity, humanity in God*—but only a supplementing of human knowledge of truth, and, at the same time, a sanction of Christian revelation.

"What other objects of our knowledge exist but GOD, MAN, NATURE?

"What other task can our intellect have than to find the relation between these three sole existing objects?

"The first thing for the human mind is, to draw the synthesis, *God in nature, nature from God* (the history of creation); then follows the synthesis, *the Divine Spirit in humanity, the human spirit from God*, or the Christian revelation through Jesus (God-man). Now, there is yet to be drawn the synthesis between *humanity* and *nature*, and thus to recognize the *tri-unity* which makes up the result of this *connection* or unifying of *opposites*. By the solving of this problem, the human mind is to see the whole truth, which in itself is one, and could only enter the human mind while the three objects of the truth to be known, and their relations with each other, were proclaimed in three successive epochs.

"This view not only does not contradict the Christian revelation, but can alone place it in its right light, and verify it as eternal truth."

"Do you believe," said Diesterweg, "that you will persuade the theologians of this, who will accuse you, as they do me, of heresy?"

"I do not dispute with the theologians," answered Froebel. "I think I am really as orthodox as themselves. I know Christ, and he knows me: that is enough for me. I do recognize that it is historically necessary that the old form of truth shall not perish entirely—at least, not till the new form has completely developed itself. No view must be entirely lost. The history of man would be incomprehensible if it should be so; for each view shows a phase of the general development, and each one proves that, in spite of all the obscurations that have arisen out of human error, the spirit of truth has at no time quite forsaken humanity. The spirit of truth is God's spirit—the spirit of the Father who never forsakes his children.

"But even the knowledge of truth cannot be bestowed upon us, as freedom cannot be bestowed upon us: it is only won by strivings of the human mind itself. Every revelation which God sends into the world, through the minds he creates, is a germ which human labor has to develop. Even the strifes and the errors of the church are not to be shunned: they even will serve to develop the germ of truth, and make it understood. Every historical crime is an experience which leads towards truth."

"Evil must come, but woe to him through whom it comes, you would say," I replied. "But, while the unavoidable historical battles for truth are being fought, the trusting soul in children must not be disturbed; for it carries the truth in itself originally and unconsciously, and hence is an ever freshly bubbling fountain in the world of humanity.

"The children find in your kindergarten, for the first years of their lives, the first child-church, in which they are prepared for their religious life. But they come afterwards into the school; and there the instruction that is not adapted to the mind of the child, mars, more or less, the good foundation that has been laid, instead of its being continued as it should be, to say nothing of the injurious influences which at present, from all sides—even from the family—are undermining the religious consciousness. You should prescribe the right religious service for schools, which must carry on that which was begun in kindergarten. The form of worship used by adults is not suited to childhood; and what is called divine service for children in schools is still worse for them in many cases."

I related to Froebel what I had heard in one of the city schools.

The teacher, after some previous instruction, said: "How happy you are, children, that you are accepted in the bond of Christians! Not all children are so happy as to grow up in the faith which alone makes them blessed. Do you know what children will not go to heaven to the Lord Jesus Christ, if they are not converted?"

The children answered, "It is the Jews, for they crucified Christ."

"Quite right," said the teacher; "only he who believes the Lord can go to him in heaven. But now there are some other children that live far over the sea, in a hot country called Africa. These children cannot go to heaven if they are not first converted; and do you know why?"

"Because the heathen children are not baptized," answered the children.

"Yes," said the teacher, "because they are not baptized. How sad it is for a poor mother whose child has died! She cannot be consoled by thinking that her dear child is now in heaven with the Lord Jesus."

And this is called divine service for children! But even if, as we will surely suppose, the above-mentioned instance is an exceptional case, the teaching and catechizing that one generally finds as a rule in the religious teaching for children is no divine service for them; for that, above all things, should awaken childlike devotion and piety. One need only look at the assembled children to feel convinced that this first requisite of religious teaching is not found in the majority of cases. It depends chiefly upon the personal character of the conductor of the service how it affects the children; but the mere biblical stories of either the Old or the New Testament are little suited to carry the child's heart up in love and devotion to God. Besides, the historical instruction belongs especially to general education, and should only be found occasionally, as an example, in the service for children. The latter should aim to connect the inward and the outward life of the children themselves.

The church songs are seldom adapted to the understanding of the younger children. Notwithstanding the single cases in which the conductor of the children's service possesses the gift of making an impression upon their feelings, another method is needed to reach the desired end. The family, and above all the mother in it, should awaken the religious feelings in the earliest days, if the divine service that is to come later is to find the heart open. Froebel's *Mother and Cosset Songs* give suggestions to mothers for this purpose which should not be neglected.

Froebel expressed the deepest condemnation of the example I related.

"As long as mothers," said he, "do not know how to administer the priestly office at home for their children's benefit, so long will their piety suffer. For the earliest childhood formal worship, even connected with the daily life itself, the peculiar life of the child, must be occasional, and, as the opportunity occurs, day by day. Family devotions and the example of pious conduct in the family life are the chief means. This our immediate forefathers understood better than we do.

"The first groundwork of religious life is love—love to God and man—in the bosom of the family. The unifying of all the circles of life, beginning with the family, springs from love; also the love of God, and the reverence for all that is highest, springs from love, which is the means of union in the whole universe, and brings out the highest *consciousness of life* in the final aim. Worship, in a child, is to feel and practise love; hence everything is legitimate which awakens or teaches love. What is suggested for this in the 'Mother and Cosset Songs' mothers must carry farther by their own application of the principle. In the kindergarten we use the same means as are employed in the established divine service—pious songs, stories, and prayer; but these must correspond to the age of the children, and must be received into the hearts we have made practically susceptible by the service to which we have accustomed them. The producing of this susceptibility is the great point for consideration.

"The development of the child requires the same series of steps in the child as the development of the human race—that is, it must be done as God himself has conducted the education of the human race. We must, on the whole, while considering the previous culture, proceed in the same path in our educating.

First, God the Creator, who makes himself manifest in his works. But the history of Creation told in Genesis in words cannot yet be comprehended by the young child. Instead of words he needs his own experience; his garden-work teaches him that the growth of plants does not depend upon himself, or upon human power, but that an invisible power governs it. This teaches him almost without words to find the Creator. Only a slight suggestion is needed to awaken the heart of the child to love and thanks to the Giver of all good things. By pointing out God's works while rambling through the scenes of nature, a thousand opportunities offer for worship.*

"All that is told in Genesis of the history of Creation is lived by the child in his kindergarten education. He learns to know the peculiarities and names of the animals, to water the ground, to take care of plants, etc., and out of all things rises the thought of a living Father who creates and animates all. We see this daily in our kindergarten.†

"The mother teaches the child to pray, and also what are the claims and commands of the Heavenly Father upon the child, and conscience awakens. Then she directs his attention to the Christ-child, and he learns how to know and to love the virtues of childhood through knowledge of the Divine, ideal child. He is

*See *Education by Work*, by Madame von Marenholz-Bulow.

†An example of how logically this kind of religious education works may justly find a place here. On some opportune occasion, a kindergartner told the children that it is the will of God that those who have greater possessions than others shall give those others what they need. A little girl asked her companions if they had apples at breakfast-time, such as her mamma gave to her, and they replied that they had not. When the child was to be taken to the kindergarten the next day, she said to her mother, "Mamma, you must give me a great many apples today for the children in the kindergarten. Auntie says the dear God wishes it because the children have not any apples." The request was granted by the mother, and the child divided the apples among the children in the kindergarten, as if it were a matter of course. There is no difficulty, if it is done in the right way, in producing at this early age obedience to the commands of God, such as "Love your neighbor as yourself," and thus leading children to practice religion.

then prepared for the second revelation, God-man, but chiefly by using and cultivating his powers in acting according to the commands of God.

"Outside of family devotion, the time for Divine worship at an appointed hour and in an appointed place, the church, connected with doctrinal teaching and the history of faith, comes at a riper age, say the tenth year. But even for that age our public worship is not appropriate. We might have a similar form, but its contents should be adapted to the age. The instruction should have reference to the beginning of the unfolding of the intellect; even the text of Holy Writ often needs an explanation couched in a childlike form, corresponding to the age, such as is seldom found in our churches. Fanaticism and confessional disputes do not, of course, belong there any more than theological questions and dogmas that are difficult to be understood. To awaken love of God and goodness, which expresses itself in acting out love for mankind, is always the most important task.

"The connection between church-life and our everyday life, carrying out religious thinking into doing and acting, having God before our eyes in everyday life, is not alone to be taught to children by words in a church, but outside of the church by practising them. The worship of God is only one-sided, is only a temporary social edification, which deserves not the name of worship, if it proves fruitless for the inward and outward life of man. This we must impress upon our children.

"Our church festivals have lost their significance for the majority of men. We can only give them life again when the young come to the understanding of them. Other festivals, for which the present age offers many opportunities, must be used for religious elevation, even for worship outside the church.

"The fitting religious service for children has grown out of the new education of itself, without any special precepts from me. New forms of social life correspond to the new spirit which has waked up in society; let us only awaken this spirit in our children, it will work creatively in this field also. But in order to do this, that dry, insipid frame of mind must be avoided which is usually created in children by incomprehensible word-teaching and catechizing."

"It seems to me," I added, "that for the religious elevation of childhood and youth the beautiful above all things—*art*—must cooperate. Music, architecture, and painting must contribute to the elevation of mind in worship, as they have been used in the Catholic church. The degeneration in religious art should not have induced our evangelical church to cast it out entirely as a means of devotion.

"To youth still in the midst of the life of the senses, it is unquestionably necessary that the impressions from without should be in harmony with the feelings from within.

"The want of art-culture in the masses works disturbingly, in the unmelodious church-singing, for example, and surely everyone is more easily stimulated to devotional feeling under a beautifully built Gothic dome than in a white-plastered village church.

"Here, the harmonious development of human gifts from childhood up, striven for by you, must bring a reform. The artistically cultivated senses of the new generation, together with the general elevation of the arts, will again restore pure, holy art, as is needed for the worship of God, and the true artistic sense waked up in the people will know how to select what will serve for devotional elevation, and to reject what awakens mere sensuous pleasure. Then men will again learn to understand that beauty and truth flow together into one wherever each is found in its original purity. The harmony which these two heavenly powers, beauty and truth, reached in the Greek world, the future will again unfold in the height of their spirituality through the Christian idea developed in its full purity, in just so far as the God-given tendencies of men are led undisturbed to their goal. But how long will it yet be before this goal can be reached through the indifference that now prevails upon the subject?"

"The more we individuals work, the sooner the goal will be reached," answered Froebel; "only keep good courage in the work."

15

Visit of Herr Bormann

In the list of newcomers to the Baths of Liebenstein I found the name of the School-Counsellor Bormann, of Berlin, and hoped with his presence to see at last a Prussian official become more closely acquainted with Froebel's cause.

Through my activity in the cause at Berlin I was repeatedly obliged to go through the experience that, especially in the circle of the schoolmen, no one troubled himself about it or even knew of its existence.

The political reaction that spread more and more in those years impressed in that circle upon everything reformatory the stigma of pernicious innovation and a lust for destruction. So much the more important was the hoped-for cooperation of Herr Bormann, on account of his office of Director of the Berlin Seminary for the preparation of female teachers. There are no places that can be of more importance to the dissemination of Froebel's principles than these institutions, where the being of the child and his educational treatment at the earliest age should form the groundwork for all teaching.

But alas! even now (twenty-five years later) this is not the case, and scientific discipline and the methods of instruction stand in the foreground, although at present the significance and importance of the *educational* is made more and more prominent.

On the afternoon of that very day Herr Bormann was in the kindergarten at Marienthal, and expressed by the most profound attention, as well as by appreciative words, his warm sympathy and full concurrence in Froebel's system of education. He not only saw the movement-plays, but examined all the play-gifts and materials for work, among which those for building particularly attracted his attention. He was specially impressed with the preparation their use gave for later mathematical study, as well as for the cultivation of the sense of form.

On our way back from Marienthal to Liebenstein he could not cease to express his astonishment at the discoveries of Froebel's genius, and at his deep knowledge of child-nature.

"This thing is of the greatest importance, and must be made known," he said. "I will write, while I am here, an article for the *Brandenburger Schulzeitung*, if you will furnish me with material for it."

The next day Herr Bormann called upon me and took away with him notes and manuscripts which were to assist him in his work. He agreed with my opinions upon Froebel's method, and promised to support my efforts for the introduction of kindergartens into Berlin with all his powers. I put into his hands all the materials of the plays and occupations, and thought I might dare to nourish the hope of being able to promote the cause in Berlin without encountering too many difficulties. The article in the *Brandenburg Zeitung*, which appeared soon after Herr Bormann's departure from Liebenstein, ended with these words: "There can be nothing more anti-revolutionary under the heavens nor upon the earth than Froebel's educational system."

The article set forth how in Froebel's method, even in the play occupations, every opportunity for destructiveness was removed, as every new form was obtained by transformations from the preceding one, but not by overthrowing or destroying it.

To those penetrated by Froebel's principles it must be obvious how the principle, that is, the recognition of life developing itself organically as the *norm* for the development of the human organism, when the model and guide of education, excludes all violent interference and every disturbance of legitimate order; and, in fact, scarcely could a more suitable means be found to prevent the budding of revolutionary thinking, and to direct the striving after natural organic development and orderly and legitimate reform, than Froebel's educational method. Certainly the application of a given rule or law must, by the formative and creative productiveness of the kindergarten pupils, awaken their sense of law and order, and call forth from the beginning an opposition to all disorderly and anarchical action.

Froebel was made very happy by Herr Bormann's recognition and by his article, which Bormann sent him, and both by writing and by word of mouth he promoted with joyful hopes the measures he had begun for the assembling of teachers in Liebenstein at the end of September. Diesterweg and Middendorff would come to it, and the former thought he should be there a few weeks earlier.

Neither Froebel, therefore, nor his friends, were at this time—the end of July—prepared for the impending blow of the prohibition of the kindergartens in Prussia.

Upon a journey to Fredericksrode and Inselberg, which we took in company with Froebel and his scholars just after the arrival of Diesterweg, Froebel was so happy and even merry that we all enjoyed ourselves highly, and his continued vigorous activity seemed secured.

16

The Prohibition of the Kindergarten in Prussia

It was on the 9th or 10th of August; the dinner had just been removed from the table at the castle of Altenstein where I was visiting, when the Duke stepped up to me with the *Vossische Zeitung* in his hand, and said, "The Froebel kindergartens are prohibited in Prussia."

At the first moment I thought it was a little raillery, such as the Duke sometimes addressed to me about my partiality for Froebel's cause.

"You are jesting," I replied. "How can it be possible?"

"Read," said the Duke, handing me the paper. And I read the rescript of the Prussian government of the 7th of August, 1851, which forbade the kindergartens.

The princely family were almost as much surprised as I was at the official prohibition of kindergartens as dangerous to society. No one was able to find any rational ground for it, and we agreed that there must have been some special exigency, and that it was a mistake of the reactionary measures, that were overstepping all limits at that time.

Startled and disturbed to the greatest degree, I went to see Froebel, who had already received the astounding news! He and his wife were deeply shocked but Froebel was quiet and collected. The view that there was some mistake which might yet be explained, and thus lead to the repeal of the prohibition, was much the more predominant with him, because the rescript referred to the pamphlet entitled "High Schools and Kindergartens," which were designated as socialistic and atheistic, and referred to Carl Froebel.

We considered what was to be done in regard to the necessary explanation, and agreed that Froebel should write to the Minister von Raumer to beg him to take up the case, and to obtain a repeal of the unjust prohibition.

The next afternoon Froebel brought me the rough draft of his letter to the minister, that I might read it and suggest any alterations.

He expressed it as his firm conviction that an examination of his efforts, which he requested, would place them in the right light; that the confusion of his identity with that of his nephew, the author of the pamphlet quoted, would be seen, and that the repeal of the prohibition that had been published would take place. Froebel also sent some of his own writings to Berlin with the letter.

The conviction that a mistake had been made, and that the prohibition would be removed, sustained Froebel, and left him the hope which was expressed by myself and others, that this occasion would draw the attention of the public to his cause, and bring out a more general recognition of it.

When the unexpected answer from the minister arrived—"that he must abide by the prohibition, inasmuch as the principles expressed could not be assented to, and in spite of the confusion of persons, concurrence with that objectionable pamphlet consisted in laying at the foundation of the education of children a highly intricate theory"—Froebel first felt the whole weight of the blow which had fallen upon the work of his life.

It was clear that they would not repeal an ordinance once promulgated, and would not give the cause any examination, but only thrust it aside. Froebel's method did not coincide with the direction of a morbid pietism, carried to a great extreme, that prevailed at that time, and the education of the people was considered the most dangerous weapon in the hands of the revolution.

Froebel's childlike faith in the truth and justice of the world struggled against such a treatment of his explanations, and he still thought there must be means to produce an acknowledgment of the value of his ideas and efforts, even in official circles. It is indeed so difficult for a pure and noble will and deepest convictions to believe in indifference, and in intentional perversion of truth by party hatred.

These were days of severe inward conflict for Froebel, which consumed his very life-marrow, but not for a moment was he in doubt about his mission or the value of his work, of whose future victory he was immovably persuaded.

At one time, with suppressed feeling, he said, "Now if they will not recognize and support my cause in my native country, I will go to America, where a new life is freely unfolding itself, and a new education of man will find a footing." This expression proves how energetic he still felt.

Another time he said, "I will battle for my cause; without battle, truth never breaks a pathway; I must not let it be struck dead by being shoved away silently. I will apply directly to the king of Prussia; he has a sense of the great and noble in spite of everything, and a mind to appreciate my ideas. You must give my petition to him yourself, Madame von Marenholz, as soon as you return to Berlin, and explain the whole affair to him at once."

He did not speak of this plan generally, and would not let its probable want of success under present circumstances weigh with him.

The letter which he addressed to the king, to petition for a new examination of his cause, was written with touching simplicity and in truly childlike confidence, as was the custom in earlier days, when the children of the land turned to the father of the land with true reverence. Some changes and abbreviations, chiefly in regard to the form, seemed to me indispensable, and Froebel allowed me to make them. After this was done he said, on reading the sketch, "The *old man*, as you let me be called there, must not be said, for years have not made me old"—a naïve expression for the eternal youth of the spirit!

When afterward in Berlin, at an audience of Queen Elizabeth, I gave Froebel's petition to the king, I scarcely felt any confidence, in spite of his acceptance of it, in the success of the step.

The feeling that prevailed at the court at that time was too much in opposition to the hope expressed by Froebel for the renewal of human society by a correct education corresponding to the actual stage of culture, to lead to the desired result.

The assignment of the subject, on the part of the king, to the Minister von Raumer himself, which took place later, with the direction to comply with the petition for closer examination of the cause, could only lead to an undesirable issue.

Although in those days of fear of whatever was new, rising to madness—a fear which in every form was a "red" spectre, I had found sufficient occasions of sad experience, and in my advocacy of Froebel's cause had run the risk of being myself taken for a "red," I was in the highest degree astonished by the views which I came to learn in my conversations with the minister. I saw that party fanaticism struck the mind with perfect blindness, so that the only means of salvation offered against the evils of the time were looked upon and thrown aside as dangerous poison.

There was nothing to be done but to wait for better days, when the light of reason should overcome the darkness that had spread abroad, and even Froebel's innocent plays for children should be freed from the interdict that had struck them down. The explanatory newspaper articles, coming from all sides, the wit of the *Kladderadatsch* about the supposed danger of the kindergartens with their "three-year-old demagogues"; praise of them in places where such institutions had been founded, sympathizing expressions from pedagogical authorities—nothing could then take the odium from the cause. The circumstance, that in many confiscated letters of persons politically compromised, the importance of kindergartens was mentioned as a new foundation for an improved education of the people, was used in official circles to justify the prohibition as a correct one; and this fact must also have served with the king to palliate the error that had occurred.

The last word of the minister was: "I shall never allow the establishment of Froebel's kindergartens."

"But will the authorities prevent families using Froebel's materials of play for their children before they send them to school?" I inquired.

"No, that is not in our power," was the answer.

"Now, then," said I, "I hope the founding of family kindergartens will afford you the proof of how unjustly the cause has been judged, which, in spite of its inoffensiveness, holds within itself a deep meaning."

And a family kindergarten, the first institution of that kind, was opened in the course of that year by our little society in Berlin, and given into the charge of a pupil of Froebel's, Fraulein Erdmann. But much as the spread of this blessed influence of the kindergartens was hindered and in part prevented by the prohibition, yet the subsequent more rapid diffusion of them might be due to the very prohibition itself. The cause was torn from its obscurity, and thereby gained an importance which it might not have gained otherwise. Even evil must serve the good.

The proscription of the government made the cause now the darling of the party of the extreme liberals, as such. Therefore for a long time it appeared in a false light and appears so still, even at the present time, with regard to its still quite misunderstood religious tendency.

Here again something has been thrown away whose right use is suited as nothing else is to work against irreligion by an early religious groundwork laid in the heart of the child. Thus is the cause of the new education more or less associated in the public mind with radicalism, although it has not the least agreement with any radical tendency.

In 1860 there was a public abrogation of the prohibition of the innocent kindergartens, but the mistrust roused against it in many quarters has never been entirely removed. The repeal was to me a greater satisfaction because my unremitting endeavors, particularly with the minister of the "new era," had helped to bring it about.

The great joy felt by the votaries of the cause at this late justification of it was, however, shadowed by the fact that Froebel was no longer alive to enjoy the triumph of the expiation.

17

Visit of Varnhagen von Ense

Before Froebel had received the adverse decision upon his last petition, and was again and more deeply grieved by it, some bright sunbeams had penetrated the oppressive atmosphere of the Marienthal and Liebenstein circles. The visits of many distinguished persons brought him recognition and concurrence; and there occurred in September of that year the long-prepared convention of teachers, to whose judgment the public prohibition gave enhanced significance.

Among other well-known persons living at that time in Berlin, I had excited the interest of Varnhagen von Ense for Froebel's efforts, which were often a subject of discussion at our interviews.

The increasing discouragement which took possession of the liberal thinkers in that time of reaction, after the sad experiences which followed the hopes of 1848, which showed that the most ideal efforts for political reform are wrecked upon the selfishness, coarseness, and roughness of the masses, together with the irritation which was produced by those measures of the authorities that obstructed all progress and all enlightenment, turned the minds of many thinkers to the necessity of a better education of the people. Diesterweg's influence and his demands in this regard, which had made him a martyr in his post of usefulness, had led some politicians who honored his public-spirited activity to regard the field of education as the one above all others in which was to be gained the right foundation for universal reform and amelioration of morals.

When I once expressed to Varnhagen that the true friends of the people—the liberals in the best sense of the word—ought to turn their eyes, during this time of reactionary measures, to other fields of action besides the political one, and especially to look at Froebel's work, he said: "We will not quarrel about whether the hen or the egg came first, but in the present circumstance it is not to be thought of to bring forward anything new in any field whatever. Do not deceive yourself; we are already in the beginning of things which are to come. After the violent gagging which is now going on, things will first grow much worse. It must be so; no new epoch is born without storm and misery. The tatterdemalion from above wakes up the tatterdemalion from below, and the wild beast in humanity will first exhibit itself. It is a blessed thought to me that at my years I shall not have to live through these coming battles."

"But," I rejoined, "after the storm comes better weather. Shall we not strew the seed which will grow then, when its fruit is to be the condition for life (*Lebens bedingung*)?"

"Indeed we must," said Varnhagen. "You know I believe undoubtingly in the progress of humanity. The good and true will and must conquer, and even what is evil must smooth the way for them. But the historical Augæan stable is not so quickly cleansed as you think. It will be longer than I feared before that is done. I see that in the circumstances of today. But it shall not on that account be said that all good, whatever name it takes, is not to be furthered to the best of our ability. Even the better education—the real education—of the people (which we have not yet) must be silently prepared for, without the help of the ruling powers—indeed, against their will. Otherwise every new seed will be trodden under foot."

"But," said I, "in the circle of the rulers, and amid their wealth of influence, are there no minds which have the insight to perceive that the universal and especially the moral culture of the people, in the most various degrees, is the only radical means against anarchy and destruction?"

"No, not at present, in those benighted circles where imbecility hinders all free outlook," replied Varnhagen. "Whom the dear God will ruin he strikes blind. As yet I cannot judge," he continued, "how far Froebel's educational idea is calculated to work determinately upon the general human development. After what you have told me of it, I might assume that such importance does belong to it; but see how slowly and unobservedly the earlier educational systems broke their way, although every votary of each thought the salvation of the world depended upon it, and fought for it with enthusiasm. What Froebel wishes to effect lies in the far future, since his education has to do especially with the newborn generation, and through it with the following ones. A consideration of our posterity is the holiest duty; but the present time has so much to do for itself, the nearest future is so shrouded in darkness, that little power and time are left for educational improvements. When your house is burning over your head, you do not think of the improvement of the interior. Therefore you must not expect to awaken a general enthusiasm for the cause for which you work enthusiastically yourself."

"All that is quite true," I said; "and I do not in the least expect there will be a general enthusiasm for a thing whose whole importance can never be seen but by a few. I know also that 'the presiding spirit is not in haste,' as Hegel says. But I believe a new idea must strike fire, if only in individuals. Froebel's idea requires our sex—the activity of women—for its success. Can they lay their hands in their laps in a time of fermentation and transition to new social forms, and look idly upon the general conflict? That cannot and must not be; and there are signs enough at hand to proclaim that there is a fermenting and working in women's souls now. The perverse and ridiculous desires for the 'emancipation of women' in our time, together with their false pretensions, testify to the aberration of newly awakened powers. As soon as these are led into the right path, the disorder will cease; the pretensions which genuine worth never makes will be silenced. All eyes will then be turned to the right way—that is, to the path pointed out by God and nature; but the voice of manly authority must direct.

"On that account, I ask the men of mind whom I meet to accept our educational cause, and to bring Froebel's idea into recognition. Means are offered by it for the redemption of the female mind, since the unfettering of the mental powers is demanded for this work in a way that has never been tried. The very highest demand of our time upon women is to work at this problem of a new education: this is their appointed part in the present struggle for culture.

"If Rahel were living, she would do me justice; she would help me with her deep insight into human nature, her great love of childhood. Her words, 'Not the cultivated insight so much as the cultivated *will* is the condition required for moral worth,' express in brief what Froebel's education is specially striving for—the perfect development of human energy."

The reference to Rahel immediately called out deep emotion in Varnhagen. He said, with increased feeling: "I must become acquainted with your Froebel; and, so far as I can, I will say the word for him. In the coming summer, I will take my vacation in Thuringia and go to Liebenstein, that you may take me to him."

And so it was. At the end of August, 1851, Varnhagen came to Liebenstein with Fraulein Assing and old Dora.

This visit was greeted with joy by the Princess Amely as well as by Froebel, to both of whom I had communicated Varnhagen's intention. The Princess Amely longed, with the vivacity and eagerness of eighteen years, for the intercourse with masculine minds, and followed the movements of the time with ardent interest.

"You will bring Herr von Varnhagen immediately to us when he arrives," she exclaimed, when we met at tea at the castle, on the evening before his arrival.

When I informed Varnhagen of this invitation, he said, "We must go to Froebel first." And we went, on the afternoon of the same day that he arrived.

We found the pupils with some children in front of the Marienthal house, playing "Would you know how does the farmer?" The play pleased Varnhagen, who hummed the melody to himself for a long time afterwards. Froebel's play-gifts were spread out upon the long table, and were thus already at hand, after the first greeting, for an explanation of the method.

After Froebel had expressed the thought that "only the history of the human race could offer the right guide for studying the nature of the mind, and for guiding it correctly from childhood up," he went on to say: "Apples were given in Paradise to the childhood of humanity, as the earliest means of knowledge. I also have apples here for the same purpose—the balls of the first gift, clothed in rainbow colors, but not of a kind to be eaten.

"In the beginning of human culture, when experience had to be of a palpable nature, and the pleasure of the senses and its results were to be tasted materially and experienced practically, the apples had to be eaten. That is no longer necessary. We can spare our children the details of experiments which mankind has passed through, if we educate them aright. They must indeed become wise through their own experience, but they need less rough experience; they no longer need to spoil their stomachs with sour apples. These balls are, as it were, ideal apples which satisfy the higher needs of nourishment felt by the mind, and not by the palate, and impress the mind through the eyes."

Varnhagen laughed heartily, and said, "Do you mean that you have to offer to human nature, developed and refined by thousands of years of culture, the means used for the development of the mind in the beginning of its existence?"

"That is it," answered Froebel; "we may restrain the sins which spring from the animal appetites when we direct the regards of the child to something that satisfies his higher ideal or spiritual wants—wants, which he as well as they bring into the world with him, and which crave satisfaction from the earliest infancy as much as the body desires nourishment.

"The spiritual unconsciousness into which the child is born is changing into conscious being from the first moment of life. The incentives which are needed for awakening the powers of the soul go out from the external world; and these must not be left to chance at this stage of human development. Chance is blind; education is to act with its eyes open. It was necessary to bring light upon the great chaos in the beginning of Creation, and God said, 'Let there be light!' Chaos still encompasses every human eye that wakes into life, for a chaotic world veiled in darkness surrounds the newborn child. The task of education is to bring light into this darkness, order into this chaos.

"But how shall this be done? The senses are to be awakened as the organs of the mind, and not as the organs of mere sensuous pleasure, or of mere desires, as in the animals. Yet that is what happens if we aim at bodily nourishment alone without giving food to the mind. This need never happen to the child of the present day.

"Now I wish to find the right forms for awakening the higher senses of the child. I must ask the whole organism of creation, the whole universe, for them. I must go back from the particular to the general, which contains the particular, and furnishes the typical or fundamental form for the manifold phenomena of creation. Then come the properties which are common to all things, and without which there is nothing knowable. I must seek objects in which the universal properties of form, color, size, weight, movement, etc., are to be perceived one by one, and strikingly shown.

"For this purpose I have not only forms for the child's eyes, which are to make him acquainted with the outward world that surrounds him; I have symbols which unlock his soul for the thought or spirit which is innate in everything that has come out of God's creative mind. If the ripened mind is to know and understand this thought, its embodied image must make an impression upon the yet unconscious soul of the child, and leave behind it forms which can serve as analogies to the intellectual ordering of things.

"What symbol does my ball offer to the child? That of *unity*. Out of unity as form proceed all phenomena, whether it is an original cell or a seed. And everything must in its development strive again for unity or completeness—the flowers and the fruits, the heavenly bodies and the organs of the human body (whose head is in the form of the ball), all proceed according to the law of the sphere. Unity as spirit, absolute unity, is God himself; the universal spirit goes forth out of the All and returns back to the All. In God 'we live and move and have our being.' We are spirit out of God's spirit, we are children of God, and therefore capable of finding and recognizing in all the works of God, within certain limits, our own mind and God's mind.

"Unity! To know God is to know the highest, is the chief end of all knowledge, and at the same time is the beginning of all knowledge. The beginning must answer to the end as the end (the result) must answer to the beginning, if completeness is to be reached. The beginning of the development of mind is unconscious being, the end is conscious being. These opposites are conditional upon each other (they are relative, not absolute); the steps of the whole development, or *growing* consciousness, lie between and unite beginning and end, that is, the unconscious being of the child and the conscious being of the mature man. Therefore must the perceptions of unconscious childhood and the conceptions and ideas of the conscious mind of man also correspond. Do you agree with me?"

Varnhagen expressed his assent.

"Am I not right, then, when from the very beginning I create such impressions upon the child's mind through material or concrete things, which, according to the analogy that prevails in the universe between spirit and body and between thought and its embodiment, are the prototypes of conceptions and ideas in the spiritual order of things?

"The child's mind unconsciously seeks, must seek, according to its organization, for the conditions upon which its development depends. He finds these conditions, and by degrees fulfils them by the help of the things surrounding him; he receives impressions from the properties of things when his eye perceives in them form, color, size, number, movement, etc. But the great abundance of these things which present themselves chaotically to his unpractised senses makes the earliest work of the human soul a difficult one, and the impressions received are therefore indefinite and confused. Now what else is the education of the child's mind from the beginning than to make easier to it the task laid upon it, the perception of single things?

"The greater the progress of culture, the more various and numerous are the particulars of the things around us—the more difficult the perception and knowledge of them becomes—the greater is the task of individuals in order to attain to knowledge and power. Hence better and earlier preparation is necessary. This is obtained when the development of the mind is spared from indirect ways, when the senses as organs of the mind are furnished from the beginning with a guide to knowing, and when the single things out of the mass come before the eyes. And surely those things which produce the most significant and decided impression of common properties must be chosen for this purpose in an orderly manner.

"If the later instruction must select, arrange, and dispose its material, then even much more carefully is it necessary to do it for these first perceptions of the child, which are to be the source and foundation of all later reception and learning.

"Only those who accept these thoughts as correct ones can understand what is the aim of my educational method."

"But how do you know," said Varnhagen, "that the right beginning has been found, and that the child's mind has not been forced to something foreign to it which works disturbingly rather than usefully; perhaps, indeed, awakening it too early, and therefore harmfully?"

"That is just what I wish to prevent, the artificial ripening of the fruit from which our generation is now suffering in the highest degree," answered Froebel, with eagerness. "Do you not understand that it is not in our power to constrain the yet unconscious mind? The nursling does not yet understand words; how then shall I force him to look at the balls or any other object? He looks around and receives impressions from what he sees repeatedly. Things impress themselves on his power of conception gradually; not, perhaps, in their totality and their parts, but in their universality, by their properties. That is a process which we can neither prevent nor bring about. It is the way designated by Nature herself to promote the development of the mental tendencies.

"Now can this process be disturbed by having the unconditional beginning of all knowing, both for the instinct of the unconscious being and for the conscious and thinking mind, presented in a distinct form and separately, instead of being left in the confusion of the manifoldness of things? Unity is always the beginning. I must have the perception of one before I can say two; and an ordered series of individualities is more easily counted than a confused mass of individualities.

"For example, will not the child's eye perceive colors more easily if he looks at the three primary colors of the balls one after the other, and then at the combinations of colors made by the union of any two primary colors (as is shown here by the green ball between the blue and the yellow), than if it is forced to discern colors in the many-tinted objects around him, in disorderly confusion?

"The necessity of simplifying the material of study in schools, in order to make it easier for the children to learn, to bring more clearness into the subjects of the instruction and therefore into their heads, is acknowledged. But the mind of the newborn child does not wait till the school period to use its organs of sense, and to perceive things that immediately surround it. The development of the mental powers begins with the first drawing of the breath upon earth, and ends with the last, and the natural and orderly support of this development is education.

"Our mind is an organism at whose command are a multitude of organs by which it makes itself acquainted with life. These organs ripen and unfold themselves gradually like other material organisms, and their more or less complete unfolding depends upon conditions that correspond to their nature. These conditions I think I have found. They are chiefly those of development: first those of cosmic development and then the fulfilling of the need of the human mind to make its inward nature objective in the material world, and to represent it in and by material."

"That is to say," I interrupted, "imitating God's world in miniature so to organize material that it satisfies the human need (the work of practical life) or realizes a thought of beauty (art), or facilitates knowledge (science), and thus forms in the actual that which makes the subject-matter of human life, and all this according to God's law of formation, or the laws of creation."

"Yes, quite right," said Froebel, and continued: "people may try as much as they please, the child's mind unfolds and ripens to the understanding of words only by and through concrete things, but they must be used consciously if the aim is education. Nothing—absolutely nothing—in the education of man must be left to mere accident. But the child must reproduce with matter what he has received into himself from the eternal world, in order to understand it. The child, that is, the yet undeveloped being, needs form (*Bild*), and form created by itself, in order to comprehend thought, or the intellectual, in order later to receive it 'in spirit and in truth.'"

Varnhagen replied: "The thought of such a discipline of the human mind in the unconscious stage of life is very illuminating to me. It appears to me to be of great significance, even though its carrying out is not perfectly clear to me. I have already been in some degree initiated into your guiding principles by Madame von Marenholz, and have seen some of your materials; and I concur in the fullest measure with all that I have seen. The discoveries of your genius claim my entire admiration. But I seek in vain for a reason for the prohibition of the kindergartens by the government. Even the mad and childish fear of all popular education, as bringing danger and destruction, cannot be taken as a reason. Your education has to do with the last born generation, who cannot possibly cut off the heads of the present, and these men do not trouble themselves about the distant future. The prohibition is indeed an incomparable folly! But you need not fear; the time of recognition will come, and all the sooner precisely by means of this prohibition. Persecution will exalt your cause, and the more so, the more foolish and groundless persecution it is. They undertook, by it, to give a thrust to the rising socialistic ideas."

It was time to break up, as we were to go to the Duchess Ida's to tea, so the continuation of Froebel's remarks was postponed until the next afternoon, when he promised to come to Liebenstein.

"That is a new Pestalozzi," said Varnhagen; "he lives and moves in his cause, and knows nothing of personal feeling. He is a peculiar phenomenon, especially in our time, so completely concentrated in himself, so free from all the influences of the world. Truly a remarkable man!"

He spoke in the evening to the Duchess also, of the impression he had received, and found her in full accord with the good hopes he connected with Froebel's educational method. The liberal expressions of my friend, the sensible and lovely Princess Amely, pleased Varnhagen exceedingly, and he said, "Frau von Marenholz was not altogether innocent of that."

On the next morning we visited the Liebenstein kindergarten, where Varnhagen watched all the plays and work of the children for more than an hour. He said, among other things, "Here also the meaning and spirit of the method must work by degrees through the rough material. It is in the kindergarten as in the history of nations and their culture."

"Yes, indeed," I replied; "the spirit of the thing can only be expressed completely by its praxis when this is really comprehended by the conductor of the kindergarten; and yet the method works in its own way fully in correspondence with the child's nature by intuition, even without that! The spirit of the child's action is transformed into flesh and blood, because the action corresponds to the inner unconscious demands. This ever-repeated forming of parts into a whole, which hovers before the child's fancy, this ordering and creating, infallibly awakens the sense of organizing. This being fundamentally occupied with one and the same objective action excites to investigation; and the impulse after truth, innate in man, must awake early, if the child comes to the knowledge of the elementary truths of cause and effect through his own experience in the handling of material things, even if at first only by small physical experiments—such as this little one is making, for example, with his blocks, which he has not placed regularly upon each other, but askew, so that his building falls over.

"It is most desirable that this view should make its way—namely, that this impulse of seeking after truth is the only true foundation of real intellectual culture. Only the love of truth can make knowledge living and fruitful which otherwise remains dead. Without an earnest love of truth there can be no religion, which each makes his own and in his own way when he elaborates what is given to him as an endowment, and transmutes it into his own spiritual property."

"Yes!" said Varnhagen, "if we had but progressed so far! But I freely admit that correct education brings us nearer to this still very distant goal. It is a condition of all progress that blind obedience to authority become a seeing one, and that everyone should arrive at a degree, at least, of intellectual independence. The light of the spirit has illuminated only the smallest part of our earth-ball, and even in this part there is still a dark mass which has not yet answered the call, 'Let there be light!'"

"I think there is no better means," was my reply, "to get rid of the eclipse of sun and moon in human history than a just and correct human education."

Varnhagen was especially amused by a little four-year-old girl who, with childlike earnestness and shining eyes, always pressed before the others when there was anything to show or explain.

"These social games really give play to the individual peculiarities," said Varnhagen; "that little thing will make a perfect coquette. She thinks everything revolves about herself."

"Yes," said I; "in such social conditions every too-sharply prominent peculiarity, that is, every fault, receives a check and is reduced to its proper limits, but without destroying the peculiarity in its development. People cannot believe how much the education of children, even at this age, is facilitated by a social condition thus controlled, and requiring the performance of duties."

Varnhagen was so pleased with his view of the kindergarten

that he begged me to give a present, in his name, to the kindergarten teacher, whose "zeal and gentle manners touched" him, as he said.

Madame Froebel also came in and answered some of his questions about the method.

As we were driving, in the afternoon, through the "grinding-grounds" near the village of Steinbach, and Varnhagen saw the wretched existence of the families of the knife-grinders, he said: "Your kindergarten, through the preparation it affords to all kinds of work, and through its power of promoting activity, would after a time make possible an easier and better mode of gaining a livelihood than this, and thus be the best remedy for poverty and misery."

Towards evening Froebel came to Liebenstein and took up again the subject of his method. Afterwards we had a long talk about many other things.

Varnhagen said: "I share your theory of regarding the universe from the point of view of an uninterrupted organic development; and I look upon the history of the world also as an organic process, which shall reach a goal appointed by God. Your thought that, according to this theory, the education of your pupils should consist, from the beginning, of plastic formation, according to the law lying at the root of all organic things, is entirely new to me, but I must recognize it as completely correct. That all development progresses according to law, is indisputable. This law corresponds to the all-penetrating spirit of the world, and must everywhere, from the smallest to the greatest, be in agreement. That has already been more or less recognized in various philosophical systems. And the still unconscious mind of man in childhood cannot do without this development according to law. Give it material, and show it how to make material forms according to a rule corresponding to this universal principle of law, or how to connect parts into a whole, and thus the way and method of organic formation will be in a measure prefigured.

"That is very illuminating; and one can understand that that which is original in every human soul can be, in a certain sense, satisfied by it, and even that originality can be called forth by it. But how much is this originality overgrown and supplanted—yes, even smothered—by what has been inherited from parents, grandparents, and ancestors! Indeed, it should be the task of true culture to cut down and work over these overgrowths, and to favor the growth of individuality and originality. But how rarely is that done! And can it ever be done completely?"

Froebel, highly pleased at Varnhagen's deep interest, replied: "As soon as we understand the complete development of the human being, even within the limits set upon our planet, this becomes possible. Humanity as such, as the thought of God, can only then appear in its full essence (Wesenheit). But every thought of God must have its full and complete realization—so also the thought of humanity, as it has come into the world through Christ. The precept to imitate Christ would be without meaning, if this imitation—I mean human perfection on earth—were not possible, and were not some time to be fully and universally realized."

"And that," I interposed, "by every individual, in the form of his own individuality. The being of man *as an individual* can only appear in an individual form, in which the common humanity is reflected in a particular way belonging to the individual alone. And humanity truly exists as a being, as an organism, only when the individual originality is expressed completely and entirely in each individual."

"You must also add," said Froebel, "that humanity, as we understand the idea of it, belongs to the earth, and must therefore rise to its attainable perfection within the limits which are affixed to it as an organism."

"That would be the promised apotheosis of the earth," said Varnhagen. "That is still far distant, if we consider our actual circumstances. But you are perfectly right. Without a popular education adapted to our time we cannot progress even to the nearest goal. This education must be a practical one, which, as far as possible, shall make everyone independent in the life of actuality. Hail to you, if you smooth the way to that for us."

Froebel replied: "Certainly the nearest goal and the initial step is to be considered first, for we have to educate for our time. Yet only he can be an educator of men, in a high sense of the word, who understands the nature of man in the past, present, and future. Without knowing the final goal of human destiny—or, at least, having a presentiment of it—we cannot take the first steps towards it. The farthest and the nearest, like the greatest and the least, are in connection; and never and in no place should this connection of all things be left out of account."

This lively conversation was kept up until late into the night; and both Froebel and Varnhagen felt in an exalted mood, and were mutually pleased by knowing each other. Froebel gave Varnhagen, at his departure, a copy of his "Education of Man" for a keepsake; and when Varnhagen went away the next day, he said his stay at Liebenstein and his acquaintance with Froebel formed the bright point in his journey of the year.

When I went to see Froebel on the afternoon of Varnhagen's departure, to carry his last remembrances, I found him surrounded by a little circle who were accustomed to assemble there on Thursday afternoons.

He was busy at the moment in explaining his educational doctrine to a strange gentleman. The expression of malicious irony and vaunting self-conceit in this rather young man displeased me immediately, and that displeasure increased during the whole conversation.

Froebel, plunged in his own thought, found no time to fasten his eyes sharply upon his auditor, but, with artless zeal, brought his cause before him.

He was saying: "We see that all development of every kind is connected with conditions upon whose fulfilment or non-fulfilment the consequences depend. That is true in the material world in the organisms of nature, and is equally true in the intellectual world in respect to the development of man, as is expressed in the history of this development—the world's history.

"But these conditions, by which all development is determined, depend fundamentally upon a law according to which the essence at the basis of every organization comes forth and is made manifest. This first law of all phenomena is the *law of opposites.* This is the endowment of every essence that comes into existence, and particularly man called into consciousness. He, in spite of his inner relation to God and nature, stands as an individual essence in the relation of *opposite* to the universe, or nature, on the one hand, and to unity, or God, on the other. The law of connection is given at the same time with the law of opposites. Connection (joining by union of members, or articulation), or the balancing of all existing objects, is the ground-law in the universe, in the visible and invisible, the material and intellectual, world.

"Everything in the organic world subsists in the membership of its parts in a whole. These parts always stand in an opposite direction from each other, and are connected or bound together by a common medium; for example, the leaves of the flower or the stem of a tree, which connects the root with the crown. The limitation in space of every visible phenomenon or thing conditions the opposite by the relation of the limits, as *below* and *above*, *before* and *behind*, *right* and *left*, etc.

"It is the same in the world of representation and thought. Every proposition demands its opposite, and both demand their connection. Thesis, antithesis, and synthesis are the conditions of all logic.

"Man, on the other side, is a representative of this law, since he stands midway between God and nature, between Creator and creature, on one side as a product of nature, belonging to the world of unconscious being, on the other side as mind destined to self-conscious being united with God, or mind from God's mind. Only because he carries within himself the essence of both is he capable of knowing both, and is at the same time called upon to make manifest the Divine in the universe, as the Good, the True, and the Beautiful. He is called, as creature, to be also creator.

"He can only create according to the law of the Creator himself, the law according to which he has been himself created, and by means of the material which nature affords him. This material he is to form and transform according to his own ideas and for his own purposes. In this way he represents his inward world in the outward world, and thereby learns to know both.

"Up to the present time man creates and still works unconsciously upon the law of his activity, as the instinct of the beast works, whose creating is only possible also according to this law. But it is the destiny of man to attain consciousness of himself and his own action. When we make the law of development in the universe, or nature's law of formation, our law of education, this consciousness may be prepared for even in childhood. It therefore lies at the foundation of my culture of man by means of educational development."

The auditor, with some apparent impatience, interrupted Froebel with the remark, "Your law, the connection of opposites, has already been philosophically treated by Hegel in his 'Dialectics,' very well known to me."

And now followed a rush of words upon Hegel's philosophy, which showed anything on his part rather than an understanding of that system; or, rather, he appeared to take it for granted that what Froebel had stated with great emphasis and pretension was nothing more than the repetition of some phrases of the precepts of that system.

"I pray you," he said, turning to Froebel, "of what use in education are such philosophical phrases? Education must in our time be practical above all things, and prepare for practical life."

With rising animation Froebel replied: "Yes, indeed, education must be practical, and especially in a time like ours. But the question is, What must we call practical? Nothing can be more practical than my mode of education, or the law lying at its foundation, which is anything but *a philosophical phrase*! I do not know how Hegel formulates and applies this law, for I have had no time for the study of his system. I must work out my educational method from my own original views, and cannot linger over the philosophical systems of others. Most of them belong to a theory of the world that is passing away, whose one-sidedness becomes more apparent every day, and requires a supplement—a supplement, however, which will not be wanting.

"But I will by no means on that account undervalue the investigations of the past, or mistake their importance. I know that what the present possesses of the knowledge of truth, is due to the work and investigations of our predecessors. Still less do I take the liberty to judge of anything that is not known, or but superficially known to me. Esteem and reverence for science as the greatest treasure of mankind is the duty of every individual.

"At present, when the question is that of rising to a new stage of knowledge, we must begin at the beginning; in almost all the fields of knowledge, we must turn back to the true source of each one. Therefore, let us go ourselves to the things themselves, instead of taking the ready-made systems, and look at things anew as far as possible with our own eyes, without preconceived opinions, without repeating what others have said, in order that we may draw from a new source, and gain a new knowledge to add to the sum of what we possessed before. The beginning of a new epoch in which we are living requires this.

"My educational method offers to its pupils from the beginning the opportunity to collect their own experiences from things themselves, to look with their own eyes and learn to know by their own experiments, things and the relations of things to each other, and also the real life of the world of humanity; this last, however, within the limits necessary for morality, and not divested of the *nimbus* of the beautiful and the ideal.

"In such a manner a greater inward as well as outward independence will be gained, which teaches one how to stand on one's own feet. But that is as far as the heavens from that apparent independence which grows out of hollow and empty pretension. That too much and too early knowledge with which youth is crammed (just as too early ripening is brought to fruit by too strong manuring of the ground and the artificial warmth of the forcing-house) prevents men from reaching a true and real independence, which is only the fruit of the vigorous efforts of one's own powers, especially by acting and doing.

"You are quite right; philosophical phrases, that is, philosophical systems learned by heart, the contents of which cannot thus be made one's own, not only are useless, but positively injurious. One's own thinking is thereby hindered, the unfolding of individualities nipped, and these turned into other than their natural paths.

"Not until the human mind has arrived at the knowledge of things and their relations, and has come to understand life and its claims in some degree, from its own experience; not until it has gained the capability of judging for itself; and not till the universal foundation for its own theory is laid, should it concern itself with the theories of others as fixed and ready-made systems. Only the somewhat matured mind can cultivate itself further by means of the systems of thought of others.

"The facts of life, of history, and of nature offer to youth suitable and sufficient material for thinking for all degrees of the capacity of human individuality; and they at the same time cultivate the judgment, so as to put it in a condition at a later period to comprehend the relations to the highest things in an abstract manner, or philosophically. The history of the human race shows plainly how the philosophic theories were at first the result of many centuries' work of intellectual culture, according to which the individual has even now to ascend these various steps in the path of experience before he can arrive at the summit of intellectual ripeness and independence, which all philosophy claims. First history, and then the philosophy of history.

"It is quite a different thing whether we look upon concrete things and facts as merely material, the things and facts serving for this or that outward purpose, or contemplate them as the outward form of spiritual contents, as the intermedium of higher truths and higher knowledge. In such a manner the inconspicuous products of the kingdoms of nature serve the investigator of nature to discover facts which lead by syllogistic reasoning to the highest scientific knowledge. In this sense the material world is a symbol of the spiritual world, and it is in this sense that education needs to use it, especially for the purpose of leading the child to the ultimate cause of all things—God."

"I cannot declare myself in agreement with the last view you have expressed," said the auditor, with ironical self-conceit, "for I am an atheist. With the practical means that you have shown me, something can be done. The technical culture for which they serve is of the highest importance."

Froebel smiled somewhat ironically at the incomparable presumption with which the gentleman said he was an atheist, and replied: "I shall not quarrel with you upon your religious convictions, or rather upon your complete want of such, and will only remark that in my opinion there is no such thing as an atheist, for the deniers of God make out some kind of a God for themselves in their own fashion, even to making *themselves* one in their miserable self-confidence.

"But if you think that my educational materials are useful, this cannot be because of their exterior, which is as simple as possible, and contains nothing new. The worth of them is to be found exclusively in their application, that is, in the method in which I use them. But this method consists in the application of that law which you characterize as an 'empty phrase.' The whole meaning of my educational method rests upon this law alone. The method stands or falls with the recognition or non-recognition of it. Everything that is left is mere material, the working of which proceeds according to the law, and without that law would not be practicable."

Froebel had risen from his seat as he was uttering these words, and spoke with the tone of the deepest irritation of offended dignity.

The conceited, puffed-up, and really ignorant young man, standing opposite to the true genius in his homely simplicity and modest dignity, made a characteristic picture of the ever-recurring misapprehension of the true meaning of things, not only by conceited fools, but also by that jejune mediocrity which presumes to take the mastery by coarse boasting, assumption, and ignorance. The great number of this class of people, who without thorough culture meddle with scientific subjects and philosophical systems, utter in loud voice the theories and thoughts of others, and give themselves the air of culture without possessing it, judge all things and everything, criticise contemptuously as long as it is not something universally recognized or in correspondence to the cant words of the time, and may well come to the conclusion that our method of education is not perfectly correct.

The reverence for intellectual superiority, pure devotion to the search after truth, sacrifice for the realization of an idea, all seem to the great mass of the youth of the present day mere folly, and intellectual acquirements have value in their eyes only so far as they serve self-seeking, vanity, and desire for pleasure, or are useful for material gain. These undeniable facts are well fitted to point out the need of educational improvements, and to show that the learning in the schools, and obligatory attendance upon these last, do not yet result in real, fundamental culture.

Froebel's words made little impression upon the young fool whom they admonished. Instead of answering them, he pointed to some of the figures and structures which he had been making, not without skill, of the blocks, sticks, etc., which were lying before him, while Froebel was speaking.

"You see," he said, "I already go to school to you, and am surprised to find how excellently this material can be used without your law. I would add to your building-blocks a few others for the higher architecture. This material is too simple for older pupils."

Froebel replied: "It is this simplicity alone that makes these building-blocks suitable for children. I have also thought of carrying the dividing of them still further, according to the same law, but that would be an error. A further division would make the legitimate use of them impossible. We can use the four boxes of blocks together for a greater increase of material. The just line of the division must be observed. The older pupils may multiply the material by their own discoveries, but then it ceases to be a means of methodical instruction. Such building-blocks as you suggest can be offered to a riper age of childhood, by which the various styles of building of nations and times can be represented, I admit, but that does not belong to my kindergarten, which can use only what is elementary. My material is all-sufficient also for the first school years. A too great variety of it would prevent the unfolding of the spirit of invention."

"Your law would hinder my invention," said the all-wise gentleman.

"And yet," said Froebel, "you have used the law yourself in the forms you have made. Any one is able to make the forms with the proper material, but every one who does it, applies my law, *even if without being aware of it*! While you lay your little sticks in opposite directions to bring out this figure, you apply *the law of opposites*, and when you use these other little sticks as connecting links of those lying in opposite directions, you connect the opposites, applying also the law of their connection.

"All formation is on the condition of uniting various parts; what is united forms, as it were, a web or texture, and that exists only by the connecting of opposing lines or threads, as, for example, the web of the spider, which only thus holds together. No organism exists without such a knitting of parts, without at least approximately forming a web, even if it is not visible to the eye. The magnifying power of the microscope shows us plainly the net-like web, whether it is upon a leaf, or upon our skin, or whatever it may be. Even the smallest cell, which is not visible to the eye, consists of a web, and everything which comes into view from the invisible point can be formed in no other way than by being produced thus from different directions, or shot forth, as in the process of crystallization. Every web also forms a net in a certain way by the crossing of the lines running in opposite directions. But this net exhibits at every crossing, or every point of contact, a centre which is to be referred to some circumference, as it were, and every square of the net is a division which offers the best means of arrangement of the different parts of a whole.

"For this reason I give my children a net consisting of perpendicular and horizontal lines, which serves as a guide for drawing all forms, and regulates and facilitates the proportions of parts to a whole and their correct and equal coordination. Painters use a net for the same purpose in their copies of pictures.

"The net affords the most intelligible image of the joining of opposites, by the opposite direction of its lines. The web of all nature's forms is always a net, and expresses the law as the *norm* of all formation. The name is of no importance, but I hold my designation of the law of the *connection of opposites* as the best, and particularly good for describing relations in the intellectual order of things.

"The inflexible dualism in philosophical theories has arisen from the one-sided emphasizing of opposites without consideration of the connecting members, that is, God and the world, without taking in man as the connecting link, etc. Our time has the task of completing this one-sided theory, since it teaches that all opposites, without exception, exist only as an absolute principle, but never as absolute in the phenomenal world, where the relative rules. The law of connection is therefore the law which our time especially needs to know!"

Froebel turned more to the others present than to the stranger with this explanation. The man was evidently not capable of understanding the deepest treatment of the subject.

To prevent Froebel from losing himself too far in his outspoken thoughts, as he often did, and thereby not dwelling upon their application to his method, I asked him to point out his law in one of his materials.

"And which of the occupations will serve best for it, in your opinion?" he asked.

"The drawing, I think," replied I, "which shows so clearly and significantly how by the application of the law of the *connection of opposites* the greatest variety of figures arises without any preliminaries, and without any other direction to the child than those which guide all his occupations and bring them to practical results. When I asked a six-year-old child in the kindergarten to carry out the directed linear figures still further, he answered, 'I cannot find the opposite of my last figure.'

"'Now, then, draw without a rule,' I said. The child looked at me astonished, and replied, 'But can't I find any more figures?'

"A better proof that the law is the very simplest and is a guide for making the child work intelligently for independent formation cannot be found! Your grown pupils say that the drawing makes the law intelligible to them in the highest degree, and some of them have said that they first acquired the power of logical thinking by this occupation of drawing."

Froebel was delighted at this testimony, and took a number of the drawing-sheets of the trained pupils, shuffled them together, and laid them in a pile upon the table, saying: "Now see whether you can find in these inventions, made according to my rule, the individual stamp of each pupil, and can put together the sheets drawn by each."

This proved an easy task. In some of the drawings lying before me predominated the radiating, the articulated, or the open style; while in others, more compact, condensed, and solid bodies showed their similarity of form.

Only a few were too indefinite to express characteristic marks; so that it was easy, in the majority of these little sheets, to discriminate between the work of the different persons.

"Surely," I said, "the free inventions of all the occupations wrought in the kindergarten show how good a means it is to call forth the individual tendencies and characteristics of each pupil. But one must be convinced of this by one's own observation in order to believe it. As long as this is not made, the cause will have opponents who will pervert it into its opposite. A short time ago a teacher called it a wooden education (*Schablonenerziehung*), because he thought the children were forced to bring out the same things with the same materials, instead of being allowed the necessary freedom in action and play."

"That is only because they do not know how my law is to be applied, which *alone* can make possible any freedom in formation. The order of the whole creation rests upon this law *alone*, and all freedom of development corresponds to this order."

He took the first sheet of his drawing-method in his hand, and showed how the lines of different lengths drawn in the net formed a right-angled triangle, consisting of perpendicular, horizontal, and oblique lines; and how thus, out of the triangles placed together in opposite directions, symmetrical figures are produced, like those which are formed by the planes, consisting of different triangles."

He said: "With my planes I give the triangle as a material surface. Here in the drawing I have three lines which form the triangle. Then the parts which are arranged by lines into a whole form a triangle as a whole, which again serves as a part to form a greater whole by the union of several triangles.

"In the further carrying-out of the designs there arise larger and more complicated figures, whose parts are then united as a whole, to be added together as parts or members of a still greater whole, like the articulations in every organism of nature. Nature follows the same course, proceeding from the simplest to the most complicated, and forms a similar articulation, since everything in it is a member or a part of a greater whole, from a blade of grass up to the universe. This articulation begins with the simplest and rises to the most complicated, the boundless whole. Everything, then, is a member (or part), and also a whole, or an organism.

"Thus I give to the child, by my system of drawing, an image and scheme of organization, and develop in him his tendency for organizing. Every productive work, every work consciously willed, is conditioned upon the union of parts according to an idea, and that is nothing else than organizing.

"All organizing rests upon the application of a rule or a law: it is therefore according to law, and can never admit of caprice. Without the application of the law, the child could not create independently, any more than he could learn to read and write without guidance. But, before he learns to read and write, he himself must learn the beginning of action, or of organizing and shaping; and for that there is need of the impression of elementary forms, which lie at the foundation of all forms also. These must make an impression upon the child's mind, in order to prepare for the later culture of the power of abstract thinking (*Begriff-bildung*), or scientific mathematics. My system of drawing shows plainly the transition from the regular mathematical forms—the skeleton of all forms—to the forms of beauty.

"You will recognize these forms as beautiful, that is, harmonious in the correspondence of their parts. The single parts you find here in their beginnings, as *mathematical* forms and then as triangles.

"We also always find the fundamental forms *as* mathematical forms in nature, but draped, in order to rise to beautiful form.

"Art developed in the same way. The Egyptian temples show us only straight-lined figures, which consequently show mathematical relations. Only in later times appeared the lines of beauty, that is, the arched or circular lines.

"I carry the child on in the same way. You can perceive in these figures how the gradual transition from the straight to the curved line takes place."

One of the teachers present, from a neighboring town, here interrupted, and said: "One sees in the kindergarten how remarkably this method of drawing develops the children, and how quickly, by the application of this simple law, they are first directed how to make forms, and then go on to the independent invention of regular forms; and that this method is the only one that can make such young children capable of drawing *without patterns*, which I never should have considered possible if it had not been for my personal observation. Besides, this combining and conceiving is the best *thinking* exercise for young children that can be found. You will be pleased, Herr Froebel, when I bring you the inventions of my children, which I have selected for the coming teachers' convention."

"Certainly," said Froebel, "that I shall! You have already done much in your school in a short time, since you introduced my method."

This teacher was one of the eager and self-sacrificing pupils of Froebel, from the neighborhood of Marienthal, who devoted every spare moment to learn of him, coming to him a long way even in stormy, cold, and snowy weather, and often going home late at night.

"The instinct of children," I added, "knows how to make Froebel's law their own very quickly; that I observe in every kindergarten I visit. The youngest children are able to make very pretty inventions, and without imagining, on that account (as many of the present mere imitators of the thing do), that the new figures they have discovered are exclusively their own possession. They see how every child can do the same thing.

"Through the children, adults will learn how to seize upon the law and its consequences, while at present there is so little understanding of it that many people presume, in their pitiful self-conceit, to deride it!

"By and by *Froebel's educational law* will be accepted as distinctly and independently as Newton's law of gravitation. Now, every schoolboy who has learned anything understands Newton's law. When Newton proclaimed it, only a few of the learned were able to comprehend it.

"The whole striving of the present time tends to make serviceable by practical application the discoveries and knowledge of the human mind. The practical application and results will prove the truth of the idea lying at its foundation, and then these will make it plain to the common understanding, which always at first needs demonstration.

"It is always the simplest and nearest principle that men seize with the most difficulty. No one thinks it strange that the instinct of beasts makes them act so intelligently, makes the migrating birds, for instance, fly toward the south at the right time, makes them choose the shortest way, and on their return the next year seek their old nests, etc. But they do not believe in the reasonableness of the idea of the human instinct in the child, and deride your idea of guiding his unconscious action educationally, and making it useful for later culture."

Froebel assented, and went on: "The time has now come to exalt all work into free activity, that is, to make it intelligent action. This can only take place when the law, according to which all formative activity proceeds, is recognized and *consciously* applied, as it has been hitherto unconsciously applied. The occupation-material of my method gives the means of the unconscious application of the law on the children's part to rise to art in such a way as to come to their consciousness by degrees and be recognized as the guide and regulator of all formation. In no other way can human work be transformed into free activity. It can only become intellectual action out of what has been mere mechanical action, when the occupation of the hand is at the same time the occupation of the mind.

"At the present time, art *alone* can truly be called free activity, but every human work corresponds more or less with creative activity, and this is necessary in order to make man the image of his Divine Creator—a creator, on his own part, in miniature."

After all the company had gone, I expressed to Froebel my great sorrow that so many useless and even harmful elements should press into his cause, while the intelligent advocates stood apart from each other.

"Have you never found any young man but Middendorff," I inquired, "who could and would devote himself wholly to your cause?"

"I once thought I had found such a one," answered Froebel, "but he left me and betrayed me in the most injurious manner."

He then related to me how much he had loved a young teacher in the Keilhau institution; how he had overloaded him with benefits, and had devoted his time to him at a great sacrifice, in order to induct him fully into his educational idea, in the hope of making of him an intelligent, true scholar and teacher who would spread his doctrine abroad after his death. With great sorrow he was obliged to come to the conclusion that there had either been an incapacity in the young man to understand the thing fully, or he had wanted the necessary self-denial for such a task. After free conversation upon the misconception of his idea, a profound estrangement had taken place between them, and the offended vanity of the pupil had separated them. His selfishness and falsehood had shown themselves more and more afterwards, and made Froebel feel that his intention was only to make serviceable for his own purposes the idea Froebel had held as so sacred a one. When the sad time of poverty and want came upon him, during which he needed so much friendly support, this ungrateful one left Keilhau, which seemed to him no longer suited to the execution of his plans. He endeavored to bring discredit upon Froebel and his institution, by the coarsest detraction and false accusations. This was his gratitude for the love and benefit that had been bestowed upon him!

Froebel made this communication to me with the deepest sadness, and with tears in his eyes.

"Must every Master have his Judas, and every truth its betrayer!" I exclaimed.

"Yes," said Froebel, "it cannot be otherwise than that self-sacrifice, which every bearer of an idea must make, should call forth its opposite, which is selfishness. Selfishness makes profit out of everything that does not resist it. 'Let him who will follow me take up the cross.' Thus it always is with those who do battle for truth; they must *expect* to be crucified!"

"To have nourished a snake in one's bosom," I remarked, "is always the most painful suffering one can have to bear. But the greatest of sins consists in betraying a new truth, which is to serve for the salvation of humanity. That is the sin against the Holy Ghost. Beware of such persons as your visitor of today, who will not hesitate to commit this sin against your idea."

How much our cause would have to suffer from its betrayers we had no suspicion at that time. For my own part, I hoped that the inconspicuousness of its outward appearance would protect it from the Sovereigns of Industry, so great a number of whom have taken possession of it at present.

Far worse, even, is the influence of those who do not hesitate to deride it and make it ridiculous, while they proceed to make use of its practical means to gain the credit of the discovery for themselves!

For this purpose they select single passages, without their context, from Froebel's writings, which in Froebel's heavy manner of expression sound not only confused and obscure, but absolutely senseless. It is at best difficult to express new views clearly and significantly, since every new thing must create its own expression of itself. But in endeavoring to express deep thoughts upon the being of man in childish plays, the danger can scarcely be avoided of making that appear ridiculous which is truly earnestness.

Besides, there are in every cause, and especially in the first attempt to carry out what is still new and therefore undeveloped, weak places and defects which can easily be used maliciously; thus, many a badly formed verse, many an example not quite well chosen, is used in that way.

They do not hesitate to call Froebel's occupation-materials and children's plays a "play-martyr system," even after numerous kindergartens with their cheerful, happy, and naturally developed pupils have given the lie to such slanders; after thousands of parents have blessed the beneficent institution, and an ever-increasing number of thinkers have recognized and accepted the idea lying at the foundation of it as a true one and inspired by genius!

No *friendly* visitor of even the numerous kindergartens conducted without comprehension of the method, and without knowledge of the science of teaching, would be induced to use the expression "a martyr system," which only exposes the malice of those who apply it.

The tactics of those critics who think they are criticising Froebel's work fundamentally, proceed, after showing that the Froebelian principles and measures are ruinous and inefficient, to speak of the necessity and timeliness of the very institutions and arrangements under discussion which they have themselves disparaged, and particularly to exalt the no-longer-to-be-delayed education for work as the true foundation of the education of the people! The discussions of this subject, reported with great emphasis, are followed by practical propositions, ingeniously invented means of cultivating the working power of childhood still in the playing age, etc., and with astonishment one recognizes in these propositions and means for the furtherance of this object the very plays and occupations of Froebel hitherto ridiculed; and, indeed, without any change or alteration on the outward, material side, but also without anything of the methodical means by which alone the result is to be reached, and of which this new discoverer has not even a presentiment!

Another mode of setting themselves up as improvers and promoters of Froebel's method consists in laughing at the law lying at the foundation of it, or casting it aside ironically (showing themselves utterly ignorant of it), and then, with the assertion that there is another meaning to it than the one Froebel gives, letting the occupations invented by Froebel without any change follow as their own invention! This is scarcely credible, but it is true. Without any conception of Froebel's idea and method of applying it, without understanding the meaning of the subject itself, they carelessly copy what Froebel has invented and what his real pupils have worked out, and set themselves up as its improvers and promoters, not thinking that the time must come when the ground and truth of it will be seen and recognized, and they will find themselves in the pillory. It is the characteristic way of such enemies to decry as "orthodox" and "imitators" those who truly and earnestly advocate the cause and as following Froebel to the letter blindly, and without any judgment and discrimination of their own. And yet every child must understand that continuous development, which everything and everyone needs, is only possible through the application of what exists according to a prescribed rule or method, or methodically. One can only improve what is at hand, and can do it then only by real understanding of the thought lying at the foundation of the discovery. It is also a heavy responsibility to take upon themselves to put off the recognition, and with it the universal application, of an innovation so full of promise for the improvement of the education of the people, and that in a time like ours when such heavy battles are impending for a new social birth; battles which the unconquered roughness of the masses threatens to make bloody. But these people will have to expiate on a large scale whatever apparent advantages they have gained for the present, when the truth shall be seen and their miserable machinations shall be revealed. They forget that this spirit, this idea, is the only living one and therefore alone capable of making a germinating seed of truth grow. But this delay to profit by the new educational system is inevitable, since the authorities and all those who have influence in this respect will be led astray by such charlatanism and the intentional fraud of individuals.

The improvement which each and all need can only be reached by means of practice, but never by those who cast aside the method on which this practice depends as "empty phrases," without observing that the fish they thought they had caught had escaped and left only sand in the net. The men without genius neither understand genius, nor are they able to separate the idea as such from the person who holds it; they think the idea cannot be holy, if they see the person who holds it err, as every man does. Yet while setting themselves up as improvers, they have not pointed out a single error, or refuted Froebel, or added to his idea an iota of anything useful and new. They speak about what they do not understand, and therefore cannot give or carry out the application of it, and so they will continue to strike genius dead in its swaddling-clothes, until there shall appear in sufficient numbers those who really do understand what it is that Froebel has found for a *new starting-point for the development of the human mind*, and also the means to start from the visible world instead of from ideas; from experience and facts instead of from doctrines; and to smooth the path of transition from the sensuous to the spiritual in the period of unconscious being without tearing away the connection, as is done now, whatever may be said to the contrary.

Besides, there can be no question at present about the want of full understanding and practical application of the method, so far as the necessary preliminary conditions for it are yet wanting. One of these conditions consists in the existing ignorance of mothers, and consequently in faulty family education; another, in the want of sufficient and special power of teaching. These wants are to be duly considered first, and the power of teaching is to be cultivated in as "orthodox" a manner, according to Froebel, as possible; that is, methodically, without the deterioration of these boasters. Only thus can the spirit of the method pass into the practice of it, make up what is wanting, and by improving the whole secure continuous development. The subject must first be set forth in its original form, and the right beginning made.

At that time, when Froebel was still actively employed for the realization of his idea, he found, among the never-ceasing disappointments, ever-recurring consolation and encouragement through a few sympathizers who, filled like himself with the love of truth, were ready for every sacrifice to it.

When at the time above mentioned he had ended his account of the betrayal of one of his pupils, he took in his hand a letter he had just received, saying, "The betrayal of the faithless one is atoned for by such noble and true men as the writer of this letter."

He read some passages from the letter, which was from Professor von Leonhardi of Heidelberg. They were the first words I had heard at that time from my true friend of many long years. Froebel related with deep feeling how Leonhardi had devoted his whole life and all his powers to advocating and saving from neglect the teachings of the late philosopher Krause. Ever since his eighteenth year he had not hesitated at any sacrifice of every personal interest, even to giving up his paternal inheritance, in order to carry on the editorship and spread of Krause's writings, by which the door of truth was first opened to him, and whose enthusiastic promulgator he remained to the last breath. To his unwearying activity, his rare power of work, and his peerless perseverance, is chiefly due that the weighty heritage of the great thinker was brought to light, and numerous disciples and advocates of his doctrine won over.

Leonhardi left even the material savings of his simple and unassuming life to the work to which he had devoted himself in the interest of mankind. His property is secured to the establishment of a Krause-foundation, whose work shall be to spread his philosophy by word and pen.

The known agreement of Froebel's views with those of Krause already made the latter desirous, as early as 1835, to connect his efforts with those of Froebel.*

This plan, which he imparted to Froebel, could not be carried out, because the scientific activity of Krause for speculative philosophy differed too much from the educational activity of Froebel, which was so entirely devoted to practical life. Yet Leonhardi continued to remain a true friend to Froebel and his educational work, which seemed to him best adapted to carry out in the sense of Krause's views the moral improvement and renovation of human society.

So Leonhardi neglected no opportunity of calling attention to Froebel and his work, and afterwards he stood at my side as the most faithful helper and counsellor. He was one of the first who supported my plan of founding a Universal Educational Union, and lent a helping hand to promote it.† Till his death he belonged to the committee and supported its efforts. Leonhardi was one of those rare men who devote themselves to an idea throughout their whole existence, with a never wavering conviction of it, from pure love for truth and humanity. The fewer such examples our time has to show of the loftiest self-denial, the greater is the duty of rescuing the memory of such from oblivion.

The affinity of views between Froebel and Krause is undeniable, although the activity of the two led them in quite opposite directions, and each of them construed an idea, that was one in essence, according to his own theory. The view that genius has picked up its ideas here and there, and has done its work cor-

*See Hanschmann's biography of Froebel.

†This may account for the widespread error that the Educational Union arose out of the Congress of Philosophers of Krause's followers. This is not the case. I invited only a few members of that Congress to join the Union I founded. See the Report of the Congress of Philosophers.

rectly only by the help of others, is one of the many perverted notions concerning the creative power of man, which it falls to the lot of genius to bear. Genius is the most original thing in the world, and born of God's mercy to receive the inspiration of truth and beauty. But genius also needs excitement and influence from without, in order to be conscious of itself and the mission which it is to fulfil. The ruling minds of an epoch are spiritually related, and affect and work upon each other, without the peculiar stamp of each being necessarily effaced.

So some of Krause's writings and his personal acquaintance had an influence upon Froebel, and here and there lent expression to his views, which he found so much difficulty in putting into words. In regard to this, it is to be lamented that Froebel did appropriate many a mode of expression from Krause's writings, by which his own were made unenjoyable and anything but clear. The same complaint may be made of Krause's writings. Praiseworthy are the efforts to purify the German language from unnecessary foreign words, and particularly to Germanize scientific words; but Krause's style combines a great number of different words into one, giving birth to real word-monsters that are ill adapted to carrying out the contemplated purpose of clearing up ideas. Particularly the idea taken from Krause about the linking together of parts, or articulation (*Gliederung*), seems to stand in full contradiction to this purpose.

But even genius is subject to error, and often carries its fundamental thought to its logical result in a one-sided manner; and from this liability Froebel cannot be said to be free.

The theory in which Froebel and Krause agreed especially is the idea of the analogy existing between organic development in nature and organic development in the spiritual world, and according to which the historical development of mankind has proceeded, obeying the same laws as those of nature and its organisms (*Gleickgesetzigkeit*). The same logic of the one all-penetrating Divine reason rules in both, *unconscious* in the one (nature), *conscious* to itself in the other (mind). Therefore are the opposites ruling everywhere, not absolute, but relative, and always find their connection or solution in the *process* of life.

Mankind, as the highest organism of creation, is destined to constitute an entity bodily as well as mentally. All the domains of human life are necessarily penetrated with one spirit; and, since they are linked together as independent organs, they must form conscious parts of the whole, which is human society.

To that end, at some future time, science, and art, as well as all the active principles of human life, justice, and religion (or state and church), must be penetrated with the same spirit of truth, and with a consciousness of the one aim of serving humanity perfected according to the thought of God, that is, "the kingdom of God upon earth." With this aim, mutual love, penetrating all individuals, must unite them into a living, self-conscious whole, which then represents a spiritualized or glorified humanity.

This is something like a popular statement of the general theory of the two contemporary thinkers. The goal which they place before man is the same—the ideal of human conditions and human nature. And both recognize the correct development and culture of the human being, and the improvement of all human arrangements, as reaching this destiny; both wish for moral improvement, for the renewing of human society.

Krause, in pursuit of this aim, set up a deeply pondered scientific system, embracing all domains of human existence, which, in the sense of his philosophy, shall enlighten men upon their own nature and destiny, and the highest aim of all social arrangements, and determine, in conformity to that, the thinking, feeling, and acting of individuals.

Froebel, on the contrary, particularly occupies himself with finding the germ of Divine reason in human nature in its unconscious era; and he proceeds, from the law that dominates it as an incontestably steadfast one, to rise to consciousness and freedom of spirit. The law of development in nature offers him the guide by which he may find the law of development in man, and for the spiritual ordering of things. This law becomes for him the *law of* *education*, according to which God guides the development of man—of individuals as well as of nations—and of humanity as a whole. He sees in creation the embodied thoughts of God. These offer to the yet unconscious mind of man (in childhood) reflections of his own being, and thereby become sensuous images of the unfolding spiritual life, which, by these symbols in the physical world, rises to spiritual consciousness.*

The conformity of the unconscious (or the life of impulse) with the reason, that determines the life of the mind, makes a synthesis between nature and mind—the material world and the intellectual world. The human being is the intermedium of unconscious nature and the all-conscious Mind, since it goes forth out of unconsciousness (in childhood), and belongs to this unconsciousness, bodily, during its whole earthly life; but, at the same time, it may be rising to an ever-higher degree of spiritual life, approaching the absolute self-consciousness of God. In short, human life is the passing-over from unconsciousness to the highest consciousness.

Krause takes his departure from thought, abstraction, in order to explain the phenomena of the concrete world in nature and culture, and ends with the ideal or prototype of all the forms of life, the realization of which is the ultimate task and final destiny of humanity. He draws up the plan, as it were, of the temple of humanity in the future.

Froebel, when he teaches how the first steps are to be taken by which to bring forth a generation cultivated in conformity with nature, in which the original idea of God is restored by man, points out the way which leads to this temple of perfected humanity, and furnishes the material for building it; and thus the first condition is fulfilled by which the highest ideal can be brought to ripeness.

To reach this end, he goes back to the fountainhead and origin of all life in its germinating time, in order to seek *there* its pri-

*What is spiritual is that which is in communion with other spirits, including God.—Tr.

mary roots and the NORM of its development. Only the life still fettered by necessity shows significantly and clearly what is the law that rules everything, because all caprice is shut out from it. It is the freedom of conscious being which conditions its opposite, unconsciousness and bondage, since only its own striving, which it needs in order to break its fetters, can lead to freedom—that is, to that freedom which recognizes law as its first principle, and submits to it *consciously*.

The highest goal of human development—the completion of full-grown humanity—demands the highest degree of self-consciousness. This self-consciousness implies self-knowledge as a condition, and self-knowledge is only attainable through self-activity. In the products of his activity man recognizes himself and his power, just as God, the Creator, manifests himself in the works of creation.

For the works of man, as well as for the formation of the organism of human society, nothing less than the law of formation which determines all the works of creation can be adequate. Therefore this law is the principle of all *human* creation; and every individual must be penetrated by it, in order to be able to contribute his part to the building-up of humanity as a whole.

The life of the unconscious, consequently human life in the stage of unconsciousness (childhood), is determined exclusively by the principle of law, the law of nature. To teach children who are rising out of the unconscious era into the conscious, to apply this principle of law which dwells in them to their own doing and producing, serves to make it objective to them and causes it to be recognized, as they grow in intelligence, as the rule of all formation. Only by such experimental knowledge is the human mind made capable of taking part, intelligently, in the new building-up of human society.

The rough, unspiritualized masses cannot do this, and they hinder those members of society who are conscious of themselves as men, from being able to work successfully for perfection.

It is therefore and must ever remain an essential condition of all progress to furnish for all members of society some degree of this intelligence in regard to human nature, human destiny, and human perfectibility. Therefore the task of the time is the solution of the problem of universal culture.

Krause strives for this solution by teaching adults, already cultivated and thinking beings, that is, the favored minority, whose part in life is to protect and increase the treasures of science for mankind.

Froebel wished to lay an educational foundation for all, within the individual limits set by nature, that all may by degrees, if only in the course of centuries, help the whole sum of human powers and tendencies to their development, in the interest of the whole human race. And he wished to lay this foundation at a time of life which, till now, had been left without that systematic support of the mental powers which we call education, namely, in the earliest childhood. The fundamental principles of his method may be summarized something as follows:

1. The period of unconscious impulse, that comes but once in life, being the beginning of the whole development of every man, is the most important moment for educational influence.

2. As the conduct and discipline of the mental powers at the school age of children are, in conformity to the destiny of rational beings, *methodical*, so the guidance of the mental powers in the unconscious era preceding the school age needs even far more to be methodical than the succeeding years, which have already reached a certain degree of intelligence, because the spiritual instinct of the unconscious period, far more than the instinct of animals, lacks all power of reaction.

3. Impressions of the concrete world made on the unconscious child, who is stimulated by them to the act of perception, form the beginning for the later knowledge, which is the beginning of consciousness.

4. Things can only be perceived in the properties of form, color, size, number, weight, sound, etc., common to all things, and to impress each of these properties *one* thing is chosen in order to exemplify it in the simplest and most striking manner; an

A B C of things is thus learned, which consists of only about half the number of the letters of the alphabet.

5. The methodical use of this A B C of things—in the first childish activity of play—affords a means of help, like those which the school applies for its various disciplines of instruction (namely, the selection of appropriate materials and their order and division. Thus, for example, in geography, the division of the land into mountainous chains, water basins, etc.; in history, the division into epochs; in natural history the division of the species of plants into orders, families, etc.).

There is no other way to give the mind a clear view of a multitude of things, than to compare multiplicity, variety, and manifoldness with unity or universality, in order to make prominent that which is common to all the parts (fundamental forms or types) which bring out this common property in the simplest manner. But if the comparatively matured mind needs this help of classification, how much more must it be needed by the child's mind in the first stages of its development!

6. Matured thinking, and particularly philosophical thinking, rests upon simple, determined fundamental conceptions; for example, the conceptions of unity, variety, being, growth, time, space, connection, relation, etc. All these are abstractions deduced from things in the world of phenomena. In other words, fundamental *con*ceptions must correspond to definite fundamental *per*ceptions, which have preceded them either consciously or unconsciously.

In Froebel's system, the perception of the form of the ball corresponds to the idea of unity. Space is designated by the limiting of space. The conception of time is expressed by the succession of facts in the past, present, and future. It makes a great difference whether such perceptions are acquired in childhood clearly and definitely, with conscious intention, or are left to chance.

7. Such things are to be offered for the first observation of the mind as will afford appropriate fundamental *per*ceptions for subsequent fundamental *con*ceptions. Thus is gained an immediate connection between conception (abstraction) and sensuous

perception. A logical chain connects the impression which originates human thinking with the end, or conception. Clear observation and clear representation lead to comparison and clear conclusions, and thus to clear logical thinking.

8. To reach this result, merely the rightly chosen objects (types) are not enough, there must also be the right treatment or use of them in order to give the first acquaintance with the material world. By such activity the first experiences and the first technics of the human hand are acquired, or an A B C of work which, together with the exercise of the sense of beauty, gives a simultaneous preparation for *art.*

9. Only a methodical mode of education, which is founded upon the knowledge of the natural progress of intellectual development, and applies to the human being the same principle of law, according to which all and every development in the universe proceeds, is a mode of education adapted to the nature of the human being on the one hand, and conformable to outward *nature* on the other.

This mode of education discovered by Froebel may be called a philosophical pedagogy, since it requires intelligent comparison of the nature of man and of his relations to the world and to God; and the highest goal of human perfectibility is predetermined by the first steps of the yet unconscious human soul.

Since the practice of this mode of education is placed specially in the hands of women, it may be called the *philosophy for women.* It is specially a philosophy for practical life, and it receives its whole significance only by an immediate application.

This shows the opposite direction of the work of Froebel to that of the purely scientific system of Krause. The task of the latter is the clearing up of the minds of thinking adult *men* upon their relations to nature, humanity, and God—the fixing of the conceptions upon everything which occupies the mind of man upon the institutions which he has been called upon to realize upon earth, and upon his own being and its highest destiny; while Froebel has to do with the guidance of the yet unconscious human soul in order to lead it intelligently to the highest goal.

The views of both these philosophers combat the present prevailing materialism without denying that true side of it which respects the reason that rules in nature, and its concurrence with the human mind. On the contrary, the ideas upon the personality of this mind, consequently of its immortality and eternal progress, and especially upon religious truth so far as it has been revealed to the human mind, are eternally and unshakably established by both Krause and Froebel.

This view of things is not only a negation of materialistic errors, but it points out at the same time the means and connection through which the opposites of mind and nature, as absolute, are resolved, without risking a single one of the truths in the kingdom of the mind. This view, then, offers to the present time a remedy against the prevailing errors which have arisen from misunderstood truth.

18

Teachers' Convention

In September of 1851 every member of our circle was occupied with gaining participants in the impending Teachers' Convention, which had been planned and prepared for the past few months, and was appointed for the 27–29th instant. Every promise of participation which came was a message of joy to Froebel. The prohibition which had been decreed against kindergartens gave only greater importance to the coming investigation of the Froebelian method by specialists, and Froebel entertained the hope of again seeing his idea brought publicly into estimation through favorable judgments of it.

Diesterweg, who had already been in Liebenstein in the early summer, came now again among the first arrivals, and Middendorff soon followed.

Many were the councils held at my residence upon the order of the proceedings, the contents of the essays to be read by Froebel, and the reports to be contributed by existing institutions, etc.

I begged Diesterweg to take charge of the part assigned to me upon the progress of the cause in Berlin, that greater weight might be imparted to it by his authority in the pedagogic world.

Rector Köhler, of Corbach (not to be confounded with the later advocate of Froebel's educational system, August Köhler, of Gotha), came a few days before the assembling of the convention and took part in our preliminary discussions. He engaged one of Froebel's pupils at that time, Sophia Seibt, to be the conduct or of a kindergarten he had undertaken to raise. This lady subsequently became his wife.

The loyalty and reliability which were expressed in the personality of this man awakened the hope of gaining in him a powerful support to the cause, a hope which was fulfilled for a short time only, as, alas! he was taken from this work by death a few years later.

Among the expected guests was Director Marquard, of Dresden, one of the well-known advocates and veterans of Froebel's cause, who had already founded a kindergarten in Dresden, in company with Adolph Frankenburg, which was excellently carried on by his wife.

Marquard was also the first who introduced the method into his school, and gave his support to the cause persistently and faithfully with much activity and self-sacrifice.

Among the teachers who came were Herr Stangenberger, who at that time prepared the lessons for Froebel's stick-laying; Herr Pösche; Herr Heinrich Hoffmann from Hamburg, conductor of a kindergarten there; two young rising naturalists, Dr. Karl Müller, and Dr. Otto Ule, afterwards editor of the widespread periodical *Nature*, and whose name is now numbered among those distinguished in science; the Consistorial Counsellor, Dr. Peter, and Deacon Müller, both from Meiningen; and many others. From the region around Liebenstein, out of city and village, a great number of teachers and some clergymen were found, and Minister von Wydenbrugk, as he had promised.

Among the kindergartners who participated (Froebel's earlier scholars), I was specially interested in seeing Henrietta Breymann, one of Froebel's favorite pupils, who at that time had charge of a kindergarten founded by the Sattler family in Schweinfurth. I had become acquainted with her at the time of my first knowledge of Froebel, and was delighted by her amiability, her talents, and her zeal for the cause. More and more intimate as time went on, we often worked together, especially in Brussels, where I invited her during my residence there to undertake the instruction in Froebel's method for a six months' course, arranged by the suggestion of a number of teachers, and at the same time to take part in a kindergarten instituted there.

Fraulein Breymann (now Frau Schräder in Berlin, wife of the railroad director) is one of those advocates of Froebel's education who hold fast to the method, and strive to overcome that which generally in its practice is merely mechanical; and to keep up its true spirit.

The institution founded by her and her sisters in Watzum, near Wölfenbuttel, was the first known to me which took up Froebel's method for part of its programme, as a necessary branch of instruction for general female culture, and carried it through successfully. Frau Schräder agreed with me in considering the training of the female sex for its educational calling in Froebel's method as the first condition of making it useful in the general reform of education. In this sense she works with her husband, who is a true follower and clear-sighted advocate of the cause, in our Universal Educational Union, which is striving specially to secure the chief end of the reform by the complete application of the method. She is also one of the decided opponents of the ever wider-spreading superficiality in the cultivation of kindergartners, which is now thought to be a purely mechanical calling, with the time of learning the art reduced to a few months, while a year is scarcely long enough for the majority of the somewhat uncultivated young girls who study it.

There were also a few kindergartners present from other places, beside the pupils then attending the Marienthal institution—Fraulein Traberth from Eisenach, Fraulein Krämer from Philippsthal, Fraulein Bohmann, and some others.

In the convention which was opened on the morning of the 27th, in the hall of the Liebenstein Baths, a warm and lively sympathy prevailed, and every individual was intent upon expressing recognition of Froebel, and making him forget the injustice of the prohibition. The presence and accord of Diesterweg, who took the chair on the first day, contributed specially to this spirit, and also to make favorable to the cause those who stood a little apart from it.

There was but slight opposition; and no discord disturbed the assembly. The majority of the participants were penetrated by the conviction that a reform of education was incontrovertibly necessary, and that the new foundation required was afforded by the method of Froebel.

After Diesterweg had spoken a few words of welcome, he opened the assembly as its chairman, and spoke of our work in Berlin. Then followed various reports from existing kindergartens by their conductors, in which Froebel and Middendorff joined. As Diesterweg had already spoken of our activity in Berlin, and as there were many discussions, and I was at that time suffering from sore throat, I declined making any special communication about my personal activity.*

The statement of his efforts, which Froebel made on the afternoon of the first day of the Convention with the most peculiar vividness and impressiveness, and with the deepest conviction of their value, made a universal impression and called out great unanimity of opinion. He did not enter deeply into the fundamental idea of his method that finds so little comprehension, but brought out especially the practical side—the early use of the child's powers for manipulation and productive activity.

The proof of the possibility of leading the activity of the child to the elements of all work in its very earliest years by playful occupations, was given by a great quantity of articles from kindergartens, plaited, folded, pricked, cut, and drawn with and upon paper and other materials, which lay spread out upon the table. They had been sent from the various kindergartens and some village schools in that region. That teacher from Steinbach who had promised Froebel the work of the schoolchildren, had laid out a great variety of figures cut from paper, the majority of which

*See further in regard to this Convention, in Hanschmann's biography of Froebel.

were free inventions of the village children, and were distinguished by their beauty of form, sureness of hand, and neatness of execution.

"How much might be gained for the universal moral improvement of the people," I said to Minister von Wydenbrugk, who was sitting near me, "if the sense of beauty and skilfulness of hand were cultivated in all the village schools!"

"Only let all the teachers be prepared for their calling as well as those whose children have produced this remarkable work of their schools, with their freedom from all pretensions," was his reply.

"Yes," I said; "what the mothers are to do on one side and the teachers on the other can alone bring the new education into life."

"But how is it possible," said an unmarried, very highly cultivated, and gifted lady who sat near me, "to be so uninterruptedly occupied with children and their plays? Are these occupations so charming?"

"Indeed," I replied, "if it were only the play and the mere outward apparatus, the occupation might well be tedious. But the idea at the foundation of it, and the contemplation of the being of man and its development in the child is an inexhaustible mine of interesting discovery. Originality alone is always interesting, and where is it to be found as in the child? Then the task of improving education is one of the most important tasks of our time, particularly for us women, and is truly worth some sacrifices. It seems to me to be the holiest duty of everyone who bears within himself a spark of genuine humanity."

As it was late, the discussion of Froebel's statement was postponed till the next day, and the evening was devoted to social intercourse.

On the following morning, Counsellor Peter opened the assembly as chairman, and Froebel's method was then thoroughly discussed.

Middendorff spoke warmly and beautifully upon the great influence of women as the educators of humanity, and invited the kindergartners who were present to take part in the discussion, with which request a few of them complied.

The discussion was principally confined to the practical application of Froebel's materials without entering further into the fundamental idea which contains the germ of the whole matter. This was quite natural, considering the superficial acquaintance with the subject on the part of the majority of those present, but it left me somewhat dissatisfied with the result of the discussion, which did not bring to light prominently what was characteristic and really new in the method.

The many plays of the children of our Liebenstein kindergarten in the afternoon of that day did not fail to illuminate the most serious faces, and to call forth the greatest enthusiasm and applause, to Froebel's great delight; and when his pupils, in the evening, under the guidance of Madame Froebel, executed some of them in the hall, the majority of those present joined in and played and sang merrily like the children. Nothing is more contagious than the love of play in old and young! Froebel himself took part in conducting, and even Diesterweg entered the ring. No gay ball could have passed more pleasantly than the social play of that evening, which turned everyone back into a child, enjoying the present moment in the most innocent manner.

Diesterweg, who took part in everything "joyfully," as he said, turned to me with these words: "Now we are all children today, Frau von Marenholz, so you must be satisfied with us!" He referred to a remark I had made—how little everyone understood Froebel's idea, because everyone forgets how he had been a child, and what was wanting to him as a child.

Middendorff said: "This is like a fresh bath for the human soul, when we dare to be children again with children. The burdens of life could not be borne if it were not for real gaiety of heart."

We were all astonished that Froebel, at his years, bore this straining of all his powers so long without being wearied, when so many claims were made upon him. But he met us again the next morning fresh and cheerful, and was particularly pleased by the "Declaration" of the pedagogues present, in regard to his educational views, that had been agreed upon among themselves.

But the judgment was in too general terms to give prominence to the kernel of the matter, and that which was really new in it. It could hardly be otherwise, as it was impossible in the space of a few hours to throw light upon all sides of the subject, and really penetrate to the depths of the idea. In spite of this lack it was of great significance that immediately after the prohibition this favorable "Declaration" was made public, and was signed by men like Diesterweg.

The points in the "Declaration" were that Froebel's educational system was far removed from all partisanship and every one-sided tendency; that it must be looked upon as a deeper foundation of both theoretical and practical education; that it promised essentially to advance school culture; and that it had proved itself particularly fitted to improve family education through the culture of women for their educational calling, which it involved.

These statements under the existing circumstances of misapprehension were of the greatest importance, and would have gained more for the cause in influential circles, if people had not been at that time so much absorbed in political matters.

After the "Declaration" was read the propositions of the Assembly were that Froebel should write an essay upon his system, publish a "Kindergarten Guide" for teachers, and establish a new periodical.

After Froebel had expressed his willingness to work for these ends, the meeting was closed.

Froebel, alas! was never able to perform his promises. The "periodical" for Fr. Froebel's cause was put under the editorship of Director Marquard, and by the cooperation of us all was published before the end of the year.

On the afternoon of the third day of the Convention many discussions were held, and the last reports of institutions were brought in.

Those participants in it who did not intend to leave the place the next day made a party to visit the surrounding country, and the two young naturalists, Dr. Ule and Dr. Müller, were invited to speak upon the characteristic points of nature in Thuringia.

On the following day, in the clear warm summer weather, this excursion to the neighboring mountains took place, and well provided with lunches, we made a halt in the neighborhood of Gerberstein, in order, after taking these refreshments, to hear the promised essays of the two naturalists.

Dr. Ule spoke of the formation of the Thuringian mountains, their supposed origin, the law exemplified by them, and upon the latest scientific theories of the development of the earth.

Dr. Müller spoke of the vegetation of Thuringia, and went on to the general development of the plant-world, pointing out the connection of their orders and families, which showed the trees of the woods and the tiniest mosses at their feet to be an unbroken chain of organic formation.

At the close of the essays, a lively discussion of them took place among the listeners, who took great interest in them.

The region lying around us on a high plateau in the woods, in the midst of broken rocks scattered wildly around, surrounded by ancient oaks, beeches, and pine forests dressed in their autumnal pomp of coloring, afforded the most fitting place in which to speak of their size and their wonders.

Although Darwin's theory was unknown at that time, the discussion of the fundamental principles of the materialistic theories of the world had begun, and the preludes to this theory which for the most part prevails now, resounded with old and new hypotheses. Every new idea which is expressed finds itself suggested in the opinions, presentiments, or suppositions of the atmosphere of the time, before it is concentrated into a focus by one mind, and then uttered in a definite form. So with the theory of Darwin, which is now turned to base uses, and is perverted, by consequences deduced in a one-sided manner from it, to the strangest caricatures of truth. Every truth becomes absurd when carried out to an extreme in a one-sided manner.

Middendorff, with his deep faith and pious feelings, was hurt by some expressions of those present, which were in opposition to his religious sentiments, and turning to me, he remarked: "How is it possible to speak of the wonders of nature, of such a gloriously built universe, of the order and connection ruling it, showing the wisdom, goodness, and power of the Creator, with astonishment and conviction, and at the same time to think so sceptically of the existence of God and all supersensuous things!"

"Yes," I replied; "one would think the investigation of nature more than anything else must lead to the irrefragable conviction of God and his eternal reason penetrating everything and ruling everything. But we see it is not so always, and that even the astronomers who investigate the wonders of the universe in all its magnificent extent can be sceptics and deny God. Perhaps the human mind is not yet far enough developed to be able to perceive the various sides of truth at once. Even genius cannot comprehend everything. Natural science and philosophy are more or less hostile to religion, although both investigate the causes of things. It is to be hoped that our time and our eagerness for knowledge will give a new impetus, that spirit and nature will come nearer to their reconciliation."

Froebel, who heard the last words, stepped nearer and said: "No, that cannot happen yet. Contrasts must come forth in their whole sharpness, in order to be connected and balanced: you are right; the mind of the individual cannot comprehend everything. We are not so far on yet. Each one must work out his own little piece of work. When the intellectual working of many races shall be brought together and rightly connected, a new result will be reached. Then even one-sided views and the contradictions growing out of them will be brought into harmony. Let the empirics work in their quarries; they will bring treasures to light which are also necessary."

"It appears to me," said I, "that the investigators of nature who work in the dark mines of the material world by the light of their own lanterns, and imagine that there is nothing brighter, no sunlight, must some time or other break through the surface above, when they can no longer deny the brighter light of the sun."

Froebel remarked: "The time has come when man must recognize his relations to nature, to the material world, and at the same time to the spirit of God which rules in them. It is on that account necessary that the investigation of mind should be specially active on that side, and also in a one-sided manner. The other sides of truth will consequently be in the dark, and disappear entirely from the eyes of many. The knowledge of the recent past is held firmly by others, and alone recognized as truth.

"These contrasts evoke the necessary conflicts which are demanded for the knowledge of truth. The truth is not changed by it; that remains one and the same, but we cannot perceive it in its wholeness and absoluteness, hence God reveals it but partially to us at different times and in different stages of our development."

"Certainly," I said, "and one part of truth cannot contradict another part, since they belong together. Therefore, it is always so strange to me that a new truth is looked upon as a destroyer of the old one. Many now imagine that they must look upon the eternal truths of Christianity as overcome and effaced, in order that a way may be opened for new scientific discoveries in the kingdom of nature, without having the conception that every new truth must confirm the old one before it can prove itself to be truth. But you are right; the contradictions arise out of one-sided comprehension, and it may be necessary to real and deeper knowledge that the doubt should come up and battle with views, often confused views, of an earlier recognized truth. The result can be nothing else than the victory of truth, or the balancing of contradictions by the recognition of every side of truth, and the necessary completion of the old view by the new one."

Middendorff replied to this: "The right faith, as I understand it, cannot be disturbed by the fragmentary and contradictory knowledge of human science. The quiet certainty of that which is written in our souls as truth, and confirmed by historical revelation, can still exist, even if science brings to light seeming contradictions to it. We know that many such contradictions have been explained, and true science must ever rectify itself by further development of its knowledge.

"I recognize, as Froebel does, the same Divine mind in nature as in man and the history of his development, and I am also persuaded that we can go no further at present without new knowledge of the relations between ourselves and our development with that of the Divine nature. What I believe and how I believe it is therefore in no wise disturbed, and I always think; surely you will also already come to recognize the law in nature and its material to be the same Divine law that rules in the world of spirit, and which is the law of an all-loving and therefore self-conscious Father!"

"Yes, certainly," I agreed; "the truths of the natural world are a part of religious truth, and it is only the transition to a higher knowledge of truth that occasions the momentary disagreement between the knowledge of nature and of God, and sets the revelation in the material world in opposition to the revelation in the spiritual world. Experience in both domains must lead to similar revelation of truth, which remains forever one and eternal."

"How beautifully our young men spoke upon the organic connection in the universe!" said Middendorff. "The harmony that is expressed in it should alone be enough to testify to the ruling of a holy Providence."

"It has never come to me more significantly," I replied, "how Froebel's education must help one to find harmony between spirit and nature. If the child's mind, through his own outward creative activity, imitates in a measure the building-up and development of the universe, in that he, starting from simple, solid bodies, perceives the material in its most elementary division and articulation; if the awakening mind of the child recognizes in the concrete world the consecutiveness in material development, and is led from the material body and its regular division to the contemplation of the surface, from this to the contemplation of the line and to the point made visible; if he learns to see the connection of all things, and nothing comes broken and isolated before his senses; if things, from the simplest up to the most complex, appear to him fixedly arranged in their natural, logical succession, from unity up to manifoldness or plurality, and his own handling of material leads to plastic formation, starting from simple fundamental forms and rising to ever high linking together of the same; and if his own formations are shaped according to one and the same law—this child's mind must, in later stages of development, arrive at the consciousness of the organic life imitated by his own hand, and will find it again in nature in its most original state of existence. And thus he recognizes the agreement between the intellectually organic linking of his own being with that in the material world.

"The different ways in which nature and mind express themselves, as visible formation in nature and invisible formation in mind (by speech), cannot disturb the perception of their analogy, and as little the less or higher degree of their position in the visible creation; and then there can be no more division and contradiction between the material and spiritual order of the universe, which are never and nowhere separated from each other, but only superposed and subordinated to each other."

We broke up, discussing and disputing on our way home, but united in the enjoyment of a beautiful moonlight evening in that glorious country.

After all the guests had departed, Froebel showed the effects of the exertion which the Convention, together with the work and fatigue consequent upon it, had cost him. Yet he was stimulated and made very happy by the concurrence of so many intelligent and sensible men and specialists, which was very plainly seen in the following weeks that I spent in Liebenstein; and it occurred to no one that this energy and strength of life were to fail so soon.

Froebel's earnest wish that Middendorff should remove from Keilhau to Marienthal, in order to devote himself entirely to the education of the kindergartners, was the more lively on account of the task he had undertaken: to prepare for publication a new statement of his system in all its relations. He thought he could not undertake it without Middendorff's help.

A correspondence on this subject with the Keilhau circle did not, unfortunately, lead to the desired result. They could not spare Middendorff from Keilhau. They thought if he left the institution, which was flourishing anew under the wise and watchful guidance of Barop, it would be in a high degree injurious. Therefore Froebel had again to practise resignation. And it seemed as if his state of feeling, after the examination and recognition of his efforts by the convention that had just taken place, was one of such newfound repose and inward satisfaction that the downfall of his hopes in this one case could not prostrate him, as it might have done earlier.

The words Froebel uttered to him on parting, given in Middendorff's little pamphlet, "Froebel's Exit from Life," which are also quoted in Hanschmann's biography, are so significant of the state of his mind that they are worth repeating: "I recognize the unity of my life throughout. Such a one has not been known for a long time. It has been able to work itself out only by rare circumstances. But it is one condition of fulfilling the demand of our time. If you go away now, stand there, as I stand here, in the same inward unity."

Many expressions of this kind showed that he was approaching the close of a life which he looked upon with repose and satisfaction, and recognized as an undivided whole. And it had been a truly consistent life; for a leading idea had determined its goal, and all its action, thinking, and striving, without any hesitation or any doubting.

Froebel and Middendorff accompanied me as far as the next post-station. We made a short stay in the shade of the wood, in order to rest; for Froebel seemed to be somewhat exhausted, which was not in keeping with his usual rare vigor in walking.

In our conversation, the "Declaration" of the lately assembled pedagogues was considered, and I expressed my opinion that that which was new, or the *new beginning* which Froebel's method brings with it, was not made sufficiently prominent.

Froebel said to this: "Let well enough alone. What we have already reached is much, as things stand. The outward and what strikes the eye is the only thing accepted at first, but a path is made for a deeper understanding afterward. I once did as you do. I thought everyone must have an insight into my fundamental idea—must understand it and concur with it. That brought me many disappointments. Now I know that it will be centuries before my view of the human being as a child, and its educational treatment, can be generally accepted. But that no longer troubles me. If the seed is sown, its coming up is not far off, and it is the same with the fruit."

"I hope," I replied, "that I shall be able to carry out the plan of a General Educational Union, such as we have spoken of. Then there will be a hope of gaining over some minds of intellectual power sufficient to understand and prepare the deeper contents of your method. I would like above all things to have a short *résumé* of your fundamental thoughts, to facilitate my own study of your writings. Will you, on the first opportunity, prepare such an one for me?"

"Why can I not write everything—long and short, theoretical and practical!" he answered. "But I will think about it, in order to meet your wish, when I have had a little rest."

In the following November, Froebel sent me a short statement of his theories, of about forty pages, in one of his letters to Berlin. This short and pregnant statement is, in spite of its quite abstract subject, written with great clearness, and was the only one of the kind in existence. For this reason it was preserved by me as a holy relic. I always carried it about with me in a letter-case, in order to preserve it from destruction, by fire or otherwise, during my absence. And this very care led to its loss! I left the letter-case in a hotel in Naples, in a locked travelling-bag, while I took a short trip to Sorrento. This bag was stolen. Every search for it was in vain. But the contents of the paper were saved in two copies of it which I had taken. One of these is still in my possession; the other my friend, Dr. Karl Schmidt, took when I initiated him into the doctrines of Froebel. He shared my opinion that the time had not come for its publication, because the want of a thorough explanation of its short propositions would only lead to misunderstandings. Froebel himself, in the accompanying letter, had also given a special direction in reference to this.

This second copy was found among Schmidt's effects, after his death, in a large portfolio, with a great quantity of material for the contemplated popular edition of a manual of the Froebelian method, which I had given to Schmidt, and was to be furnished with some additions by himself. This portfolio, according to an assurance of Schmidt's widow, who had concealed it, was put out of the way, and has never been found again.

The contents of the "Froebelian letter," as we were accustomed to call it in our little circle, were imparted by me to some of my pupils, particularly to Frau Schräder (formerly Fraulein Breymann), with whom I have often perused and discussed it. The authenticity of the copy is therefore demonstrable.

After I had had a residence prepared in the upper story of the Liebenstein kindergarten building, in order to occupy it the next summer, in the hope of being able to watch the little pupils of the institution better than I could do before, I bade farewell to Froebel and his household, to take up the work in Berlin for the winter.

The picture of idyllic rural and domestic repose which Marienthal afforded at that time, and the protection and care in which I left Froebel, in view of the watchfulness and fidelity of his wife, made the parting easy, and free from any presentiments that it would be for the last time.

The letters also which I received in the course of the ensuing winter from himself and his wife breathed only content, and spoke of well-being, with the exception of a few trifling ill turns. We were in continuous intercourse upon our mutual work for the cause; and Froebel was always greatly pleased with the smallest success gained in Berlin, and constantly expressed the most touching gratitude for it. This success consisted at that time only in the sympathy I won for the method by my regular lectures, in consequence of which the number of our members increased, and in the undisturbed progress of the kindergarten established by our Union, which was more and more visited, and more and more won the recognition of the parents of the pupils.

Thus ended the year 1851, the last throughout which Froebel lived.

19

The Year 1852

In the beginning of this year Middendorff wrote me that he thought the birthday of Froebel ought to be specially celebrated, since the latter had always regarded the entrance upon his seventieth year as the most important period of human life, the time for the complete survey of one's own as well as of human life in general. Middendorff thought the scholarship fund I had undertaken to raise for the assistance of needy young women who wished to cultivate themselves at Marienthal for kindergartners would make the most fitting birthday present to him. At the same time he asked me if I could possibly come to Liebenstein on the day, which would be the 21st of April.

If anything in my activity for the cause ever gave me trouble it was this collection! Since the issue of the fatal prohibition, the majority of those who had taken an interest in the cause had fallen away from it. How could that be called good which had the official ban? Even those who had actually promised aid and immediate assistance to the cause had withdrawn, especially some influential officials who no longer dared to show their interest under existing conditions. I was often made to feel that people intentionally kept out of my way that they might not hear anything said of the forbidden cause, or they only uttered evasive phrases if they were reminded of their former promised support. In all this it was plainly to be perceived that no one could see any adequate motive for the measure that had been taken, and were therefore doubly embarrassed.

Nor were there wanting apparently just complaints of the

method as it appeared externally at that time. More than ever were heard the most senseless objections which were sought after without the least knowledge of the subject, in order to cover up the mistake the authorities had made, whether consciously or unconsciously.

Under such circumstances, success in begging for material support was not to be thought of for a cause whose aims were ideal, or whose fruits were only to ripen in the distant future. So the contributions of those who aided my small fund were only sufficient to educate one scholar.

Moreover, my intention to go to Liebenstein on the occasion of the birthday festival, and carry a little work as a present, was frustrated by serious illness, and I was scarcely able to accompany my offering with a few lines.

I received from Middendorff a full description of the festival, which he afterwards published for the friends, together with his account of "Froebel's Departure from Life."

It was destined to be Froebel's last birthday; a few months later his soul celebrated its birth into another world! The last days of this long life of trouble and labor flowed on serenely and beautifully, and his letters were full of thanks for all the proofs of love which he had received. He wrote, "It was indeed very beautiful; you ought to have been here!"

Middendorff's description of the festival is deeply touching, and gives one a glimpse of a human existence which, wholly unselfish, belonged to humanity alone, and whose influence was so powerful that even the simplest souls in the group of his pupils were elevated and made capable of true devotion by it.

The idea of the festival originated with Middendorff, but everything was arranged with the pupils and with Madame Froebel, and their plans were respected, and guided Middendorff even in his poems for the festival. The whole breathed the childlike, poetic spirit of Middendorff, and of the fresh young circle that surrounded Froebel.

Middendorff said the festal song of the scholars at sunrise

waked Froebel, who then with profound emotion spoke to them, recognized the day, and thanked them. As he stepped out of his chamber into the lecture-room, he stood still on the threshold, taken by surprise, admiring, with his eyes beaming with joy, the beautiful decoration of the room, which was adorned with flowers in flowerpots, festoons, and wreaths, and the table richly covered with presents of all kinds. Again the song burst out from the semicircle of scholars dressed in white holiday garments, ornamented with green wreaths, which expressed the meaning of the ornamentation, and pointed to the blessing which would go forth to the world of childhood out of Froebel's work. Then Madame Froebel handed out her birthday present, and the scholars followed with an orange tree bearing flowers and fruit, which Froebel had often pointed out to them as a symbol of the united ages of man in leaves, buds, flowers, and fruit borne at the same time, representing childhood, youth, manhood, and old age.

Then the many gifts which lay spread out upon the table, and which were sent by pupils and friends from various parts of the world, were brought forward and examined. The most striking of these were a copperplate engraving of Raphael's Madonna with the child John, a Bible with illustrations by the best artists from the *Cottaschen Offizin*—both accompanied with a beautiful poem—also a likeness of Pestalozzi and a work upon the "Mythology of the North." There were also the works of children in kindergartens as well as those of teachers, and many from the scholars at Keilhau, all accompanied with cordial words of love and honor, in poetry and prose.

From the near and far came tokens of harmonious efforts to honor and make happy not only the gray old man but all around him.

In the afternoon the children came from the kindergartens of Salzung and Liebenstein, and accompanied the offering of the little gifts they had prepared with a song, whose childlike, expressive words, sung by the clear little voices, deeply moved Froebel. He laid this song, with some of the other poems, into a letter which he sent me after the festival.* Then followed the children's plays, which made Froebel as happy as they did the children.

He wrote further: "After the children were on their way home, at sunset, came the postman with a load of letters. Blessings and festal gifts continue to this day to come from all the countries round—from the north, from the south, from the Lower Rhine, from the Baltic, from great places and from small places." And heartfelt, touching words were those with which Middendorff accompanied extracts from the letters, which testified to the powerful and lasting influence of Froebel's teaching upon receptive minds. They had all received a lifelong impression, a direction to higher aims than the selfish enjoyment of existence—a power for self-sacrificing action in behalf of the ripening of childhood, and a consciousness of their womanly dignity through duty fulfilled in their chosen calling.

In the evening the teachers of the neighborhood assembled with Pastor Rückert and his household around Froebel; the pupils acted a dramatic farce, and then, by the wish of all, returned to the representation of the kindergarten games, conducted chiefly by Froebel or his wife. Before the parting, a closing song was sung, and a green wreath placed upon Froebel's head by one of his pupils. In a happy and exalted mood they then separated.

Middendorff adds to his highly poetical account, from which only a few facts have been taken, the following words: "So the day ended as it began, in beautiful unity, with thanksgiving, love, and joy. Those who attended the festival will never lose the remembrance of it. For not only in form, but in reality, he has seen, felt, and sympathized with the all-sided, consistent life. He has known by experience that the expression, 'All-sided unity of life,' by which name we have designated the training-school at Marienthal, is no empty sound," etc.

*It was inscribed to "Friedrich Froebel, the founder of the German kindergartens, April 21, 1852, offered with sincere gratitude by the kindergarten in Salzung."

Middendorff's little account of Froebel's last birthday and end deserves to be preserved in a larger edition for the circle of followers, since it gives such a true and warmly colored picture of the life, work, and death of Froebel as that of one of the "just."

Middendorff writes later that, after this festival, Froebel's life was happier and more tranquil than ever before, and that he enjoyed his existence like a child; afterwards that he was disturbed by various communications in the daily papers, in which the contending religious parties represented Froebel as their intellectual sympathizer, although he had never inclined either toward the Christian pietists of that period, with their hypocrisy and transcendentalism, or to the transitory superficial radicalism supported by the free societies. His own understanding of religion and of Christianity was a far clearer and deeper one than these extreme opinions of a time of transition to new and higher views.

On account of his cause, and not for personal justification, Froebel felt in duty bound not to leave these false assertions uncontradicted. The bodily weakness which had come upon him was increased by the composition of an article written for this purpose. He could no longer, as formerly, collect and write out his thoughts tranquilly.

When he sent me the little essay for my criticism, and for the management of its publication in Berlin, I felt bound to beg him to abstain from publishing it. The article contained no *new* points upon his religious views; it was, rather, the same statement that he had made in his former writings in a far clearer and more objective manner. Both contending parties—still contending down to the present time—would have found opportunity again to express their views, although Froebel bound himself to none of them, while acknowledging what was the right of each one.

Painful as it was to oppose Froebel's justification of himself, yet Middendorff and Diesterweg agreed with me that it was better to prevent the publication of the article in question. Froebel himself seemed to see this, and requested me to send back the manuscript.

It is surely, in most cases, not advantageous for great minds and thinking men to publish every scrap of their writings and every unimportant letter. Their biographers should study thoroughly everything they can find access to, and select all that appears necessary, but not those indifferent letters which show the heroes of mind in their nightgowns, and tear away every veil before profane and unappreciative eyes. To the public belong only the ideal forms of those who have accomplished something, not the everyday garment which every one wears who is called a man.

No one could look more piously upon the bearers of divine ideas than Froebel, to whom such an idea was entrusted; no one could recognize the great and eternal significance of the Christian idea with more *complete* conviction, or love its sublime messengers with more reverence than he.

Jesus was to him the eternal type of man, the model for the humanity of the future, and the Messiah of the fundamental truth, "God in humanity."

Whatever other fundamental truths God might send into the world, no one will ever obliterate those contained in Christianity; but these must be freed and purified of the mere overgrowths and dross added to them by the erring human mind. For *all* truth is *eternal in itself*, and can only find confirmation and completion by new truths; the human eye cannot see *absolute* truth, it can only approach it. And even those inspired by God can clothe it only in an earthly garment.

Froebel used to say, when he expressed his views of Christianity: "The fundamental idea of Christianity, that we are God's children (or that God lives in humanity), expressed in the New Testament by the words, 'You are of Divine lineage,' explains the relation of man to God exhaustively for all times."

Those views of modern times which regard the historical view of Christianity as a myth poetized by the popular mind, as it advances with every new turning-point in the world's history, in order to designate the consciousness of the period in the instinct of the people—those views could not interfere with his own convictions, but he also saw in them a self-contradiction. On the contrary, this conception of the eternal fundamental idea of the

Christian theory can serve only as a confirmation and attestation of it, since every great and general truth only impresses itself on the popular mind so far as it clothes itself in a poetical form understood by it. This form grows indeed with the idea and makes it difficult to separate the pure thought from the letter; indeed, it may in time lead to the most absurd conclusions.

Yet this legend, poetized by the popular mind, is insofar the confirmation of the truth of a fundamental idea, because thereby is expressed the agreement of the childishly undeveloped conception of the idea of a given period with that of the conscious human mind standing upon the summit of the consciousness of the time.

Then, no truth can be received until the mind of the people to whom it is proclaimed has become ripe for it. This ripeness appears in different degrees of knowledge, from instinct or intuition in the popular mind, up through the clear self-consciousness of the cultivated mind, to the divine consciousness of the *one* mind which has been chosen by God to proclaim the truth in question. Just as little can the modern view of nature in any way prejudice the fundamental idea in Christianity. Froebel also acknowledged that it was a *problem of the time* to look upon the relation of man to nature and the organisms below him in a new light, and give it due place. The partial views and erroneous conclusions coming to the surface in such an investigation are temporary, and will be corrected later. True knowledge always rectifies itself in the course of its further development.

But whatever new thing may result from the increasing knowledge of the human mind, whatever apparent contradictions may come to the surface with the truths recognized by it, the *objects* of the truth to be recognized remain always the same, namely, *God* (or the Cause of whatever is); the universe here (or what man has found and which has not arisen out of himself); *man* (as a link in growing *humanity*). Outside of these we know nothing, and no human knowledge can go.

But these three subjects can be apprehended only through their mutual relations, namely,

1. The relation of the material world (as the first thing perceivable) to *God*, and of God to the world, with which the earlier pantheism busied itself, and also monotheism in its first phase (the Mosaic history of Creation).

2. The relation of *man to God* and of God to humanity, which is the chief subject-matter of Christianity and its result—the establishment of God's kingdom upon earth.

3. The relation of *man* to the world, or nature, and of this to man—which constitutes the chief object of knowledge for the present.

Froebel's conviction went on to the view that the knowledge of one of these relations between the objects named cannot possibly annul or even alter the others, and it is necessary for the education of the human race, under God's guidance, to understand that these relations must be seen *one after the other* by the human mind, which is not capable of seizing the *whole* truth at once.

By this conviction the opinion and the belief are not excluded that God sends his truth into the world by minds especially chosen for that purpose, or that the revelation of truth comes at certain turning-points of their development immediately through *inspiration.* But that truth which has been already given must be first made their own through the labor of the human mind, science, in order to gain a real recognition of the idea containing the truth. But the recognition of each of the three conditions named forms the *synthesis* between two of the three objects designated.

According to this view no truth, or fundamental idea, which always comes from God himself, can ever be really lost, even if it is covered up for a long time. The final result of the new truth will always confirm that which went before and show it in a better light.

The faithful votaries of Christianity have, according to this view, nothing to fear for the subject-matter of their belief, so far as its *spirituality* is concerned, either from the modern theory of nature, or from the historical view, which shall have separated legends from ideas. All investigations by the human mind can only serve to uncover the truth; and the contradictions and errors inevitably bound up with it, even if they are advocated by several generations, have their compensation, and must help the light of Divine truth to shine forth more and more clearly. And this comes to pass when the kernel of truth is freed from the envelope in which it must always come into the world for the weak eyes of man. Froebel was of the opinion that the recognition of truth in the present phase of development is not to arise from *self-contemplation*, from which the great majority of philosophical systems hitherto have arisen, and by which no firm foundation can be gained, since they rest on subjective theories. This firm foundation can only be gained from the immutable principle of law in nature, since this alone is objective to us. Only in the life of unconsciousness, or instinct, which is yet fettered by necessity, can firm ground be found, from which, rising to the consciousness of the human mind, its self-contemplation finds a secure, firm basis; not indeed to identify spirit and matter and to place on the same level the spiritual and natural life, or to let the spiritual life arise out of matter, according to the present materialistic theories, but to find a *point of union* for both domains, which *must of course be discoverable in the creation of one and the same Creator.*

Froebel finds this point of union in the one universal law of creation, to which the manifold and various laws of both domains—that of mind (God) and that of nature (matter)—are to be referred, and indeed in the analogy between the two. This law he calls the law of the "connection of opposites," which is expressed in the material world in the law of gravitation, and which also finds its application in the spiritual world in the compensation of ever-recurring opposites—in the restoration of equilibrium. The everywhere perceptible analogy between the thought and its material appearance logically demands the identity of law in both domains as held by Froebel.

While speculative philosophy moves in the domain of abstraction and the absolute, educational philosophy, since it has to do with the whole man, must consider the real and ideal, the concrete and the abstract, the relative and the absolute in connection, for these opposites always in fact appear united in the world of phenomena.

Froebel's educational system concurs with this view of the actual idea of the time, and with the inquiries growing out of it, which aim at finding the unity between the intellectual and physical world, or between mind and matter, the real and ideal, etc., and thereby get rid of the inflexible and one-sided dualism. Education cannot and should not be dualistic, since it has to support and assist the development of body and mind equally, and to look upon their harmonious culture as its goal.

Even if the two fields of activity—philosophical knowledge and educational action—are entirely separate, yet children must first read the book which God himself has given humanity to read in its childhood, namely, the world which he has created, and in which he has manifested his divine thoughts.

Froebel would awaken and strengthen the eyes of children that they may learn to read this book aright. Scientific speculation leads to error, if this foundation is wanting. If its task has heretofore been to separate the spirit of things from their hull, and thereby to make them understood, the problem yet remains of again uniting the spiritual contents with their phenomenal form, from which they have been separated, that is, of finding the synthesis between these opposites. For the solution of this problem Froebel's educational underpinning is an absolute necessity. His method will prevent men from ever again seeking the impossible, that is to say, from standing the pyramid on its apex, by offering abstract teaching to the child's mind, and to youth philosophical systems, for which all preliminary conditions are wanting.

The pupils of the new education will be better prepared than the young have ever before been for taking a synthetic view of things, as the present time is striving to do.

This will at least smooth the way for a union between the natural sciences and intellectual science, and will by degrees bridge over the abyss yet separating the human being and the kingdom of the spirit from the rest of God's creations.

The sketch here given of Froebel's views finds its completion in his writings, although not in the summary way in which it is offered here. Although these writings present no complete system, and although their contents are in some confusion, and are difficult to understand on account of their very heavy style of expression, they are yet a mine of new thoughts full of genius, which only need to be put in order and supplemented by an understanding mind, to be assigned as a whole to their place in science.

20

Last Days of Froebel

Towards the end of the winter, occasional letters from Froebel and his wife informed me of slight attacks of illness and consequent suspension of work. In spite of this, the instruction of his scholars and other busy work was but rarely interrupted, and his accustomed mental vivacity was apparently undiminished.

At Whitsuntide of that year he received for the first time an invitation to participate in the Teachers' Convention which was to meet in Gotha. He wrote me very joyfully upon the occasion, and took it as a proof that his cause had secured increased estimation in the teachers' world.

Middendorff gave an account of the Convention as he received it from Froebel's wife. When Froebel entered the Convention, in the midst of a discourse, the whole assembly rose. At the end of the discourse the president of the meeting gave him a hearty welcome, followed by three cheers from the whole assembly. Froebel thanked them in a few simple words, and immediately taking up the subject in hand, which was "Instruction in the Natural Sciences," was listened to with profound attention.

After the Convention, Froebel was made specially happy in the garden of a friend of nature in Gotha, where he examined almost every group of flowers, and happily and gratefully acknowledged all the good things that were offered him.

In the kindergarten of Gotha he explained the intellectual significance of some of his occupation-materials. In the evening he took part in a reunion of the friends of his cause, although he was somewhat exhausted by the excitement of the day; he spoke of the importance of the kindergarten for the female sex, and the duty of teachers to learn to understand it on its own theory, and prepare for its introduction into the schools.

While he was on the journey to Gotha he had been rather quiet and reserved, but on the way home he appeared cheerful, well, and communicative.

On the 6th of June came the attack of his last illness, and Froebel thought he saw in it a crisis that would end in recovery. During his last illness his repose and cheerfulness never left him for a moment, and he took part in and enjoyed everything, particularly when flowers were brought him. He once said on such an occasion, "I love flowers, men, children, God! I love everything!"

The highest peace, the most cheerful resignation, were expressed, not only in his words, but in his face. The former anxious care to be active in his life-task resolved itself into trust in Providence, and his spirit looked joyfully in advance for the fulfilment of his life's idea.

On the Sunday before his death, a favorite child came to bring him flowers; he greeted her with unbounded delight. Although it was difficult for him to lift his hand, he reached it out to her, and drew the child's little hand to his lips.

The care of his flowers he recommended in these words: "Take care of my flowers and spare my weeds; I have learned much from them." And in his very last hours he asked again for flowers. The window must be opened frequently, and he brightened up visibly at the aspect of nature, and often repeated the words, "pure, vigorous nature"; and at another time, "Always hold me dear," also, "I am not going away, I shall hover round in the midst of you." He spoke much about truth to Barop, who had come with the teacher Clemens, saying, among other things, "Remain true to God."

He asked them to read his godfather's letter, which in Thuringia, according to old custom, was given to the baptized child by the godfather, and contained the confession of Christian faith. In some places he exclaimed, "My credentials! my credentials, Barop!" especially at the passage in the confession "from this time forth our Saviour will confide in thee in justice, grace, and mercy." For the third time he cried out aloud, "My credentials!" at the words, "Let my son hear! look upon and hold with immovable truth to thy soul's best friend, who is now thine." It was as if he would say, "To him have I been consecrated from the beginning of my life, and I have never in my life neglected this bond."

One could see how earnestly his Christianity dwelt within him, little as he was ordinarily accustomed to speak of it. Thus he said in the Teachers' Convention at Rudolstadt: "I work that Christianity may become realized." Another time he said: "Who knows Christ? But I know him, and he knows me. I will what he wills. But we must hold to his testament, the promise of the Spirit." He repeatedly admonished the friends around him in Keilhau "to preserve unity, concord, and peace; to lead a model life, as one family, in a united striving." "Have trust in God; be true to life!" And ever and again he expressed love and thanks to those around him. At midnight of the 21st of June the last moment approached. His eyes, which had been closed for rest, were partially open. He was in a sitting posture, as if his wish to find his last rest sitting up was to be fulfilled. His breathing became shorter and shorter, till, at half past six, he drew two long breaths, and all was still.

So quietly, without a struggle and without a death-throe, ended a life which had at no moment served selfish interests, but was devoted wholly and completely to humanity, and to childhood in humanity.

Middendorff added to his communication about Froebel's last moments: "It involuntarily drew us who stood around the deathbed to our knees. We felt near the consecrated one. Never was the awe of death so effaced to me. I had felt something similar to it at the death of a beloved child. Nature made her last struggling efforts, and then stood still untroubled. The mind, clear to the last, fervent, joyful, and loving, went home like a child to its pure source; a life well-ordered in all directions, united within and without, was fulfilled and closed. What he loved so much, and so often gazed upon on a clear evening—the going-down of the sun—he himself represented. As the sun sinks to our eyes, so sinks to our eyes the light of his being; and as, at sunset, I have no thought of its passing away, but only of its receding from view, and thereby know the certainty of its return, so I felt here in sorrow the certainty of the eternal duration of life. Yes, true is the promise—'Death and lamentation shall be no more.' As he often, when plunged in meditation, penetrated to the light of a new thought, so his mind, freed from all limitations and absorbed in his inmost soul, in his own being and life, penetrated to a new existence—to the light of another day.

"O, what stillness, what deep stillness, now! Consecration and holiness breathed around me. I felt joy in the midst of my pain! He who stood so near to nature, and not only saw, contemplated, and investigated it, but who was sunk in it as a child in purest love on the breast of a mother—he had followed its teachings, trusted implicitly its laws and holy commands, had not been deceived in his hopes; and how it had rewarded his love. In his illness, he had been as quiet and gentle as a lamb. He scarcely allowed an expression of pain to be heard; no murmuring, no unwillingness, was perceived. True son as he was to Nature, so was she his true mother, who took him softly and lovingly into her arms.

"But how could he have trusted her so well, if he had not clearly known who she was—if he had not known who inspired her and penetrated her, who governed her and wrote her laws, held her together in unity and self-consciousness, and kindled intelligence of her in the human mind? How could he have been so serene, if he had not known himself to be a son of that Almighty One—if he had not recognized and known the first of men who lived this unity of the Son with the Father, and had not felt himself one with him in all his striving? How could he have been so cheerful, if he had not carried within himself the knowledge that the consciousness of the Sonship of this only One would break forth by degrees in all sentient beings, and thus the conscious unity and salvation of the minds for which he lived and struggled would surely and certainly appear? Therefore were his last words to his friends the prayer with which he closed his work upon earth—'God, Father, Son, and Holy Ghost. Amen.'

"My soul was full of thanksgiving for the favor vouchsafed to me that I could close the eyes and bestow the last cares upon him to whom my dying father had commended me, and who had received me upon his breast. How grateful it was to my heart that it was my duty to be so near, at his last moment, in his last battle, to him whom I had accompanied so long in life, with whom I had fought the battle, with whom I had, for a time, worked and suffered the heaviest trials! Chiefly was I thankful because I saw this life end as it had begun—because I saw that he was what I had heard and believed him to be, and that he remained wholly in unison with himself; for to the last moment was revealed this repose springing from inward concord—this clearness, truth, and unity. As he himself characterized it, 'One must himself perfect his life to a ripe fruit.' And so his life dropped as a ripe fruit from the tree of the life of humanity. So can and also will be fulfilled what he said: 'The age of ripeness is coming.' And again: 'The fragrant flower has withered, but the fruit has set which will now ripen. Behold in it three in one—the connection with the earlier time, the steady advance to the present, and the seed of the future.'"

Of the burial-service Middendorff said: "The bier, adorned with garlands of flowers and a laurel crown made by the wife and pupils, stood in the place where lately Froebel's bed had stood. All gathered round to look once more upon the beloved friend, and to gain an ineffaceable impression of the dear features. No trace of pain was to be found upon the countenance; a holy earnestness and inward cheerfulness shone forth from it. It was a look of introspection united with a light, blissful smile. The countenance showed an extraordinary tenderness. The lips were slightly open, as if his mouth would pronounce the secret of the other world—as if it said, 'I see in light what I have here seen darkly. Believe, follow the truth; it leads to freedom, to bliss.'

There is something striking in standing before such a countenance; the soul becomes a prayer. We sank upon our knees. 'O might we all die like him, and rest in the grave with such a certainty!' was the expression of one of the bystanders. The bier was carried out first through his workroom, where he had labored with unwearied industry, often half through the night, for those near and far, under the impulse of the living idea in himself and his all-encompassing love for humanity; past his beloved flowers, of which he took such care, and which, as if from gratitude, made plain to him the highest truths, like his yet dearer pupils, the children; then through the sitting-room, where Pestalozzi seemed to call to him from his portrait—'Slowly, step by step, will be laid the sure foundation for the temple of pure humanity'—and the divine Madonna looked at him as with thanks that he had so deeply divined her heart's desire, and shaped it into deed and love for all; and finally through the lecture-hall, where his scholars had listened with rapt attention to his words, which kindled them to their high calling—where strangers from north and south had thronged together, and from whence they had gone possessed by the might of truth. As one said, 'He does not preach like the learned, but his speech is powerful'; and many of these have widely borne the seed with his motto, 'Come, let us live with our children!'

"The garlanded bier was set down in the spacious vestibule, to be strewn with wreaths and flowers by the numerous children. All, even the smallest, tried to show their love and gratitude to him once more.

"But not only children came; friends, known and unknown, pressed forward to show their esteem and reverence; the teachers of the country round about, one and all, kindergartners and those he had befriended, came even from a great distance, invited by their own hearts to that solemn day.

"The teachers united in a solemn song, in moving tones. Then the train was set in motion towards the churchyard of the village of Schweina.

"A heavy shower fell while it was on the way, so that we were obliged to stand under shelter for a long time. Parson Rückert remarked, 'Even his last journey is through storm and tempest.'

"When the procession was again set in motion, and passed over the bridge of the brook, Ernst Luther, a descendant of the great reformer, whom Froebel and his brother had educated gratuitously in Keilhau, out of regard for his ancestor, said, 'Thirty-five years ago today he here led me by the hand through Schweina.'

"The bells of the village church began to toll; it was so earnest and sacred, as if these solemn peals called him to come up into the land of the blessed, and said with their voices that the night had passed, that we should hasten to follow his onward, conquering banner, and build the new world by means of the children! At the gate of the churchyard the teachers took the bier upon their shoulders, to carry it to the place prepared for it.

"The newly laid out churchyard, situated outside the village upon an eminence, has a singularly beautiful location. The town lies half concealed in verdure, at the foot of a tower which rises up alone, like a finger-post pointing to heaven; the whole glorious country lies spread out before the eye like a living picture. At the left, Altenstein, with the summer dwelling of the ducal family, stretches out its high hand with noble grace, as if protecting the young colony, showing by its act that it truly reverences the cross which is erected in memory of Bonifacius, the earliest promulgator of Christianity here. Directly in front stands the old castle of Liebenstein whose name has a good sound near and far for its healing springs; and on the right, shaded with lofty poplars and surrounded by green meadows and waving fields of grain, with the murmur of clear waters streaming from the rock of Altenstein, the quiet, lovely Marienthal, the seat of peace, of untiring work for the worthiness and the unity of life, consecrated by him who had now come to this spot for undistributed rest and harmony.

"Notwithstanding the storm and the rain which still continued, a large part of the community had assembled, and mothers and fathers, maidens and youths, and numerous children stood around the open grave. The venerable old burial-hymn, 'Jerusalem, thou lofty city,' was sung. Then Pastor Rückert began his address at the grave, and at the moment the rain ceased. The address began with the following words:

"'Up to the lofty city of God soars the spirit of the man whom we now, grieving, gaze after; far above mountain and valley it soars over all and hastens from this world. Loved, honored, admired, praised by some, misunderstood, misapprehended, calumniated, condemned by others, he soars over all. The body which for seventy years served this rare spirit as a vigorous instrument, after the last spark of this richly active and remarkable life has gone out, shall now rest here in the churchyard of our community, which with pride counted the great man among its citizens; in sight of this mountain which he not long ago climbed with eagerness, of this house of God where he celebrated with us piously the feast of Pentecost, of the lovely Marienthal where the noble old man had found in the evening of his days a peaceful refuge for his philanthropic activity.

"'Blessed are the dead who die in the Lord from henceforth, saith the spirit, that they may rest from their labors; and their works to follow them.' These words belong to our dead also. . . . Yes, this is one who died in the Lord. He has lived in the Lord, therefore he has also died in the Lord, sweetly and happily.'"

The following passages from this discourse may be added here:

"The fame of knowledge was not his ambition. Glowing love for mankind, for the people, left him neither rest nor quiet. After he had offered his life for his native land in the wars of freedom, he turned with the same enthusiasm which surrenders and sacrifices for the highest thought, to the aim of cultivating the people and youth, founded the 'celebrated' institution at Keilhau among his native mountains, and talked, and planted in the domain of men's hearts. And how many brave men has the educated, who honor his memory and bless his name! . . . But then the thought came to him that the educators of men must imitate the creative and productive divinity in nature, which prefigures and determines the future plant in the tenderest germ, shields and protects it carefully, out of the smallest and simplest, gradually and step by step develops the highest and the noblest; that the body and soul of the tender little one shall be brought from the earliest childhood under a more intelligent and more careful nurture than has been done heretofore, when children were sent to school already corrupted in body and soul; and that, above all, this loving nurture should be trusted to the tender hand of women, whom the heavenly Father has created for this maternal calling; and to found such kindergartens, and to train such kindergartners, was henceforth his whole endeavor, from which he hoped with full confidence for the future salvation of humanity and the deliverance from manifold bodily and spiritual ills. . . .

"To this high aim he now sacrificed all his powers, his property, his time, his repose. And perhaps children of his own were denied him by the decree of the Eternal Wisdom, that he might not be bound and limited by cares for his own, that he might see and love in the poorest human child the child of God, and in the eye of every child might read the command, 'Thou shalt take care with all thy strength that the divine image be not defaced or distorted; thou shalt, with all thy gifts, work and help that it be preserved and shaped more purely and beautifully, and that not the least of these be lost.'

"For this he labored now; he moved about unceasingly teaching and working, imitating the Master, who had nowhere to lay his head; gathered unto himself little children, and laid his hand upon their heads and said, 'Suffer little children to come unto me, for of such is the kingdom of heaven.' For this he labored into the late evening of his life, and thereby the venerable old man himself was made young again amongst the playing children. For this he lived, for this he suffered, and regardless of the cry 'Hosanna,' or 'Crucify him,' he took his cross patiently, and bore it after his Master, and submitted trustingly to abuse, calumny, and persecution, and Christ-like, pardoned the deluded ones who knew not what they did, since he knew well that the disciple was not above his Master. However, the mental excitement and effort which these struggles cost him contributed to break up the vitality of the vigorous old man. . . . So have we too, among whom he spent the last years of his life, learned to know and to love this guileless soul, this pure, childlike nature; you will all bear witness, even if you did not hear his last pious words, this our dead died in the Lord, for he lived for the Lord. Henceforth, lack of understanding and misunderstanding will no more afflict thee. Just souls are in the hands of God, and no pains touch them. Thou hast now found peace, and heaven, which thou didst foreshadow among thy dear little ones in the vale of earth, now surrounds thee with its purified indwellers, whose image our innocent children are. . . . The fruits of thy toil wilt thou there enjoy; from the abode of holy spirits thou wilt look with transport upon the plantation which thou hast founded upon earth. And here too shall thy works not perish. Works like these, instituted out of pure love, to God and to man, without selfishness and ambition, are wrought in God and cannot perish. Thy work will be continued. If thou art now laid to rest, others will rise up and carry on the work. The seed which thou hast sown will, ripening in quiet, always bring richer and richer harvest for the salvation of mankind. May the earth which rises over thy grave, pious soul, rest lightly upon thee, and when moss and turf grow green, and flowers bloom over this heart which beat so warmly for its brothers; when the little ones with whom thou didst play shall have grown gray, then will posterity bend its steps to this pleasant burial-spot, and crown it with garlands, and some strong man will tarry here thoughtfully, thanking and blessing thee, and the spirit within him will say, 'Here a great, noble heart rests from its work; it has labored for the earliest childhood and for the latest future; labored in hope, and its hope was not lost—his works follow after him.' "

I quote again from Middendorff's letter:

"The teachers sang the song, 'Rest softly,' etc. Then the coffin was lowered into the grave, which was filled with flowers. The heavens had withdrawn their dark curtain, and the sun shone down into the open grave. I stepped forward and said: 'If thy ear were not closed and thy mouth not dumb, thy lips would now open and thou wouldst exult over what thou hast heard, that that of which thou wert so certain has already been fulfilled, even though in a small circle—the *acknowledgment* of the truth proclaimed by thee. . . . Even thy last journey was through storm and tempest, as has been already said. Thou hast taken the storm and the heavy way for thy companions, and hast reminded us what journeys thou didst make through thy whole life in night and tempest, and what heavy ways thou hast travelled for us. Thou permittest us now to proclaim the not-to-be-forgotten truth that he who is with thee, and will follow thee, must be ready to follow thee through storm and through toil and hardship; must be ready for what thy life has taught, '*Through conflict to victory*!' Thou hadst not merely the courage to pledge thy life in war, in peace also hast thou pledged it again and again, and joyfully hast sacrificed all to thy cause.

"Thou didst often say, 'I like the storm; it brings new life'; the lightning which on our way here flashed out of the cloud shall remind us that the darkness which still obscures the time can be rent and illuminated by a mighty ray; it reminds us how thy words, thy inspired action, fell like a fire-flame into the dark heart, summoned the sleeping conscience to awake, and made clear to itself the darkened mind. Does not one (the descendant of Luther) stand here by my side, who feels now in his heart, with burning thanks, how thou didst lead him many years ago in the path of a worthy existence? Will not many of those present confess that thou hast thrown into their minds a kindling and illuminating torch, hast opened up to them new ways of culture, and hast furnished them the means of turning the kindled thought into act? and for how many maidens in the night of an embittered existence hast thou lighted the star of a better hope, and cast the saving rope into the dangerous breakers and drawn them to the green shore of child-nurture? . . .

"Thou callest upon us: 'You are my last witnesses, be my true disciples and heralds; be the true little band which shall always increase, and which the greater one shall join. Think of me and my words; He who was with me will be with you, and will give you courage and strength as he had vouchsafed it to me, even to the grave. . . . Thank me by silence and action, by a deeply penetrating insight and a united creative practice.' . . . There stand the mothers with their nurslings in their arms, their children by their sides, who bear witness that thou hast smoothed the way to the minds of men not only by the fire of thy speech, but also by the tones of song with which, like the delicious, caressing wind and the fresh morning breeze, thou hast imbued the hearts of the mothers.

"Now a song I had written for the occasion was sung, which was followed by the sacred hymn,

Rise again, thou shalt rise again.

"The pastor said, as he threw a handful of earth into the grave, 'May God grant to each of us such an end as that of this just man.'

"As the bystanders repeated this act, Luther cried with a loud and agitated voice into the grave, 'I thank thee, too.'

"The scholars threw flowers upon flowers into the grave; one took her bouquet from her breast and threw it in; then I cast in my song also, as the last gift.

"Mutually consoled, we separated quietly, and with inward confidence, to go in our various directions; and over the minds and feelings of all spread the wings of an exalted peace."

Thus Middendorff ended his communication, which certainly deserves not to be forgotten, and perhaps leaves upon others the same elevating impression which it has made again and again upon me, and upon many followers and pupils.

Only on this day of his burial did I learn the sad news, for which I was somewhat prepared by a short letter giving notice of his illness. My own illness and domestic circumstances had delayed me, but I was on the point of starting for Liebenstein when the afflicting news was brought me at Pilnitz by Director Marquard. We, his disciples and scholars, could scarcely believe that that life recently so strong and serenely happy was ended; that the new education had now lost its champion. It scarcely seemed possible to insure its continuance without him. It seemed in the first moments as if all sank together, and to the thousand unspoken questions which we still wished to ask, the answer could never come. . . .

"What will now become of the cause?" were my first words to Middendorff, when I arrived at Liebenstein on the 2d of July, 1852, and everything there, still more in Marienthal, seemed deserted and dead.

"We will work with all our powers," answered Middendorff. "Truth is not lost."

The residence in the house of the Liebenstein kindergarten, in which I intended to pass the summer months—for many years, as I had hoped—in order to learn more from Froebel, and to labor with him in his work, was now useless, and would have to be given up. Mature consideration by Middendorff and Froebel's widow showed that the continuation of the institution in Marienthal was impracticable. It could not continue without Middendorff's direction and instruction, and that was indispensable at Keilhau. After much parley we all agreed that the removal of the kindergarten training-institution to Keilhau could not be prevented, and must take place in the late autumn, after the course for the present scholars should be completed.

Until that time the present pupils were to be taught in Marienthal by Middendorff and Madame Froebel. Among these pupils were some gifted and intelligent natures, especially Ruwada Goose, whom Froebel particularly esteemed, who took hold of the subject with great zeal, and who has always remained true to it, and is at present occupied as the directress of a kindergarten of her own in Wilhelmshafen. She was descended, on the mother's side, from a Turk, and possessed a peculiar, quick power of apprehension that particularly attracted Froebel.

Middendorff devoted his whole time and strength to this instruction through the summer, assisted by Madame Froebel, who taught the scholars the practical occupations. Although deeply afflicted by the sad, irreparable loss of her husband after only one year's married life, she fulfilled the task, now become so much more difficult, with the greatest conscientiousness, firmly resolved to devote her whole strength to it in order to preserve and promote the work already begun. At the same time she remained an affectionate, motherly friend and guardian to the pupils.

Froebel's grave was still without a monument, and we consulted, immediately after my arrival, how that should be cared for. After long consideration, Middendorff proposed Froebel's Second Gift; to place upon the grave, one upon another, the cube, the cylinder, and the sphere. I was of the opinion that the three objects should be so placed that the sphere should rest upon the cube, and the cylinder should lean upon them, in order to avoid the impression of stiffness; but we adhered at last to Middendorff's proposal.

Unfortunately, the amount contributed by Middendorff, and the equal amount added by myself, did not suffice for setting up a monument of large size, and of granite. We were compelled, therefore, to be satisfied with sandstone as material, and the objects of a smaller size, hoping that the time would come when a monument worthy of Froebel, as a benefactor of mankind, would be erected. On the plain gravestone, provisionally erected by us, Froebel's motto was engraven, "Come, let us live with our children." On a walk to the churchyard we enjoyed anew the splendid prospect from Froebel's grave, and thought that no monument could so adorn the place as nature had done.

On this spot Middendorff related to me many particulars of Froebel's last moments: how he had never in his life been so tender; how joyfully he occupied himself with the future, when in moments of hope it appeared to him again and again that he might recover; how deeply convinced he was that his work would live, would develop, and would bring the expected blessing—the blessing that new and better men would be raised up by a new and better beginning of human life.

"It is certainly permitted to spirits in the other world to have an influence on the work they have left behind," I said, "through the men of like thought who were associated with them in life. Besides, one can scarcely imagine a future life in which there is a change from the earlier to entirely new interests. Still less can one think of a higher existence without activity. Therefore I believe that God grants to mortal spirits, after their death, a part in the government of the earth, so far as they deserve it. Perhaps God shares the government of the world with the higher spirits—those called 'angels' by the popular belief—and they descend to us like the sunbeams, and influence our spirits as they awaken terrestrial life."

"I, too, think as you do," said Middendorff. "The idea of a complete separation between here and there would contradict the unbroken continuity of the world, and the union of all life, through the all-pervading spirit of God."

The instruction of the scholars now claimed all Middendorff's interest and took all his strength. With what love and tenderness, moreover, did he address the young maidens! With what inspiration did he awaken their enthusiasm, always referring to the departed friend who had devoted his life to putting into practice the idea committed to him by God!

But besides taking part in the theoretical instruction, he played the movement plays, prepared by Madame Froebel, with the scholars, and often, also, with the children in the Liebenstein kindergarten. Whoever saw him there was charmed by the touching, childlike simplicity of the white-haired man. The visitors whom I brought to Marienthal, or into our kindergarten, often said to me, "If one knew nothing of Froebel's education, and only saw Middendorff playing with the children, he would be won over to the cause."

The physician at the Baths of Liebenstein, whom I questioned in regard to Froebel's last days, said, "I have seen many men die, but never anyone who looked into the face of death so cheerfully and so calmly as Froebel."

"One day," he continued, "he asked me what I thought of his condition, and whether he could live a short time longer. I thought I ought to speak the real truth, and was able to do so, to him. I advised him not to postpone his last directions, since the failing of his powers left little hope of recovery. He took my words with the greatest calmness, and I did not notice the least change in his countenance.

"When I went to him on the following noon, they told me that he had added some last directions to his will that morning. At the door of his chamber I heard a low singing, like the chirping of the birds which were singing out of doors, and when I entered, I found Froebel sitting up in the bed, which was pushed up to the open window, looking with glorified joy on the landscape before him and singing softly to himself. To my remark, 'You appear to be better, Professor, and to be more cheerful,' he replied, 'Why should I not? I enjoy beautiful nature even in my last moments.' I never found him, on my visits, impatient, complaining, or even discontented. He was a rare man!" So spoke his physician.

Middendorff's favorite recreation after severe labor was to walk in the beautiful neighborhood of Marienthal, and he was accompanied by the scholars, and often by Madame Froebel and myself. He came to me frequently in the evening, and we then discussed how Froebel's work could be best continued by us. The giving up of Marienthal was the hardest thing, especially for Madame Froebel, who had become attached to the place.

Middendorff often said, "You, Madame von Marenholz, must undertake the spreading it in foreign countries; we others cannot do that, and, you know, Froebel always desired it."

"I see plainly," I answered, "that this will be necessary, if people continue to misapprehend and persecute the cause in Germany, and yet I would much prefer it if we could establish something regular here at home, and then be able in other countries to point to a model institution here. But my courage fails when I hope for that, when I consider the condition of affairs at Berlin, where the reaction is always on the increase, and people think our cause must be cast among the things 'which shake society in its foundations.' You don't know how absurdly the fear of being out of favor with the ruling class shows itself, when I ask people to undertake the defence of our educational cause.

"For these reasons it appears to me that we must seek to gain over foreign countries, so that we may open the way from them for the cause in Germany. How sad that it is so, and that there is so little independence in our own country! As soon as my personal affairs permit, I will see what can be accomplished abroad.

"I think it must be possible some time to establish an International Educational Union, which may gradually unite all civilized nations in the maintenance of Froebel's method. The care of parents for the education of their children is the same in all countries, and ought to overcome all differences of political and religious views and interests."

This idea of such an educational union was, even at that time, often discussed by us, and never was forgotten in my activity. I looked upon Berlin as the starting-point for its consummation, and therefore my activity in foreign countries always brought me back there. But, alas! the favorable conditions which existed there later did not then permit the accomplishment of this plan. Hostile opposition from parties from whom I had the fullest right to expect every encouragement, rude interference from incapables, and the like, induced me, after some attempts, to desist and to give up Berlin.

What failed there succeeded, in 1870, in Dresden, from which the General Educational Union now casts out its net, to plant the educational idea of Froebel on all sides. The Union at present counts twenty branch unions, and gives, in the institution of its *Froebel-foundation*, an opportunity to many poor girls to get instruction in Froebel's educational doctrines, and by its application in families and in kindergartens to occupy themselves usefully and happily, and at the same time to find their means of livelihood.

The next century will perhaps see realized the idea of an international association, for the purpose of true human education.

In our time a narrow *particularism*, both of race and of individuals, which understands no interest but personal ones, impedes the complete accomplishment of this idea.

The summer of 1852 passed very quietly. I mingled but little with the summer visitors, among whom there were this year no distinguished or well-known notabilities. Diesterweg could not come, and the Duchess Ida, whom I saw almost daily, broke up her stay this year earlier than usual, in order to go with her daughters to a watering-place, and thence to Holland to her husband, Duke Bernhard Von Weimar. Few visitors came to Marienthal this year, and our circle was very small. But Middendorff's fresh spirits and almost always quiet, cheerful disposition enlivened it, and kept everyone in good temper.

But we had a visit from an old friend, Dr. Schewe, who had been in Liebenstein two years before, and had then visited Froebel in Marienthal, and examined his head. Froebel had never given any attention to phrenology, but was nevertheless of the opinion that it could not but be true that the organs of the human brain should show the stamp of the mind, which they served as an instrument.

When, at that time, I informed Froebel of the visit of Dr. Schewe, whose acquaintance I had made during the previous winter in Berlin, and from whom I had received some instruction in phrenology, Froebel expressed his pleasure at being able to know something more of the subject. He listened to Schewe's explanations with lively interest, and agreed with him, that education might derive great benefit from this branch of knowledge, if its results were completely and scientifically established. Froebel said: "What we use is in some way or other influenced and changed by the use, or else is used up. The special kind of work which we perform affects the form of our hands decidedly. The hand of the musician is differently formed from that of the wood-chopper, etc. So it appears to me natural that the work of our brains and the motions connected therewith should affect its form. Dropping water wears away the rock. But it is the mind which puts the substance of the brain into motion—and the brain cannot conversely produce the mind. The brain, after it is developed, is a more or less well-suited organ for the mind, just as this or that material is suited for catching and holding the sun's rays."

Froebel was very eager to know the result of the examination of his head, which Dr. Schewe made in my presence, and assented to most of his conclusions.

It seemed to me strange that Dr. Schewe ranked the organs of observation, which, indeed, assist the general powers, above the higher faculties of thought in Froebel. To my question, how genius made itself apparent in the organs, Dr. Schewe said that it could not be defined; that many things must concur for it, but yet that single qualities must predominate strongly, as was the case with Froebel. He had seldom seen so strong powers of observation, especially the mathematical sense, or the sense of form and number; and, likewise, the sense of activity (*Thätigkeit*) and that of firmness and perseverance was large.

Froebel said, in reference to genius, "That is the burning-glass in the brain, which catches the rays of the sun immediately."

Dr Schewe expressed to us his sorrow on account of the unexpected decease of Froebel, and again asserted his willingness to contribute as far as lay in his power to the spread of Froebel's educational method, of the correctness and great importance of which he was fully convinced. This promise he fulfilled by using every opportunity to call attention to the subject, and, later, by his participation as a co-worker in the periodical, *The Education of the Present*, established by me in 1861, which contained, in its first two volumes, a number of articles on "Phrenology and Education," by Dr. Schewe.

When, in the middle of October, I returned from a visit to the reigning duchess of Meiningen, in Meiningen, where, under the auspices of the duchess, the first kindergarten in that place had been opened, I called one afternoon in Marienthal, but found the house empty, in spite of the cold and rainy weather. I was told that Middendorff and his scholars were on the hill behind the house. From this hill Froebel had been accustomed, almost every evening, when the weather was fine, to see the sunset, that most beautiful natural spectacle, as it seemed to him, which he always looked upon with true devotion.

I went to the hill and saw from a distance the smoke rising from a fire that had been kindled. Approaching nearer, I saw Middendorff with the scholars standing in a circle around the clear-blazing fire. He had an open book in his hand; the scholars were throwing dry chestnuts into the fire, to make it crackle; and all were singing Körner's "Battle Song" with full voices. Then it occurred to me that it was the 18th of October, and that the day was being celebrated here.

And this festival was in no way a pastime, which they were enjoying, but was celebrated by Middendorff with solemn earnestness, as it was also at Keilhau, annually, in order to awaken in the young souls the love of their native land. He thought girls ought to be educated into patriotism equally with the boys, if not to bear the sword later, at least for other necessary patriotic deeds in times of war.

Middendorff now made a little address, in which he spoke of the great victory, with enthusiastic reminiscences of his own war life, and showed that if the women wished to bring up brave sons for their native country, the feeling of love for it should not remain foreign to them, and they must also be fitted to kindle courage in their own souls, which in times of danger should awaken in each one the necessary desire for self-sacrifice and self-denial.

We then sang several battle-songs of victory from a book that Middendorff had brought with him. In the evening Middendorff told us of some of the campaigns which he had made with

Froebel and Langethal in Lutzow's corps. Among other things he told us how a maiden had served in this corps as Jäger, had fought bravely, and had prepared good food, and how her sex had not been discovered until she was wounded. But he spoke especially of Froebel's coolness during the campaign and in battles. Once, when their Jäger corps was lying in a ditch behind a hedge, and under the fire of the enemy, whose balls were passing over them, Froebel turned to Middendorff, who was lying behind him, and asked him whether he knew how many seconds faster the musket-balls moved than the balls from the flintlocks. While he was in immediate danger of his life, Froebel had the coolness to solve this mathematical problem.

On the marches, under the hottest July suns, when most of the men in the corps were trying to get rid of everything they could do without, to make their knapsacks lighter, Froebel collected all kinds of stones, herbs, and mosses for his study of nature, and filled his knapsack with them, so that one could scarcely lift it, on account of its weight. At the bivouac-fire Froebel brought out his treasures, to serve as the subjects of conversations on natural history. Still oftener he talked with his friends of his "idea," and how they must work together for it. Already in this time of youth the enthusiasm for a better education of men arose among Froebel's friends.

Middendorff was an example of the rarest devotion and faithfulness to the friend whose life-companion he had been through forty years, and to a humane idea, whose discoverer that friend was, and whose humble shield-bearer he remained after his friend's death, carrying on the work he had left behind, even to his last breath of life. What a contrast his life and work forms to that of so many of the present so-called advocates of the cause, who, led by merely personal motives, have no conception of the high priestly office that Middendorff filled so unassumingly, and with so much humility.

On the next day Middendorff brought me again a little packet of letters, which contained words of sympathy and admiration and love, in remembrance of Froebel, from distant friends and scholars. Extracts from these letters, which we together selected as we read them, were contained in Middendorff's little pamphlet, "Froebel's Departure from Life." Here are only a few aphoristic passages out of them, which all express the highest recognition of Froebel.

"From the feeling of an indescribable sorrow arises, like a flowery island out of a stormy sea, the great, blessed conviction, that over this world of blooming and decay, over flying generations and sinking ages, there reigns an unattainable, a Divine One. A personality which, like Froebel's, is rooted in the soil of immortality, lives for all times, fairer, nobler, truer, after the finite form of existence has been stripped off, and the defects and limitations of the earthly form have been overcome. To our glorified friend too will the words of our national poet apply, that what life has only half given to the great, after ages will give *wholly* and undividedly. For the misunderstanding and the scorn with which he was rewarded here, for the pains amidst which he brought beauty into the world, for the homelessness which was his lot on earth, a double home has been given to him through death—the higher world, to which he has returned, and a home in the fairest and best hearts of his people. His childlike countenance will beam in undisturbed brightness through the coming ages, his image will be crowned with the pure hands of thankfulness, in gratitude for his giving himself as a sacrifice to his people and his spirit to the common welfare of all."

"The way which he has gone is the way of nature. Death is transformation, the beginning of new life. Froebel himself called it '*the enlargement of life.*' Froebel's death is the beginning of a new life of humanity; the dawn which opened for him will be transformed into a day which, beginning in the mothers and children, will flow out through them over all the earth. Froebel will live in the kingdom of heaven upon earth—in the kindergarten, the garden of God, the kingdom of peace and bliss, untroubled childhood." . . . "He rests not; he works and strives still among the many in whom he has awakened and fostered a striving like his own."

"The more I think over his life, the more it seems to me finished, and that, as such, it has reached its completion. Froebel, too, can say, 'It is finished.' His life-thought will live in manifold forms, and in various shapes."

A scholar wrote: "How Froebel was loved—more than anyone I ever knew! He reaped love because he sowed love. The news of his death moved me as deeply as if my father had died; and was not Froebel my father—a second, a spiritual father, who awakened in me my life-idea, my true soul? What educational science has lost in Froebel learned men will have told you. They know that with him a new era in it begins—that he has earned for himself an undying name in the history of that science. But we know that his work cannot perish. It comes from too great a depth in the soul of man; it answers too well to his needs."

Another letter: "How I thank the dear God that he permitted me to live for six months near him! Gladly would I give up every happiness that I have enjoyed, rather than the residence at Marienthal. Those hours will live eternally in me. I regret every moment that I did not spend with him when I could do so. . . . His spirit will lead me to work in harmony with his idea. Every thought of him is a reminder of it."

All the writers of these letters have only gratitude and love for their departed and (in their hearts) ever-living teacher and friend. Middendorff said: "We will raise a *living* monument to him. Let each of us lay our hand to it, work in his place as we can; then will the power of the whole world be unable to prevent the growth and blossoming of the new seed, and, even long after we are dead our thank-offering will shine in the world."

When I went to Liebenstein the following year (1853), in May, the Marienthal institution had already been removed to Keilhau for several months. Letters from Middendorff and Madame Froebel spoke of a good beginning, and gave hope of a successful continuation of the training institution for kindergartners.

Diesterweg and Middendorff came in the second half of May to the meeting of the General Convention of German Teachers. The latter had been especially invited, in order to represent the kindergarten question, which was placed on the order of exercises.

It was undeniable that in this convention the chief interest was too much directed to the special questions about schools and instruction to admit of due consideration being given to the age preliminary to the school, and it would be unreasonable to expect anything else from teachers in general. For one thing, there was at that time such abundant material presented for the reform of school affairs, which was recognized as necessary—a material which is even now far from being worked up—and Froebel's educational doctrine and its connection with the school was so little known, even the importance of kindergartens was so little recognized, and they were so incompletely carried out, that it was conceivable that the much-occupied school-directors should not pay much attention to the subject. *Instruction* lay near their hearts. They left it to the family to care for the first education, which could not be their affair. This was, in a word, the opinion of the great majority. Only a small number (especially in consequence of Diesterweg's, Richard Lange's, and afterwards Carl Schmidt's initiative for Froebel's cause) showed a lively interest in the cause. This was evident, not only in the Salzung Teachers' Convention, but also in those which followed later. So in Köthen, where Carl Schmidt spoke for the cause with so much zeal and enthusiasm. Here, and likewise in Gera—at both which conventions I was present—we could only attract a small house for our subject, which I tried to help along by some remarks, together with some practical demonstrations, in a small private anteroom after the public address.

But however much interest was aroused among teachers from time to time, leisure and strength to devote to the necessary studies were always wanting for a thorough knowledge of Froebel's method, over and above the exacting schoolwork.

This obstacle still continues to exist, in spite of the fact that the immediate connection of school education with family education, and the impossibility of being able to improve the one without the other, is becoming more evident every day.

Surely there can be no other remedy than to follow the example of Austria, which has introduced Froebel's method as a required branch of instruction in the seminaries for the preparation of teachers. As children ought to lose no more time, and should be provided before the school with the preliminaries for it and for life, so must the teachers be taught Froebel's educational method as the prerequisite for their calling, which consists in practising it. The individuals among teachers who have learned Froebel's method thoroughly have become thoroughly convinced, and faithful, devoted followers and advocates of it. This oft-repeated experience encourages me to hope that the time will come when Froebel, the reformer of education, will find a place in the gospel (*Evangelium*) of the teachers by the side of Pestalozzi, the reformer of instruction.

Some members of the Salzung Convention made various objections to the contents of the report made by Dr. Schulze on the kindergarten, and to the views expressed by Middendorff, which they thought too general and not sufficiently positive. Middendorff was much excited at this, and with great liveliness gave a detailed statement of the nature, the aim, and the success of the kindergarten, its connection with the school, and its influence on the culture of the national character. The deep conviction and the real warmth of heart with which he spoke never failed, and did not fail now, to make a great impression; but, nevertheless, the contents of his speech were only understood partially, and not in their whole depth. Most of the auditors were unprepared for Froebel's theories; and Middendorff, like Froebel before him, was too little acquainted with the present drift of thought among teachers—with the watchwords and the prevailing efforts of the moment—to be able to strike the right tone—to find an echo, apart from the somewhat digressive form of expression customary with him, which had grown upon him through his rural retirement and the influence of Froebel.

In spite of much concurrence on the part of individuals, the Convention, as a whole, did not bring the success hoped for, as far as the kindergarten cause was concerned; and Middendorff could not regain his natural cheerfulness. We mutually expressed the conviction that years must pass before the school-directors would recognize Froebel's work in its whole significance. Diesterweg also said, "It does not go so fast as one would like."

In July I met Middendorff and Madame Froebel again in Keilhau, where, during my stay in Blankenburg in Thuringia, I often visited them. In the small band of pupils were the ladies Thekla Naveau and Leonore Heerwart, who were afterwards active for the cause. All the young ladies were inspired with the greatest zeal, and clung with devoted love to Middendorff and Madame Froebel, who, on their part, devoted their whole powers to do the unfinished work of Froebel.

Here, on the scene of Froebel's first activity, one could reflect upon the life that once held sway here, and must concur with Froebel that it would not be easy to find a more lovely and homelike place than Keilhau in which to bring up youth to the duty of life, in undisturbed rural quiet.

But now one saw, instead of Froebel's little farmhouse where he and his pupils had to struggle at first with the greatest privations, several stately buildings which enclosed a large courtyard, surrounded by the steep mountains and beautiful woods of the rather narrow valley. There were beautiful, spacious apartments and schoolrooms, and a large hall in the main building. Exemplary order and care for the bodily and mental needs of the pupils were evident. The watchful guidance, the sharp practical oversight, and the somewhat strict discipline, but at the same time loving care, of the director, Barop, were everywhere apparent.

Barop received me with great friendliness, and told me many interesting particulars of Keilhau and Froebel's earlier activity here. Also, the former variances which had arisen from Froebel's disregard of the material and practical conditions of life had disappeared, and had given place to a profound recognition of his idea, and the importance of its fulfilment. Barop's communication made many things very clear to me which had not been entirely intelligible before, and led me to realize again how severely genius has to battle and to suffer before it can fulfil its mission and gain its just appreciation. Barop's character of firm, incorruptible honesty, and of an energy so rare, inspired me with great respect.

This cooperation of the united families of Middendorff, Barop, and Christian Froebel for one aim made a great impression upon the observer; and as regards unselfishness, self-sacrifice, and courage, might rarely find its equal. The activity of each individual bore the stamp of scrupulous sense of duty, and at the same time of the most entire absence of pretension. Each one was ready to give help in everything, even outside the circle of work personally assigned him. The old Christian Froebel, our Froebel's eldest brother, I found in the washroom occupied in mangling linen, his weak eyes preventing him from taking part in many kinds of work.

Heinrich Langethal, Froebel's war comrade, and his true coworker in the foundation and the earlier direction of Keilhau, had not at that time returned to Keilhau, so that I was unable, to my great disappointment, to make his personal acquaintance. Later we came into relation with each other by correspondence. At the present time this blind old man, almost ninety years old, is occupied in teaching at Keilhau, having been carried back there by the never lost memory of the time when he with Froebel and Middendorff had striven and labored here for the new education amidst the greatest privations and conflicts,* a new proof that it is striving, laboring, and creating, and not the passing enjoyment of the moment, that sanctifies the places of men's abode to grateful remembrance. Like the men of this circle, the women in it were unceasingly active, without looking to the right or to the left, living only for an unselfish, faithful fulfilment of duty. The wives of Barop and Middendorff, two sisters, and daughters of the brother of our Froebel, set the example of this. From the first moment, one felt at home in this circle, and

*See further in Hanschmann's biography of Froebel.

at the sight of the simple and unassuming life of the sprightly, unfettered pupils who did not feel repressed here as in so many of our education institutions. And in this instruction also, as far as was possible, Froebel's principle of self-activity was observed, that is, of keeping the pupils as active as possible by independent thinking, while the teachers were, on the contrary, more passive.

One forenoon a troop of young boys came from outside, marching into the courtyard with botanical boxes, and with bunches of flowers and grasses in their hands. To my question where had they been, the answer was, "On a voyage of discovery"—so they named their excursion in the neighborhood, which they usually began at sunrise, and on which they botanized and collected all sorts of natural objects, that were then explained and elucidated by Middendorff in the lesson in natural science. There were among these, with other stones, some slates with impressions of antediluvian animals, in which the region was rich.

The day was fair; we went into the garden; the collected treasures were displayed, and then the instruction began by answers to the very pertinent questions asked by the scholars. Then followed the connection with the subject of the previous lesson.

In this way the instruction in all the branches, at least for the lower stages, was directed to giving greater self-activity to the scholars. As with the body, only that nourishment is of any use which hunger demands, and which can be digested without overloading the stomach, so with the mind, no more information should be given than it has strength to receive without strain and really to assimilate. How many of the children of our schools, especially of the higher ones, can do this?

Froebel's principle that experience (empirics) must keep pace with knowledge in children and youth, is surely the only correct one, and the only means of bringing about the actual necessary school reform.

Experiences in the domain of practical life can only be gained by a life of action, and it is indispensable that for this purpose the school should give the necessary time to practical work and to experiments on the plane of actuality. To solve this problem without neglecting the necessary acquirement of knowledge is the most important task of the school in our time.

Even in Keilhau this was not attained for a long time. The beginnings, which were made there under the earlier direction of Froebel, for combining the elements of work, that is, of productive work with learning, were too one-sided to last. The relations of life into which the majority of the pupils were to enter, the examinations required for their obtaining situations, the thousand prejudices which oppose all innovations, had always compelled the Keilhau institution to take into account the life of actuality, and had made it impossible to disregard the complaints of the parents of its pupils, who were unwilling to have the proper, customary school-learning shortened and supplanted in any way by practical work whose importance for the purely educational side of culture was incomprehensible to them.

But although the *garden-work*, for which each scholar had a piece of garden-land assigned to him, was kept up, and some *workshops* were used by the pupils out of school-hours, yet Froebel's plan and arrangement for the earlier direction of the educational institution could not be fully preserved. As Barop very truly said: "We are not so far advanced that the scholar and the state official should have time and skill for garden-work, or should possess manual dexterity and practise such occupations. So long as life does not use these things and cannot make them serviceable, their educational use will not be recognized. We can only advance very gradually on the way to reform mapped out by Froebel; we must keep pace with the slowly advancing reform in social affairs in general, and with the overthrow of prescriptive prejudices. We can only educate for the immediate present. That is the reason why here in Keilhau we have been obliged to give up many things which can certainly be taken up again at some later time."

"And it must not be forgotten," I added, "that the reform aimed at by Froebel is in its whole extent entirely impossible so long as children shall not go from the *kindergarten* into the elementary school reformed and modified *according to his princi-*

ples. Without the preparation for productive activity—which is also a gymnastic of the mental powers—gained in the former, it is surely impossible to combine practical work with the literary school to the extent that Froebel intended to do. But *agriculture* might be added to various bodily exercises, like gymnastics, etc., for the sake of physical health. A counterpoise must be given throughout to the excess of mental exertion."

"You see here," said Barop, as we were looking at the garden of his pupils, "that full opportunity for that is furnished to our boys."

These little gardens were situated on the slope of the hill behind the family garden, and offered a variegated patchwork of plan and decoration according to the fancy of their young owners. There one saw stones piled upon each other to represent a druidical altar, meadows for clay cows and sheep, shrubs cut into fantastic forms, imitations of mountain chains and river valleys modeled in clay, canals and ponds with fishes and frogs and little wooden canoes, etc.

Beyond this was a long avenue of cherry trees which had been planted by the first pupils of the institution, as at that time the raising of fruit was especially attended to.

On one of their playgrounds the pupils had built a complete mock Robinson Crusoe's establishment. Robinson's hut with all kinds of implements, his castle which used to be stormed in playtime, defended from within by a small band of boys, his canoe made out of a trunk of a tree, etc., were represented.

Sometimes they asked permission to bivouac in this place on summer nights; then a fire was built, they encamped around it, and cooked coffee and potatoes. On the steep hill they exercised themselves in climbing, and with the sweat of their brows brought down, by the help of homemade machines—coltstaffs, sliding rollers, etc.—heavy blocks of stone, wood, and other things for use in the gardens.

Such play-work is well suited to strengthen the body, to give dexterity in many practical operations, and serve as a counterpoise to the abstract studies. To these are to be added the usual short pedestrian tours in Keilhau which, with the older scholars, became journeys, and in which, through suitable instruction from the teachers who accompanied them, much knowledge of all kinds is acquired, and they are made acquainted with actual life.*

How happy youth were made by such excursions I observed personally, when two years earlier Middendorff and one of the Keilhau teachers came with a little band on a foot-tour through the Thuringian forest to Liebenstein. The gay singing and frolicking troop of boys delighted everyone who saw them. Quartered and entertained in the upper story of our kindergarten house in Liebenstein, I had an opportunity to observe their merry and yet not extravagant impulses.

But much as is done in many directions to lighten the strain of school-time, and to make it less injurious to the body, it is far from sufficient, and very much must be added in order completely to reach the desired end.

The school-gardens instituted in Austria under the protection of the government, and furthered with unceasing pains by Professor Erasmus Schwab, are worthy of all praise as the beginning of a more practical and natural education of youth; and form, moreover, a continuation of the Froebelian kindergartens.

Not only the education of boys needs such supplementing by means of practical working exercises, that of girls needs it in other respects even more, that young girls of all conditions may not enter so unprepared upon real life after the school years. This may apply to marriage, or to some special calling. Besides the preparation for household duties and the needs of everyday life, the necessary preparation for the future educational calling is especially to be provided for; and Froebel's kindergarten, with its plays and occupations, and his theoretical educational doctrine furnish the necessary means for this.

As Middendorff, as usual, was accompanying me a part of the way back to Blankenburg, over the Steiger—a mountain of con-

*See school and youth gardens in my work, *Education by Work*.

siderable height lying between the two places—the languor of his appearance frequently struck me. Evidently the double instruction in the training-school wore upon him. Madame Froebel also thought he exerted himself too much. Sometimes he had severe headaches, from which he suffered more and more, and was prevented from giving the theoretical instruction to the female pupils. It gave me pleasure to take his place sometimes when this was the case. I had already had practice in it in the circle of young girls and ladies who had attended my lectures in Berlin.

On such an occasion, Middendorff once said: "You must take my place in the instruction, Frau von Marenholz, if I leave the world."

That was the first time that the thought occurred to me that our cause might soon lose him.

He expressed special pleasure when I gave him a little pamphlet, "The First Education of Mothers, according to Froebel's Method," which I had written and printed in the previous winter; and it was the first one written on the subject, with the exception of smaller essays and newspaper articles.

"I am very much pleased that we have this now," he said, as he held it in his hand, "and I have found a thought in it whose expression has a special value in my eyes. It is this: 'that experience of nature and the material world must always give additional confirmation to the knowledge and revelation of spiritual things.' For that is an undoubted truth which was fully understood by Froebel. In this way mankind must build the bridge between these two contrasts in their own nature, and our education will prepare minds in childhood 'to feel themselves at one with everything in the great world of space,' as Froebel says in his *Mother and Cosset Songs*."

"I had so many questions especially in reference to this to ask Froebel," I said, "which must now be unanswered. As we were once speaking of the future life, he said, 'That is a mere phrase, and a theory which rests upon appearances. Just as we now know that the sun only apparently goes round our earth, and that the converse is true, so we shall know at some time that the present life (*Diesseits*) and the other life (*Jenseits*) lie in the same universe (*Weltraum*), in which there is no real separation, and in which everywhere there exists the closest, most unbroken connection. Think of my words: Separation is only for union there. The sun sheds light and warmth on all that lives upon the earth, and not only upon the earth, but also upon the other planets that belong to our system, and there too its beams awaken and preserve life. It is the centre of the great organism to which we belong.'"

"Yes," answered Middendorff, "Froebel often spoke of this linking together (*Gliederung*) which binds all that exists. He had a very peculiar love for the sun, and he unwillingly missed seeing it set, here at this place as well as on the hill behind the Marienthal house."

It occurred to me, after Middendorff's death, how often during my last visits to Keilhau he recurred to the continuance of life after death. He probably felt the diminution of his strength, which undoubtedly suffered from overexertion.

On the evening of the above-mentioned conversation we had entered so deeply into it that I could scarcely accomplish my return over the mountain on the steep slope without danger. Since the shorter way over the Steiger was only passable on foot or on a donkey, I availed myself of the latter method and rode, accompanied by a boy as driver. The moon set early on that evening, and it was necessary to make haste in order to arrive at Blankenburg before night. In spite of all the urging of the youth, his donkey would not go, and a closer examination resulted in the unpleasant discovery that the poor beast had lost two shoes, and every step on the stony ground was painful. Nothing remained to be done, under these circumstances, but to dismount and go on foot, and the driver led the animal by the bridle. Thus we arrived about the middle of the night at Blankenburg, whose scattered lights were our guides in the darkness, in connection with the instinct of the donkey, who always objected when we were about to take a wrong direction.

In the little city of Blankenburg, where Froebel had founded his first kindergarten, and as often as it had perished for want of support had founded it anew, I found the interest somewhat cold, although such an institution existed there. Froebel's and Middendorff's names, however, excited a lively interest in most of the people, and they usually accompanied the mention of them with the expression, "A dear man, Herr Froebel! How zealously and painfully he worked here!" And they said of Middendorff, "When Herr Middendorff plays with the children, it is a pleasure to look at them," etc. There seemed to be no trace of a deep understanding of the subject among the cultivated people, so far as I had an opportunity of investigating. So it always is with genius and with those who scattered blessings. They are not understood, and must begin their work without help and without recognition, and be contented if they escape scorn and mockery, or even persecution.

The last subject which I talked of with Middendorff in Keilhau was the foundation of education unions, and the spread of kindergartens in foreign countries. There were great difficulties still in the way of both of these objects, but I promised to do what I could, and, as soon as my circumstances would permit, to make an attempt to introduce kindergartens into foreign countries. This plan was carried out in the fall of the next year, through a stay in London, of which I have given an account, together with that of attempts in other countries, in my *Education by Work*.

In the end of November of this year I received, in Berlin, the entirely unexpected news of Middendorff's death on the 26th of that month! A brain stroke—caused, the physician thought, by an abscess in the head—had, without any previous sickness, put an end to his life. He carried on until the last moment the work he had undertaken for Froebel's cause, without sparing his body, in addition to his occupation of teaching in the Keilhau institution. He did all that this duty he had undertaken required with so much joyfulness and pleasure, that no one perceived the strain which it cost him physically.

His end, like Froebel's, was a happy one, but without his being conscious of it, while Froebel met death with full knowledge and with calmness. Like him, Middendorff enjoyed, a little while before, a natural spectacle. The day before his death the first snow fell, and he expressed again and again his pleasure at watching the whirling flakes.

But the kindergarten training institution was now without a head. In Keilhau there was no one who could undertake its direction. Madame Froebel wrote with great sorrow of being obliged again to give up the plan made with labor and pains. She had lost in Middendorff a firm support and a true friend and protector, and saw that she could not remain in Keilhau without him. She therefore accepted the invitation of school-director Marquard, of Dresden, to carry on with him and his wife the training of kindergartners in a school institution connected with a kindergarten. But this arrangement was not a lasting one. In the following year Madame Froebel went to Hamburg to continue her activity for the cause there permanently in connection with the Union.

As it is usually the case that only after the death of those who have brought anything important into the world, their efforts attain great success, so it is with the kindergartens, which have continued to spread since Froebel's death; a result, however, which has not been reached without great toil and struggle. The beginning of my activity also for the cause, now twenty-seven years ago, was connected with many difficulties, and immediate results were often transitory. Within the last twelve years kindergartens have been more and more recognized, and will now undoubtedly be accepted in all civilized countries.

At the same time the complete carrying out of Froebel's educational idea is far from being assured. Until the continuation of the kindergarten into and by the side of the school (school and youth gardens) shall have been generally accepted, until the preliminary steps to the kindergarten itself have been realized in the family circle through mothers and governesses educated according to Froebel's method, and especially until all this is done in a really methodical way, instead of in a wooden way and mechanically, the educational reform prepared for by Froebel's method cannot reach its full completion.

One may say that Froebel has found the point of Archimedes for the new education, the new beginning which promises a new result. His idea could be understood only imperfectly by his contemporaries, and by only a few, because this idea belongs to the new theory of the world which time is preparing, and can only show its whole fruitfulness when this theory, cleared of error and misconception, shall have become completely naturalized among the cultivated.

The Unions, which in these days undertake all improvements in society, should especially undertake the advancement of this cause, and the chief share in its practical carrying out falls to women.

The "General Educational Union" has been formed through my exertions as a point of departure for these efforts; it can already show a favorable beginning, and desires aid from all those who recognize an improved education of man as one of the first requisites for improved conditions in human society.